# ENCYCLOPAEDIA OF WOMEN IN SOUTH ASIA (AFGHANISTAN)

# ENCYCLOPAEDIA OF WOMEN IN SOUTH ASIA

*(In 8 Volumes)*

## Afghanistan

## (Volume 4)

*Editors :*

**Sangh Mittra, Bachchan Kumar**

**KALPAZ PUBLICATIONS**

**Delhi-110052**

Encyclopaedia of Women in South Asia *(Afghanistan)*
*(International Studies, Women)*

Rs. 7000 (Set)

ISBN: 81-7835-187-0 (Set)
ISBN: 81-7835-191-9 (Vol. 4)



Published in 2004 in India by
Kalpaz Publications,
C-30, Satyawati Nagar, Delhi-110052
E-mail : Kalpaz@hotmail.com

*Laser Typesetting at* : Shree Vaishnavi Creations, Delhi
*Printed at* : Mehra Offset Press, Delhi

# Contents

# 1

# Historical Background, Geography and People

Afghanistan is a landlocked country with mountain-ranges from west to east which connect it to upper Asia. Towards the west and south run long ranges which restrict trade and travel and have discouraged any foreign aggression since times immemorial. Arid basins without any outlets in south and west isolate the country from their neighbours by the rough desert character. The northern plains are part of the big Central Asiatic lowlands with the Amu Darya as the border while the Indus forms the border in the east. The area covers about 65,000 sq. km with various types of landscape. The political borders as they are today are the result of Anglo-Russian politicking and the relations between the Czar of Central Asia, the Persians and the British. These borders are not based on the historical or ethnic unity and hardly on geographical features.

The northern border runs along the Amu Darya, the north-western one was demarcated by the British in 1886. The Wakhan tongue, 300 km long was mutually accepted by the British and the Russians to separate the two big colonial powers and this came about with the exchange of areas north and south of the Amu Darya. Along the Wakhan, the borders of Afghanistan and China meet for a brief 70 kms, earmarked in 1964. The border on the east is the one that is active with the Durand Line dividing the Pashtun population between Pakistan and Afghanistan. The frontier runs in the northern part along the mountain ranges, cuts through thickly populated areas, not taking into account the direction of the valleys or the narrow passes. The border along Baluchistan and Iran crosses deserts and salty steppes. Only the Hilmend oasis is populated and is divided between Iran and Afghanistan. Inside Afghanistan there are many small mountain Daryas but they cannot be used for navigational purposes.

The Hindu Kush ranges start in the western parts of Afghanistan with peaks as high as 5,000 m. The central ridges reach above 6,000 m and the ones in the east are the highest at above 7,000 m. The other mountain ranges are not so high, but the Safed Koh in the south measures 4,800 m. The Paghman mountains rise up to 4,700 m, and the Koh-i Baba even higher at 5,100 m. Central Afghanistan is nearly inaccessible highland dotted with several ridges, while eastern Afghanistan comprises many elevated valleys between the high mountain ranges. Many valleys are cut deep into the ranges and are rather well irrigated as against the extremely arid southern and western parts of the country. Only the northern and eastern regions receive enough rain or snow to allow dry agriculture. The central highland is covered during the winters by several meters of snow permitting agriculture in the valleys and pastoral use of the highlands during summers.

Thus the population is concentrated in the high-up valleys, the basins in Eastern Afghanistan and the Darya oasis in the north and southwest. Well-irrigated regions do not form more than 10 per cent of the total area, and they account for four-fifths of the population. More than 80 per cent of the country could be used by nomads and small farmers; the rest is barren inhospitable land that does not have any human population. In 1965 there existed only four cities that could boast of a population of more than 75,000 inhabitants; Kabul with 435,000, Qandhar and Herat with 100,000 each and Mazar-e Sharif with 75,000. The upper parts of the mountains consist of chalk and lime. Since times immemorial wind and water have played their part in forming bizarre landscapes without any arable land of human use. The movement of the mountains still continues, sometimes resulting in massive earthquakes. The mountainous country with its hostile landscape, limited arable land, extended deserts and high alpine mountains presents limited opportunities for agriculture and trade, but its mountains are rich in minerals and its northern plains in oil and natural gas. There are reserves of about thirty billion tons of coal, and Daryas in the eastern parts could be dammed up for hydroelectric power generation.

The high-grade iron ore mined near Hajigak pass near Qandhar in the north-eastern region and near Kabul is of strategic importance. In the area of Herat tin is found and in Central Afghanistan deposits of lead and zinc could be extracted. The Loghar valley has about 500,000 tons of chromite and gold could be washed at the Daryas Kokcha and Amu Darya. Minerals are found in the north-eastern mountains too. Besides copper, uranium and other such radioactive ores are also found. Sulphur could be mined in the north, talcum near Jalalabad and mountainous salt at many sites. Since more than 5,000 years lapis lazuli and many other semiprecious stones are mined and exported.

The high mountains hold an extreme climate characterized by big swings in temperature in different seasons. The direct sunlight without any clouds increases the temperature to round 40°C in places like Herat in summers. In the lowlands and basins in the south it varies between 30°C to 50°C. Western Afghanistan experiences strong dry winds in summers due to the arid northern storm that destroys all vegetation. Even the highlands experience arise in temperature in summers, as in Kabul, which is 1800 m, above sea level, the temperature in July reaches 25°C. In Ghazni which is 2200 m, above sea level the temperature touches 23°C and sometimes 34°C. The temperature falls during the night. There is therefore a big difference in temperatures during the night. There is therefore a big difference in temperatures in the valleys and mountains during the day and night. Winters could be very cold in the north, while the southern parts of Afghanistan seldom experience frozen nights.

The climate and water determine the vegetation and agriculture of a country. In southern Afghanistan, subtropical plants like pomegranates, figs and cotton are grown up to 1600 m and grapes, rice and several types of fruits up to 2300 m height. Up to 3500 m height wheat and barley can be cultivated. The rainfall differs in different parts. In Farah in Seistan it is 75.1 mm, at Qandhar 224.8 mm and at Herat, 231.2 mm. On the plateaus of east Afghanistan there is more rainfall at 3000 mm and at Kabul 248.6 mm. The plains in Central Afghanistan get 400 to 500 mm, the eastern slopes receive a maximum of 800 mm, while the upper regions receive between 1,000 to 1200 mm, mostly in the form of snow in winter several metres deep which is difficult to cross. The precipitation is limited to the period between October and May. Only in the high mountains there is rain and snowfall during the summers.

The aridity of the region ensures more evaporations compared to precipitating so that irrigating depends more or less on melted snow and ice. Pools are formed in troughs where Daryas end. Massive evaporation makes them brackish or even salty. Water of the Daryas used for irrigation is frequently diverted to irrigate the fields. Thunderstorms and gales are not uncommon in this region, when there is rainfall. Water runs down the valleys destroying whatever comes its way. The conditions in high mountains are also very inhospitable, where snow and storms in winter isolate the villages every years for six months. Life in the deserts of Seistan is also very tough because of the externally high temperatures, deserts storms and paucity of water. As against this, life in the Darya oases, the alms and the valleys is much better with a pleasant climate. In the low-lying areas of Afghanistan are the deserts and semi-deserts. The mountainous areas have forests that are green in summers. This is followed by alpine thorns and juniper forests in the north. The aridity of the region limits the forests to regions with 250-300 mm precipitation. Water from ice and melted snow that permeates into the soil allows lasting vegetation. But this is possible in very limited areas. The forests are open woods with pistachios, ash trees and other that are green in summer. In Central Afghanistan they are limited to a height of 2900 m and in the basin they end at even lesser height. These forests at that height consist mainly of herbaceous plants, and some bushes and brushes. There are beautiful green meadows with flowers like tulips and lilies. The semi-deserts and steppes have different kinds of vegetation covering one-fifth of the whole country, mainly saxual and calligonum bushes. The forests along the Darya valleys are rich in willows and poplars. However, a large part of Afghanistan is barren lands with rocks, sand and salt.

The condition of the female half of the population is a case of human rights and has to be analysed historically. The position of women in the traditional Afghan society is very different from that in the civic structure and the contradictions in Afghanistan of today are only one of the facets of the conflict between the traditional village life and that of the Europeanized city of Kabul. The traditional division of labour and life in tribal communities developed through the centuries and differs from region to region. For example, the job of milking the animals and weaving textiles had always been a women's job and is still done by the women among the Durrani's, while in the Ghilzai, it is a man's job. Ploughing and harvesting was generally a male job, but in Nuristan all work in the fields is done by women.

Land could be owned and inherited by men only and had to be defended by arms in many cases, as fertile soil is rare. A woman could hold her own business, but in public had to be represented by a *wakil,* a representative, her brother or uncle. Marriage is negotiated by the parents of both sides but a girl can force a family of the man she loves to marry her by entering his house demanding the 'shingeri' marriage. Divorce is rare and polygamy depends on the wealth and therefore limited to 5 per cent of the male population. When the husband dies, the woman normally asks his brother or uncle to take her in leviratical marriage, because after her marriage she had left her own clan. Infant mortality is very high and the main reason is the lack of medical care. Outside her house a woman has to wear a *chador* or *burqa,* a tent-like coat that covers the woman from head to toe. In the small villages there was no such compulsion because the clan of relatives lived together. In fact such practices were a part of religion and customs and were never questioned. It was even possible that women took up arms to defend their family and property. During the Anglo-Afghan War of 1880 women fought along with men, something that is unimaginable today. The seclusion of women started after the exiles interacted with the people of western Islamic countries like Syria, Egypt and Turkey in the early 20th century.

The reformer Tarzi had lived in Damascus with his family. When he returned, his daughter Soraya was married to Amanullah and influenced him with the ideas of liberalization and women's rights. She started the weekly "Irshad-e-Niswan" in 1921, the first journal for Afghan women edited by Asma Rasmya Tarzi and the same year the first school for girls was opened. The sister of the king led the "Women's Protective Association". But tribal revolts forced the officials to close the school and to stop these reformist ideas. The impact of the women's rights was very limited, anyway, as hardly 800 girls had been to school till 1928. In that year Amanullah sent a group of girls to Turkey for education as nurses and teachers.

A year later rebellions started against women's equality, their education and the abolishment of the veil by the clergy and the tribesmen. The king withdrew these laws but was forced to emigrate nevertheless. The tribes went back to their old lifestyle and the new dynasty had to go slow on the reforms. A regular school for girls was not opened until 1935 and the chance to go for higher education to the university came as late as 1950-51, when separate classes for girls were started in the faculties of medicine, sciences and humanities.

The next step towards women's emancipations was taken by Daud in 1959 with a decret that allowed women to give up the veil voluntarily. About 10,000 women followed the appeal over a period of time but this was limited to the city educated elite. The beginning of industrialization gave women a chance to work in shops starting with porcelain manufacturing in Kabul. The first female member of parliament was chosen in 1964 while Kubra Nurzai became the first female minister for health and remained in office from 1966 to 1969. During the presidency of Daud, schools and universities were opened for girls which soon met resistance again. In 1970 two mullahs fired at the 'naked' legs of a female teacher and some 5,000 girls dared to demonstrate on the streets against such a criminal act.

In 1953, *Merman,* a new journal for women appeared and in 1959 a former private women's union was officially made the "Women's Institute" in order to encourage women to take responsible jobs. However, all these steps were limited to Kabul and the small educated elite of the country, which was a sharp contrast to the conservative lifestyle of the women in villages. This same educated elite was responsible for bringing the PDPA to power in 1978. Their leftist faction, the Khalqis had the same goal as Amanullah and repeated his mistakes by trying to push Afghanistan into 'modernism'. They did not learn from their mistakes or history and failed not because of their wrong intentions, but because of their lack of understanding of the Afghan society. Their decret number 7 issued on the 17th of October, 1978 announced the equality of women. A literacy campaign for all illiterate persons was ordered by law and set in force along with crude propaganda which again saw people resisting it. Even women demonstrated against it and were ruthlessly put down. When the Parchami government of Babrak Karmal was installed by the Soviets, they tried to Islamize the education and reform the system but it was too late. The war, however, was not fought regarding women's rights. In the cities, especially Kabul, more than 200,000 women worked in offices, schools and factories, but they were threatened by the Mujahiddin who argued that unveiled women to be corrupt and sinners.

An extremely conservative ideology took roots in the camps of refugees, especially in Pakistan and gave rise to new problems. There were about 345 villages of refugees with overcrowded small huts. The neighbours were not relatives, but often members of alien clans or even ethnic groups. The seclusion got worse. The only chance to meet other women was a visit to the "Basic Health Units". The male members often left their families to fight in the war and the younger ones never learnt to work but dreamed of becoming warriors. There were hardly any positive changes in these camps. Non-governmental Organizations and the UNHCR were, however, able to reduce the death rate among children but tuberculosis was widespread.

Educational programmes suffered from seclusion. Some courses or workshops for sewing, embroidery or carpet weaving by Turkoman women could be arranged, but only under strict *purdah.* All elements of civic freedom vanished. 'Dignity' forbade any attempts to start schools for girls and of the 729 schools with 112,000 pupils which the Pakistan Commission of Refugees opened, there were only 74 schools for girls with 7,800 pupils. The Peshawar parties declared their support for Islamic education but madras as were opened largely with Dari and Pashto as the medium of education and such disciplines as geography, sciences, arithmetic's. Even in the capital Islamabad there are no more than 200 pupils in the two high school for girls and in Quetta there is only one school for girls. No party except the Hizb-i Islami of Hekmatyar declared its policy of equal rights for men and women, although within Islamic laws. The Revolutionary Association of the Women of Afghanistan, a 'left' organization was formed in 1977 but the founder Mina Kishwar Kamal was murdered some five years later in Quetta.

Information about the behaviour of the victorious Mujahiddin outside Kabul are scarce. When they took over Kabul, there was widespread murder, rape and terror against women forcing Amnesty International to protested publicly, but without any result. There was no difference between the Turkish troops of Dostum and the Pashtun Mujahidin of the Peshwar parties. There have been continued human rights violations in Afghanistan and hundreds of thousands fled forming a new wave of refugees. Most of the European countries are refusing asylum to the Afghans. The Supreme Court of Germany, for instance, decided that there cannot be suppression by the state without law. But these western officials are unable to understand the Islamic juridical system where there is no division between state and the church. The later does not exist and the jurisdiction is in the hands of the *kadis* who decide as per the Muslim law based on the Quran. The majority Hanafites take the Quran alone as juridical source and the sentences of the judges cannot be disputed as the have religious sanctions. Which in effect means that as far as female rights are concern, there is complete subjugation. This can be seen from a *fetwa,* an Islamic decree, issued by the 'High Court of the Islamic State of Afghanistan', the government of the Mujahiddin led by Rabbani, on the 27th of August, 1993. Excerpts from which are reproduced here, and it reads: "The veil of women belongs to the principles of Islam. Who disregards it is godless, who rejects it takes a sin upon himself. The Islamic veiling is the first religious command for women, who have to stay in their house and safe place, that her beauty outside and inwards will be covered before alien eyes and will be left immobilized. "In Anwar-al Mahmud. p. 117, Vol. I it is described in detail, that the way out of doors for women to school—under the protection of religious education—is nothing else but a disgusting act of offence. This means that for Islamic women a departure even in groups form their houses to visit a school is not acceptable, even when the teacher is a Muslim and follows the strict Islamic code of dressing.

Experience has demonstrated that this had and has an abhorrent and bad influence on the morals of women and brought results which were against the Islamic decree.

In the commentaries to the commands of Islamic is written:.... *do not let your daughter learn to read or write.*

According to this tradition it is negated and forbidden,

i.e., in the whole principles of law, the education and alphabetization of the woman was declared as *haram*! (forbidden by religious tenets)....

This fetwa mentioned sixteen conditions for conduct of a woman who wants to go out of her house, some of them are quoted below:

"11. She should not walk in the middle of the road.

12. She shall not leave the house without the permission of her husband.

13. She should not speak to an alien man.

14. Should a discourse be necessary for religious reasons, she should do it in a low voice and without laughing.

15. She should not look at alien persons.

16. She should not have any exchange with alien persons"

The *fetwa* is much abused by the Taliban who handle the millions of inhabitants of the capital as if they were in a backward village.

The condition of women in the cities is especially bad because most of the men are out fighting. There are hundreds of thousand of widows who have no means of livelihood and being uneducated and with so many restrictions they cannot work. They have been reduced to begging on the streets of Kabul. Will these women ever revolt against the atrocities being inflicted on them in the name of Islam? It is time they voiced their distress and brought some sanity to the crazy war being fought which does not seem to end.

Of all the customs those relating to marriage were socially the most important. Except among well-to-do people, marriage took place relatively late because of the high bride price and the enormous expense involved in marriage ceremonies. Parents betrothed their daughters fairly early but refused to allow them to marry unless they received a larger sum than had originally been agreed upon. In 1884 the amir fixed a very low figure of thirty rupees as a bride price and declared that should a man's wedding be pending for want of money he should borrow the fixed amount from the state treasury. Apparently this ruling was not enforced, since high bride prices were still demanded. This demand was deep rooted and, possibly, liked with the seclusion of women, a significant factor in Afghan society. Polygamy, which was permitted by the Shari'a, had become only an upper-class phenomenon. Also, the rise of parallel cousin marriages and the custom of bride exchange (*badal*) between two families, which were common in Afghanistan, were probably a consequence of the demand for a heavy bride price. In both cases marriage expenses were lowered to the minimum level. Marriage expenses were so high that many families seeking brides for their sons became impoverished. Neither custom nor religion was against intermarriage; people preferred to marry within their own tribes, particularly their nearest relations. The Pashtuns frequently took wives from other ethnic groups, but the reverse was rarely the case. Until the amir's reign the marriage contracts drawn up by the mullas in accordance with the Shari'a, were not registered. The amir made it a law that they should be registered in government documents. Also, he fixed the amount of *mahr,* as distinct from the bride price, payable by husbands to wives. In reality, wives rarely demands this sum. Originally it had been an indefinite amount of property but by the amir's time had risen to a disproportionate sum. The amir in 1883 decreed that the *mahr* for members of the royal family should be between three thousand and twelve thousand rupees, of the nobility between one thousand and three thousand, and of the ordinary people between three hundred and nine hundred.

In theory both husbands and wives under certain circumstances had the right to seek divorce. In practice, however, they rarely did so, mainly because divorce was considered a social disgrace.

Burial expenses, like those of weddings, were very high. In addition, among the well to do it was the custom to assign recites (*qaris*) to read the Quran over the graves of the deceased for several days after their death; the amir abolished this practice. The amir also prohibited the use of hashish, which was common among the inhabitants of Badakhshan and Herat. In the city of Herat alone, at one time sixty-eight persons, including some elders who had smoked it, were imprisoned for life and their release was made conditional upon their abandoning its use.

Traditionally in Afghanistan the position of women was (and still is) inferior to that of men. In some respects Amir' Abd al-Rahman made woman still more subservient to men, but in others he improved their condition.

In Afghanistan, as in other agrarian societies, the position of a woman varied according to the woman's age and the norms of the social and ethnic groups to which she belonged. Everywhere, however, women's position economically and legally was inferior to that of men. To begin with, except for elderly widows, women did not dispose of property, even their own, although they were entilted to do so by law. In addition, women could not own much. According to the Shari'a, daughters, for instance, inherited only half the amount received by the sons on the death of their father.

The other major source of women's property, beside inheritance, was the *mahr* they were assigned by their husbands at the time of their marriage contract. In practice, however, they seldom, if ever, laid claim to *mahr*. Men, however, were absolutely responsible for the support of women in their families, and women enjoyed a far greater degree of security than did men. Only when men failed to support their wives or when they proved impotent were women entitled to seek divorce, whereas it was much easier for men to divorce. Nevertheless, divorce happened very rarely. Usually marriages lasted for life, contributing greatly to the stability of family and of society. Some peasant women helped their husbands in the fields, and others served the well-to-do households for payment. In general, however, women were not expected to earn a living, as this work was considered a slur on their husbands. A Pashto saying illustrates this well: "To hell with a woman's earning, and a donkey's load." The economic dependence of women on men was complete.

From the fact that a woman received half of man's share in inheritance and because two female witnesses were equivalent to one male witness in the Shari'a court, there had arisen the belief that two women were equal to one man, in the same way that Pashtun males held that one Pashtum equalled ten Hindus in strength. This false consciousness, reinforced by the beliefs that women were intellectually inferior (*naqis-i-'aql*), were weak by nature, and were open to temptation, made men deny them positions outside their homes. The term "woman" had been assigned such a low position in society that when a man intended to insult his opponent he simply called him a "woman." Nevertheless, in their homes women had great influence over their children as well as over their husbands. Within these bounds men greatly respected them, although they expected them also to be dutiful and obedient. Women were expected to look after the needs of their husbands, whom Pashtun women referred to as *Khawand* (lord). Some upper-class women reveived a little education, but in the main women occupied themselves in cooking, sewing, milking cows, weaving, spinning, rearing children, and so forth. Servants to some extent freed well-to-do women from this drudgery, but even rich women still remained inside the walls of their homes. Like other women, the well-off called upon their relatives on social occasions only. Occasionally, women went to local shrines for entertainment, but, here as elsewhere, women were separate from men. According to a recent writer the division of the females and males into separate worlds is more pronounced in Afghanistan than in many other parts of the world. To an extent this division had been true of the unmarried females of the urban middle classes, but it would be incorrect to assume that it was universal. Women did enter the men's world; but, when they did most of them, especially those of the upper classes, veiled themselves.

Women were more secluded in urban centres than in rural areas. Indeed, among some people in the rural areas, for instance among the Hazaras, women were not secluded at all. Some of them, however, sold their wives for asses. Among the Pashtuns, particularly the Ghilzays and more particularly the *powindas*, women were less secluded. The Uzbeks, however, shut their women out of view with jealous solicitude. According to Schurmann, division of labour more than anything else accounted for the seclusion of Afghan women.

Kafir women were neither secluded nor veiled before their conversion to Islam. Unlike women among other ethnic groups in Afghanistan, Kafir women had considerable freedom. If caught in adultery, their partners were fined, but the women themselves were neither beaten nor abused. Unmarried women were said to have little or no restriction on their having sexual intercourse with the opposite sex, and the Kafirs received their fatherless grandchildren with no apparent contempt. The condition of the women, however, was deplorable, since they were overworked, underfed, and treated by men with a tolerant contempt far worse than actual ill usage. In spite of their conditions, Kafir women provided a contrast to members of their sex in other ethnic groups, where women were regarded as a source of pleasure for men in addition to their generative functions.

In time of war women in Afghanistan carried supplies to men in the battlefields. In the Kabul area many of the women during the Second Anglo-Afghan War used to go out at night after a battle and mutilate the bodies of the dead and kill the wounded and the dying. It is generally held, though historically not established, that the Afghan victory over the English at Maiwand was largely the result of the encouragement of the reluctant ghazis by a maiden called Malalay. Her story has become widely known, and she has become the symbol of female courage, as the following popular couplet indicates:

Lover! If you were not martyred in Maiwand
By God, then they want to keep you for a disgraceful life.

In the reign of the amir, a large number of women lost their husband in wars or had husbands and guardians who were expelled from the country or were employed by the government and lived away from their families for most of the time. Consequently, among other things, adultery became frequent. The amir considered adultery the worst sin, and to deal with it he punished both parties to the act with death. Women who were accused of adultery were often put in sacks and exhibited.

The amir inflicted these severe punishments on adulterous wives because like other Afghans he believed that "the honour of the people of Afghanistan consists in the honour of their women. "It was the slight of this "honour" by Alexander Burnes which, according to the amir, ignited the First Anglo-Afghan War. According to the amir the religion of Islam entitled men to control their wives and to kill them if they were unfaithful. Among other things the men's control of women meant that the latter were not allowed to go out of their houses without the consent of their husbands. Time and again the amir impressed on his subjects that the Christian powers would if they occupied Afghanistan deprive them of their hold over their wives because, said the amir, "according to their laws women enjoy liberty" and "under them no husband has any control over his wife." In the amir's view, the occupation of Afghanistan by the British had emboldened the women and it was his duty to see that they kept the honour of their husbands.

With regard to the right to property of women and their right to support by their husband, the amir applied the prescription of Islam by compelling husband to grant freedom to their wives if they were unable to support them. Also, he compelled husbands to give their divorced wives the *mahr* that had been agreed upon at the time of the marriage contract.

The sale of both Muslims and non-Muslims obtained by kidnapping was, on a limited scale, practiced in Afghanistan in the nineteenth century, but slavery as an institution was dying. Slaves were only attached to families and were treated well.

**Kabul, the City where even the Sunrise and Sunset have been Upset for a Long Time**

By Sajida Hayat a RAWA activist who has recently visited Kabul, January 2000

Having been away from my country for a long time, I recently took a trip to Kabul City, the heart of injured Afghanistan. I was a child when we had immigrated to Pakistan as refugees. I don't remember much of anything from my country. The only memories I have, are of a few places such as my house, school and our dear neighbours' houses.

But did the reports and the pictures I had seen prepare me to understand how damaged the country is, or how miserable the people are? I had only heard stories, but had not seen the reality of it. The stories changed to reality when I travelled to Kabul.

From the first moment of having crossed into Afghanistan at Torkham (the eastern border between Afghanistan and Pakistan), I had to wear a head to toe covering called the *burqa*. A three-inch square opening covered with mesh provided the only means for vision. This bag which covers from head to toe is so gloomy that you feel like throwing it away.

The Taliban themselves are absorbed in moral corruption. They have forced the *burqa* on women so that women do not witness their evil doings and savage actions. They say that people should not so much as set their eyes on women, but they, themselves, do not abstain from dong anything they want. A woman who defies Taliban orders reaps a whipping, insults, abuse and many more adjectives like these. I saw the real faces of the Taliban. They had long clothes, long hair with a turban on their head, eyeliner on, and a whip in their hand. When I saw the whip, I was filled with horror. I was not thinking of myself, but of the mothers and sisters who are whipped for revealing their ankles or a part of their hair. The physical pain of being whipped last for a while, but the emotional pain of the insults and hatred is fatal as. I saw more an more Taliban. I said to myself, that apart from their savage and inimical actions, that just by their strange appearances alone, they seem as if they have come from another planet.

A huge part of Kabul is in a state of tragic destruction. I have seen many pictures of Bosnia. Kashmir and many more war-destroyed places, but they do not compare with mournful Afghanistan, the forgotten tragedy of the world. The scenes of *burqa,* turban and beard are not only very strange, but also very unpleasant and painful. It seems like you are walking in an open air living museum. It is quite hard to find any difference between a literate and an illiterate person, but the difference between a Talib and an ordinary person is very clear and visible. The fatigue from 20 years of imposed war is apparent in the people's faces by their indignation and aversion to the Taliban.

Shopkeepers, drivers, passers-by and all the people express their indignation in different forms. "We are driven to exterminates in our day by day searching for necessities of life. They [the Taliban] create problems, violence and fear. We are very careful that women do not get into our taxis without their kinsmen. Otherwise, there is the danger of insult, contempt and a whipping for both of us," a taxi driver said.

When my friend and I wanted to take a taxi, the driver would not take us, because there was no mahram (a close relative) with us. Is the world aware of these insults and contemptible things, which have been created by a puppet minority? During my excursion, I saw some buildings that attracted my attention. Most of them were destroyed by rockets and bullets. Some looked okay, but were locked up. I asked my friend what those buildings were used for? She said that they were ministeries of education, information and culture, embassies, and schools. I thought to myself that in a country where there is no economy, education, hygiene and basic facilities, there is no need for embassies or other administrations. Destroyed houses and buildings can be seen everywhere. Bombs, artillery, and the blind rockets of the fundamentalists have collapsed them. Hundreds of public buses have been plundered and stolen by the fundamental miscreants and then driven to Pakistan to be sold. Seeing these scenes makes you wonder and makes you sad. If they impose their rules and laws on our innocent people, why the hostility also against inanimate objects? There hostility against civilization is evidenced everywhere. The Taliban, themselves, are arrogantly driving around in the best and most modern cars.

We passed by a ruined building. I asked my friend what it was in the past. "Khoshal Khan High School," she said. I did not believe it, because I remembered it very well. If not for it's bullet perforated signboard I would have thought she was mistaken. It really was the same school I had seen years ago. But it was so damaged by rockets that it was hard to believe that it was the same place. That school used to be a place of learning and knowledge. Afghan children were trained there and it was there that they learned about science and technology. Unfortunately, the minority of those children are now in the deplorable state of being refugees. Some of them beg for a loof of bread to stay alive, while others are suffering from mental disorders—the gift of continual war. I have heard that most of our youngsters in the western provinces use opium, heroin and other narcotics to try to forget the sorrow of the rampant barbarism. University and school students (especially girls who have been ostracized) have a profound rancor against the Taliban and the fundamentalists which can only be relieved by the removal of these traitors.

I met a young girl on the bus. " I was a second year student at Kabul Medical Institute, but a long time ago the doors of knowledge were closed. This is a big disaster. I don't know about my future. Where can I go? I damn the Taliban and fundamentalists," she said. I went to one of my friend's house. When her 12 years old daughter knew that I had come from Pakistan, she embraced me and wanted me to take her to Pakistan and get her into a school. Her mother burst into tears and said, "Although my daughter is too small to leave me, nevertheless her education is very important. Take her with you."

When I entered Merriam High School (a high school for

girls), there were about 30 families now living in the classrooms. It was the third years since they had been displaced from their houses, due to protected fighting in the northern provinces. Almost all of the women had become beggars. They were begging from people who themselves had nothing to eat. Their best income came from washing clothes, but is not easy. "Our children collect sticks, wood and papers from the streets to warm the water," they said. 20,000 Afghani (20 American cents) is paid for the washing of too many pieces of clothes (it requires washing from morning to evening). A loaf of bread costs 20,000 Afghani. Therefore, working from sun up to sun down is not even sufficient to provide bread, never mind other things. "Some girls who were student in this school before it had become living quarters for the 30 families, come to look at their old school. They find comfort in seeing the classrooms, school campus and they reflect on the wonderful memories of time spent at school. "We feel ashamed when we see them, but there is no other way and it is not our fault. Where do we go? Our houses and properties have been plundered or burned up. There is no place to go and take refuge there. We are helpless. We had never planned to become beggars, " the other women said. A middle aged woman came and said," We experience death every day. I wish we were not alive. I wish we died instead of enduring this gradual death. If it were not prohibited by our religion, I would commit suicide." The children of these refugees were begging or collecting sticks, wood and papers just to be able to afford at lest a loaf of bread to stay a live. Knowledge and education do not have any importance for them. They are the children of war. They were born in poverty and misery. Most of them are not familiar with peace and comfort.

There are thousand and thousand of women who have been banned from social activities and from working outside their houses. Only a small number of women have the right to work outside. They are doctors and the Taliban need them for their work. This serious state of affairs has pulled women into begging and prostitution. Famine, poverty and starvation are found throughout Afghanistan. Meat is not available for the majority of people. Fruit is rarely accessible. Children do not smile and are not cheerful. The dust of war and poverty has covered their nice faces.

I visited some beggars. When I asked them about their previous life, I found that some of them were teachers and government employees.

"Fundamentalists killed my husband. Our house and properties have been plundered. I have three small children. I was a teacher. If not for my children, I would kill myself," a woman who is now a beggar said. Most of the shopkeepers and vendors have masters degrees from the university or are people with a high level of experience in professional work. I talked with a clothing vendor. He said," If I do not this, I must beg, steal or commit suicide. I was a teacher at Kabul University. I could not envision this unfair situation. As a teacher of many years, it was my dream to train the generation that would build the future of our country. Nevertheless, this generation is drowning in starvation, poverty and misery. This unfortunate generation is only familiar with guns, blood and savagery. They feel death every moment. For them life is meaningless. All traitors deserve to be executed publicly."

When there was fighting between the Taliban and the Northern Alliances, I was in Kabul. The result of that fighting was the displacement of thousands of people to other places, especially to Kabul City. I talked with some families just arriving from the northern provinces. They said, "We left our houses and properties and escaped with only the clothing on our bodies." Some of those families were coming with a pot, cow, donkey or some other personal property. Some of them were crying because they did not know where the rest of their family members were or how they were doing. There are a huge number of unexploded mines still in Afghanistan. According to a report of the United Nations, ten million mines have been planted in Afghanistan during the recent two decades. The continual danger of these explosives threatens the lives of everyone. They have already killed or maimed more than one million people.

I talked with a cobbler. He was about 65. His feet and some of his fingers had been cut off. I thought he was the victim of a land mine. When I asked him, he started telling me his tragic story. "My misery and sorrow are not just limited to my disability. A rocket exploded in our house a few years ago. It killed my younger son and left me in this condition. My wife and daughter were not in the house at the time. When they returned to the house and saw the scene, they could not endure it. They went into a terrible shock from which they have not yet recovered." He became overwhelmed with tears and could not talk any more.

One day my friend and I went to a bazaar to buy something. I was not used to wearing the *burqa,* since it was so very gloomy. So, I was wearing it so that my face was revealed, when suddenly a woman came toward me and shouted that a Talib was coming. "Please cover your face!" she said. I saw the reaction of the Talib from behind the *burqa.* He walked close beside me and his horrible and dreadful appearance made me shudder with fright. I thought he would whip me, but he contented himself with saying some bad words. It was the first time that I experienced a Talib's anger and it was very frightening. The other women in the bazaar later came and said to me," You are very lucky that he was not a member of *Amr-e-bil marof and nahi an monkar* (the highly critical police of the Taliban)."

That was my view from behind the narrow window of the *burqa* during my short stay in Kabul. The pen is inadequate to describe the felonies and crimes which are beyond imagination. It is regrettable that the press are banned from publicizing the atrocities which occur in Afghanistan which the world has never seen before.

I wanted to stand on a mountain peak and shout about the ignorance of the world for our country. My mother told me about Kabul City before the war. She always told about the nice sunrise and sunset of this beautiful city. And now when the poor and helpless people come outside from their houses before sunrise and look for a loaf of bread until night, the sunrise and sunset have lost their beauty and meaning. Although the scenes of violence and savagery pressed my heart, the poem of an Iranian poet strengthened me.

Though the night is dark,
Keep your heart brave,
Dawn is close.
The anger of the woman who is whipped,
The aversion of the girl who is raped,
The disgust of the man who is insulted for not having a proper beard,

The crying of the woman who is begging and pulled to prostitution,
The educated who are expelled from their respectful jobs with insult and contempt,
The pain of the mother and father who sell their child,
The child who begs for a loaf of bread,
And finally the rancor of the people who are witness to the destruction of their beloved country,
Will explode the palace of oppression one day.

# 2

# Education and Employment

Afghanistan, as a traditional multi-ethnic developing country, with its attempts for modernization of education and the set-backs in providing access to education, as well as the contribution of the international community to the development of education. The role of families, local communities and enlightened leaders and governments has been essential for the development of education. The expansion of education in the 1960s and 1970s showed that, under conditions of peace and tranquillity a modern education system, with equal access and opportunities for all, could be developed in the context of national values and heritage. There is no contradiction between Afghan cultural values and modernity. The conflict during the last two decades had a devastating effect on Afghan society, and its social and economic infrastructure including education.

In the year 2000, enrolment in primary education barely reached the level of 1978 (less than thirty percent), with the percentage of girls significantly reduced. There is some secondary education, but there is no significant technical and vocational or higher education in the country. Local communities and non-governmental organizations played an important role in sustaining basic education for Afghans in rural communities and refugee camps. A recent UNESCO report concluded that the strong and growing demand for modern education for boys and girls, and the willingness of the community to participate are the key to the future.

Islam came to Afghanistan during the seventh century and ever since it has provided the spiritual, philosophical and cultural context for the Afghan people. The Islamic tradition permeated every aspect of Afghan society and way of life. Religious leaders have been able to influence the political, social and cultural life of the community. Thus, educational development during much of the twentieth century reflected the religious and traditional nature of society. The nature and form of education and its expansion have also been influenced by the changing political context in the country and by the social and economic policies of successive regimes and governments, as well as by parents' aspirations for the education of their children. In view of the multi-ethnic composition of Afghan society, cultural and linguistic policies were an important factor in the development of education.

Economic constraints have been a major drawback for the development of education. Cultural co-operation with a number of foreign countries contributed to the expansion and qualitative improvement of modern education in Afghanistan. In the second half of the twentieth century, international organizations played an important role in stimulating educational developments worldwide by setting norms and targets and by providing technical and financial assistance.

In the nineteenth century Afghanistan was adversely affected by the rivalries of external powers (the British and Russian empires) in the region and, at the same time, Afghan society experienced periods of conflict leading to the unification of the State and successive wars for independence. The vision of political leaders and the aspirations of Afghan people for socio-economic and cultural development of society were shaped by an agrarian economy and commerce, tribal and ethnic social structures, and a profound Islamic tradition.

Education and training for Afghan children and young people in rural communities and towns was provided at home, in the mosque and in religious schools, and through informal on-the-job training and apprenticeship. A few modern schools (western style) were established in the early years of the twentieth century with the objective of training teachers and clerical staff for the civil service. Following the independence of Afghanistan from the United Kingdom in 1919, the political leaders (led by King Amanullah) considered education as an important means of social and economic development and modernization.

The establishment of diplomatic and cultural relations with a number of countries including Turkey, France and Germany, and the availability of foreign teachers, expertise and scholarships for Afghan students, contributed to the development of modern education in Afghanistan. For the first time, a number of Afghan male and female students were sent to Turkey and other countries in Europe to study. The government policy promoted social progress through education. In January 1929 King Amanullah abdicated following civil strife provoked by external forces and supported by ultraconservatives in the country. Some historians believe that the government's modernization programme including its education and cultural policies were too progressive for a traditional Afghan society. Soon after the departure of King Amanullah, the city of Kabul was captured by Habibullah Kalakani who was against modernization. This was a setback for education in Afghanistan, as all modern schools were closed.

In 1929 Nader Shah took over as the King of Afghanistan. Once again the schools were reopened and attention was given to the development of education. A Constitution promulgated in 1931 referred to the responsibility of the government for the provision of universal primary education for Afghan children. Nader Shah was assassinated by a student in 1933, and his son Zaher Shah, at the age of nineteen years, became the king of Afghanistan. In the 1930s the development of education in Afghanistan was limited for a number of reasons. Based on the experience and lessons of the 1920s, there was a slowing down of the modernization programmes including educational development.

The political priorities in the 1930s were the maintenance of internal security and the consolidation of the State, taking into account the tribal and ethnic nature of Afghan society. Social and economic measures including the education policy aimed at sustaining a traditional agricultural society. The majority of rural communities had no schools and continued the education of their children, in the traditional way, at home and in the mosques. By 1940, with an estimated population of about ten million people, there were 60,000 pupils in 324 schools with 1,990 teachers throughout Afghanistan. In the

1940s attention was given to the development of a few secondary schools and the beginning of higher education, but there were no plans for a systematic development of education.

**Second World War**

During the Second World War (1939-1944), in which Afghanistan remained neutral, some schools were affected by the departure of foreign teachers. Furthermore, the machinery and laboratory equipment for schools and training institutions could not be imported. Following the Second World War, two major political decisions contributed to the development of education. First, there was some political reform (including the formation of a relatively liberal government headed by another uncle of the King), and the beginning of a short-lived democratic movement, with a new Constitution and an elected parliament. The new Constitution made primary education compulsory for all Afghan children (boys and girls), wherever the government could provide the facilities. Second, the government decided to coordinate and reinforce national economic activities, and undertake a number of projects including prospecting for oil in the north of the country, and a major irrigation and hydroelectric project in the Helmand Valley.

These projects and other developmental activities required technicians and specialists, who had to be trained inside Afghanistan and abroad. Thus the government's social and economic policies stimulated the development of education in Afghanistan. Nevertheless, the expansion of primary education remained modest. By 1950, there were 368 primary, secondary and vocational schools, and one teacher training school with a total enrolment of 95,300 students. The post-Second World War period (the 1950s) witnessed political changes in Afghanistan which had an impact on social and economic development including education.

**New Policy**

This policy was adopted by a new generation of royal family members and their advisers, and General Mohammed Daoud, a cousin of the King and a former Minister of Defence, was appointed Prime Minister. This political decision had important consequences for the future of Afghanistan. Bilateral cooperation was developed with the USSR in the training and equipment of the Afghan military, and the social and economic sector including education.

The new government initiated the five-year economic development plan in 1956, which included a systematic planning of education. Afghanistan received technical and financial assistance from a number of countries, including the USA and the USSR for its social and economic development. In 1964 a new Constitution was adopted in Afghanistan, which provided some measure of democratic reform within a constitutional monarchy. The government, headed by a former minister, and mainly composed of technocrats, was made responsible to an elected parliament. Social and economic development planning continued. A new education law, and a law for the development of higher education, were enacted. Attention was given to the development of education at all levels. There was an increased public demand for education, expressed through members of the parliament. As a result of social pressure, secondary schools were established in all districts, in some areas without adequate facilities. Provision was made to admit an increasing number of students to the University of Kabul, particularly from the provinces.

**Primary Education**

Primary education and teacher training programmes expanded with bilateral and multilateral assistance. A number of university faculties were developed in cooperation with the USA, France and Germany. A Polytechnic Institute was established with the assistance of the USSR. In 1973, Mohammed Daoud (who was in retirement) overthrew the monarchy, with the help of leftist parties and officers trained in the USSR, and the Republic of Afghanistan was proclaimed.

A seven-year economic and social development plan was launched in 1976. The government's education policy did not change. Special attention was given to the development of technical and vocational education including agricultural education. Despite economic limitations and technical constraints, successive governments in the 1960s and 1970s gave high priority to the development of education. An important political and social priority was the balanced development of education and the provision of opportunities for students from provincial and rural communities.

As a result of the steady development of education, before the coup d'etat of 1978 and the formation of a communist government in Kabul, the student enrolment in schools and other educational institutions in Afghanistan was over one million. The communist government in Kabul had a political agenda for the transformation of Afghan society Education was considered an important instrument for promoting the communist ideology and its social structure in Afghanistan.

The 'Fundamental Principles of the Democratic Republic of Afghanistan', adopted in 1980, clearly reflected the government's policy on education, which included literacy programmes, the expansion of basic education and the development of vocational training and higher education. The promotion of mother tongues (other than Pashto and Dari) as media of instruction for ethnic minorities was one of the declared priorities. Soviet advisers assisted the government in the reform of the education system.

The structure of education was adapted to be closer to the Soviet education system. The Russian language was introduced in schools with the intention of replacing English as a foreign language. In spite of these measures for the promotion of education, they had little success, as the majority of Afghan people revolted against the communist ideology and resisted foreign domination. As a consequence, the education system, especially outside Kabul and provincial centres, was largely destroyed.

**Islamic State**

With the formation of the Islamic State of Afghanistan in 1992, the first priority was the establishment of security and the consolidation of government institutions. The government had the enormous task of building a national education system, based on the religious, cultural and historical traditions of Afghan society. Programmes and structures reflecting communist ideology and practices were eliminated. Attention was given to the development of basic education for children and young people in primary schools and community centres. While there was no unified national curriculum, religious education constituted an important part of education throughout the country. In rural areas and conservative parts of the country, equal opportunities for boys and girls were not provided.

Since the emergence of the Taliban (Pashtun religious students) in 1995, girls' schools were closed in the areas under their control. As a result of ethnic fighting throughout much of the 1990s, schools and educational institutions in the urban centres have also been damaged. The Afghan values and way of life are based on the Islamic religion and tradition. Religious schools have always been popular in rural communities, which form the bulk of Afghan society.

**Religious Schools**

Religious schools were the main centres of learning, which produced the religious and community leaders. With the development of modern education in Afghanistan, the teaching of religion remained a fundamental part of general education. The Arabic language has been taught in schools to facilitate the reading and understanding of the Holy Quran. Efforts were made to reconcile traditional learning with the requirements of modern life.

In the 1940s subjects such as science and social studies were added to the curriculum of traditional religious schools, which were the main source of teachers for religious education, and incorporated in the formal education system. The development of eduction reflected the Islamic tradition with regard to the education of girls, which was historically conservative and oriented towards home and family life. In 1980s the communist regime modified the traditional and cultural aspects of the school curriculum, reflecting the new government's political and cultural policy. Many people felt that Afghan culture was seriously threatened. Islam has been the basis of Afghan culture and a major unifying principal among all ethnic groups.

The curriculum of primary schools organized by the mujahidin (Islamic resistance parties) for children inside Afghanistan, and for Afghan refugees in Pakistan, included a substantial amount of religious education. The struggle against the communists (jihad) was included in some schools as part of their religious education and training. An important factor in the development of education for Afghan society was its ethnic diversity. The Afghan people consist of Pashtun (38%), Tajik (25%), Hazara (19%), Uzbek (6%), Turkmen, Nuristani and Baluch ethnic groups. During much of the nineteenth and twentieth centuries, the Pashtun people governed the country. Thus the government's social, economic and cultural policies were influenced by the dominance of Pashtun ruling families and tribes.

In the field of education, since 1945 two national languages (Pashto and Dari) were used as the media of instruction in schools, depending on the region where the majority of the inhabitants spoke Pashto or Dari. The second national language was compulsory in all primary and secondary schools from grade four to twelve. Since the 1930s special attention was given to development of Pashto (the language of the Pashtun people) as one of the two official languages in Afghanistan. The Afghan Constitutions reflected the prominence of the Pashto language and the responsibility of governments for its promotion and development.

The other important language in Afghanistan is Dari, which is spoken by the Tajik people and some other ethnic groups. In fact, Dari or ancient Persian, is also spoken in slightly different dialects in other countries in the region including parts of Iran and Tajikistan. Dari is a developed language with a rich, ancient and modern literature, and has been used in the royal courts and governments in Afghanistan. There were two objectives in the promotion and development of Pashto. Firstly, it is the language of the largest ethnic group in Afghanistan and needed to be developed.

Secondly, the governments in Afghanistan felt a national, political and cultural responsibility for the use and development of Pashto, which is also spoken by the Pashtun people in the North West Frontier Province of Pakistan. Other ethnic languages, such as Uzbeki, Turkmeni, Nooristani etc., were not used in education for political (national cohesion) and practical reasons, involving additional resources, the development of textbooks, teacher training etc.

**Communist Regime**

The communist regime in Afghanistan (in the1980s) proposed to use, in addition to Pashto and Dari, other ethnic languages (mother tongues) as the media of instruction in some schools. While the educational value of the mother tongue for children is evident, the new language policy did not succeed, as it was politically motivated, and also required significant logistic (textbooks, teacher training, etc.) and financial resources.

The Arabic language has been used extensively in religious schools. It has also been in the school curriculum, with a view to assisting in religious education. The secondary school curriculum provides for the teaching of a foreign language as a compulsory subject. The most widely taught foreign language in Afghan schools has been English, except for the 1980s, when the Russian language was introduced. French and German were taught in several secondary and vocational schools. The University of Kabul had departments for the study of foreign languages and literature (Arabic, English, French and German).

The teaching of foreign languages played a significant role in the training of Afghan specialists abroad and the development of modern education including the teaching of science and technology in Afghanistan. In the 1960s several faculties of the University of Kabul (medicine, science, engineering, economics, law and education) were developed in cooperation with the USA, France and Germany. The Kabul Polytechnic Institute was established with the assistance of the USSR. The cooperating countries provided expertise and equipment and trained the Afghan counterparts.

These Afghan institutions of higher education applied the standards, curricula and structures of the cooperating countries, adapted to the educational and training objectives and possibilities of Afghanistan. English, French, German and Russian textbooks and literature were used in the corresponding faculties. This cooperation, which was beneficial and enriching for the development of Afghan higher education, had cultural and political implications. The higher education institutions in Afghanistan needed foreign technical assistance, and were unable to promote and develop a purely national system of higher education. Experience showed that the cultural influence of this policy was very significant, as it contributed to the diffusion of diverse ideologies and the subsequent polarization of Afghan society.

Social structures and tradition as well as economic limitations have influenced the pace of educational development in Afghanistan. The staunchly conservative people in the rural areas, where eighty-five per cent of the population lived, were not interested in, and in some areas were opposed to, modern education during the first half of twentieth century.

These people desired a traditional education for their children, largely based on Islamic religion and ethics with some skills in literacy and numeracy. Except for mosques, there were no other community institutions for the promotion of education. There were informal tribal and community councils, generally conducted by tribal or religious leaders, to discuss security matters or social and economic (agriculture) affairs and to deal with local governmental authorities. The objective was to continue the traditional structures and way of life and protect tribal and community interests.

The situation changed in the 1940s when a few schools were established in provincial centres. Modern schooling was gradually introduced in some parts of Afghanistan, but the pace of development was slower in the south and eastern parts of the country among the Pashtun tribes. In both rural communities and provincial towns, in some parts of the country, there were serious reservations and opposition to the education of girls in the 1940s. With an estimated population of about eleven million people in Afghanistan in 1950, there were 90,640 boys and only 4,350 girls (five per cent) in primary and secondary schools.

## Girl's Education

The first girls' school was established in Kabul in 1932. Ten years later (1941), the first provincial girls' school was established in Kandahar. In 1940, the female school enrolment in the country was 900. By 1970, there were 92,500 female students in 231 village schools, 166 primary schools, 46 middle schools and 16 lycees throughout Afghanistan. An additional 1,860 female students were enrolled in vocational education, teacher training and higher education institutions. The enrolment of girls constituted fourteen per cent of the school enrolment in the country. Coeducation in primary schools was introduced in the late 1950s. Secondary education for girls and boys was organized in separate schools. A Women's Faculty with scientific and literary departments was established at the University of Kabul in 1947.

In 1958 under the Prime Minister Mohammed Daoud, measures were taken to facilitate gradually the participation of women in the social, economic and cultural life of Afghan society. This policy had important consequences for the development of education for girls and women. In 1960, the Women's Faculty was integrated in the corresponding university faculties and coeducation at the higher education level was established.

In the 1960s several Afghan women were elected to Parliament and served in the government. An increasing number of girls and women chose the teaching profession and contributed to the expansion of education in the country. The promotion of girls' education continued through out the 1970s and 1980s. The policy of the mujahideen (in the 1990s) towards the education of girls and women has been conservative and restrictive, not only in relation to the progress of the previous decades but also in comparison with other Muslim countries. This policy and practice have adversely affected the schooling of girls, particularly in rural communities. The mujahidin government did not send a delegation to the fourth World Conference on Women, which was held in Beijing in 1995. Since 1995, the Taliban (Pashtun religious students) closed girls' schools in areas under their control. The most important factor hindering the development of education in Afghanistan was the technical and financial limitation and overall economic situation.

Afghanistan is a landlocked country (with an estimated population of 12.3 million in 1960, 20.8 million in 1990, including 4.7 million Afghan refugees in Pakistan and Iran, 24.5 million in 2000 including 2.6 million refugees), with mainly an agricultural economy and unexploited natural resources. The GDP per capita increased from US $60 in 1960 to US $160 in 1976 (estimated at US $600 in 1995). The gross domestic product in Afghanistan increased from 12.5 billion Afghanis in 1953 to 90.0 billion in 1976.

The expenditure on education constituted about ten per cent of the national budget. For purposes of economic assistance, the United Nations placed Afghanistan in the 1960s among the twenty-five least developed countries. Social and economic development planning in Afghanistan began in 1956, and continued until 1978, when the country was plunged into a tragic war and the consequent destruction of its social and economic infrastructure, including two thirds of all schools. In view of the limitation of resources and different priorities for development, the Afghan governments could not accelerate the development of education.

**State and Education**

According to the Afghan Constitutions education was the responsibility of the state and it was provided free from primary school to the university. The great majority of the public did not have the means to participate in the cost of education (the annual public contribution to the building of community schools was of the order of two to three per cent of the education budget). The economic development priorities of the country (transport and communication infrastructure, mining, industrial and energy sectors, and the modernization of agriculture) required trained manpower, which necessitated more investment in secondary, vocational and higher education than primary education.

Consequently, the development plans for the expansion of primary education were limited because of economic and technical constraints such as teacher training. Following the Second World War and the establishment of the United Nations, the promotion of social, economic and cultural development became a priority of international cooperation. The Declaration of Universal Human Rights, adopted by the General Assembly of the United Nations in 1948, recognized education as a human right.

UNESCO was created in 1946 and Afghanistan joined it one year later. Ever since UNESCO has promoted educational development worldwide, particularly in the developing countries. It has also adopted a Convention Against Discrimination in Education, based on nationality, race, colour, religion or sex, as well as other international instruments for the promotion of basic education, technical and vocational education and higher education. Afghan officials and specialists participated in UNESCO conferences and technical meetings dealing with the policy, planning and development of education. The international and regional meetings facilitated the exchange of information and experiences and the formulation of appropriate policies, norms and methods for the development of education. The intellectual and promotional work of UNESCO has influenced educational policy and development in Afghanistan. In the 1960s the United Nations Development Programme and the World Bank recognized the relation between investment in education and economic growth. Thus the international organizations provided increased technical and financial assistance for the development of education. The first UNESCO mission was invited to study Afghan education in 1949.

Over the years a number of educational projects, particularly in primary and basic education, teacher training and educational planning, were developed in Afghanistan with the technical assistance of UNESCO, and other international organizations such as UNDP and UNICEF.

The focus of UNESCO in Afghanistan has been mainly in the area of primary education, including the education of girls, with a view to the promotion of the right to education and the achievement of universal compulsory education. Neutral Afghanistan appreciated the increasing role of the United Nations system in developmental activities including education. A very important contribution of UNESCO to the development of education in Afghanistan has been in the area of teacher education.

**School Teacher's Academy**

In 1964, new structures for teacher training, including an Academy for the Training of Teacher Educators were established in Kabul. The Academy was the first postgraduate institution of teacher education in Afghanistan, which trained teacher educators for the primary teacher training colleges which were being established throughout the country. In the 1990s, UNESCO assisted in the establishment of a number of basic education centres in rural areas with the support of the communities concerned.

A new concept of basic education, decentralized and community-based, which offered flexible and functional programmes for young people and adults, was introduced in

Afghanistan. The non-governmental organizations (mainly from Europe and the USA) played a significant role in promoting and supporting education in Afghanistan during the last two decades of conflict, particularly in rural communities. In the context of bilateral economic and cultural cooperation, the Afghan education system received assistance from many countries in the form of advisory services, technical and financial support and fellowships.

In terms of the impact on orientation and the development of modern education in Afghanistan, cooperation with Turkey, France, Germany, the USA and the USSR was significant. Turkey had a historical role in the initial development of medical education in Afghanistan. France and Germany were involved from the 1920s in secondary education (especially in two lycees in Kabul), the teaching of French and German, and the development of higher education. Germany has also assisted in the development of mechanical and crafts schools and an institute of industrial management. The USA cooperated with the Ministry of Education and the University of Kabul between 1954 and 1978 in curriculum development, the teaching of English, teacher education, technical, agricultural and engineering education. The USSR assisted from the late 1960s in the development of a Polytechnic and a number of Technicums. Egypt cooperated with the Faculty of Islamic Studies, and religious schools. In addition to bilateral support for the development of higher education in Afghanistan, during the period 1950 - 1980 many hundreds of Afghan students were trained as specialists at universities in Europe, the USA, the USSR and other countries such as Egypt and India. These specialists contributed to the social and economic development of Afghanistan.

In 1960, UNESCO conference on Primary Education, taking into account the economic conditions of member states and population growth, recommended that the developing countries in Asia should be able to achieve seven years of universal compulsory primary education by 1980. This plan was revised in 1962 in a conference held in Tokyo, since several Asian countries, including Afghanistan, could not hope to reach the targets of the Karachi Plan before 1990. In 1964 a team of UNESCO specialists studied the long term projection of educational development in Afghanistan, and concluded that by 1980, the enrolment ratio for six years of primary education (seven to twelve years age) would be between a minimum of thirty-seven per cent and a maximum of fifty-seven per cent, and that universal compulsory primary education could not be achieved before the end of the century. The actual enrolment ratio for primary education attained in 1980 was thirty-six per cent. The war and destruction of the last two decades of the century was a major set-back for education in Afghanistan. The enrolment ratio for primary education in 2000 is estimated to be thirty per cent. Adult illiteracy has been a major problem in Afghan society. The teaching of literacy has a history going back to 1906 when an Afghan educator developed a method and six books including a teacher's guide.

**The Communist Regime**

In the 1980s, the communist regime in Kabul made adult literacy a high priority with the establishment of a National Commission, headed by the Prime Minister, and increased resources. However, due to the political nature of the literacy campaign and fighting in the country, the objectives could not be attained. In 1985 according to UNDP sources the average literacy rate was estimated at twenty-one per cent. Adult literacy at the end of the decade (2000) is estimated between twenty and thirty per cent. Despite the constraints, there was progress in the expansion of education. Between 1950 and 1978, the student enrolment in different types and levels of education increased from 96,000 to 1,037,800, a tenfold increase.

Female enrolment during the same period increased from less than 5,000 to 167,120, representing a thirty-threefold increase. There were 6,000 students in eighteen technical and vocational schools; 5,400 students in sixteen teacher training institutions; and 16,000 students enrolled in higher education. This rate of increase was comparable to the development of education in some other countries in the Asian region. There were also efforts to improve the quality of education. A modern European curriculum, adapted to Afghan society, was applied in secondary schools. The education system was diversified, and a number of innovative projects, involving international cooperation in the field of teacher education, technical and vocational education and higher education, were initiated. In the 1980s Afghan society suffered great human and material losses as well as major demographic modification. In a UNDP document the devastation of Afghan society was described as follows: "War has killed at least a million people, maimed and disabled many more, created an army of orphans and widows, turned half the population into internally displaced persons and refugees, including six million outside the country". The continuation of ethnic conflict and fighting in the 1990s resulted in more destruction and the displacement of the population.

At the end of the century there were still 2.6 million Afghan refugees in Iran and Pakistan, and several hundred thousand Afghans in Europe, the USA and other parts of the world. During the last two decades of the twentieth century much of the education infrastructure was destroyed, and the country did not have a unified curriculum or a national education system.

The majority of educated Afghans, including university professors, doctors, engineers and other specialists left the country in the 1980s. In the year 2000 about thirty per cent of Afghan children were enrolled in primary education. The education of girls decreased during the 1990s. In the absence of a national education system, the international and Afghan non-governmental organizations contributed to the provision of basic education for children, particularly in rural areas with the support and participation of local communities. The most profound impact of the tragic war in Afghanistan has been on Afghan children and youth and on the social, cultural and political evolution of the country. The children who were born during the last twenty years in Afghanistan, and in the refugee camps of Pakistan and Iran, and who were lucky to survive, faced much suffering and hardship.

The great majority of these children and young people did not have proper food and shelter or any schooling. Some of the children, who were able to have a basic education, went to a variety of schools run by different Afghan and foreign authorities and organizations. The curricula of these schools have been diverse and limited, without unifying national and cultural objectives for Afghan society. The schools run by the mujahidin inside Afghanistan and in the refugee camps emphasized traditional and religious education, as a reaction against communist ideology.

During the Islamic period, many centres and circles of learning were established in cities such as Balkh, Herat and Ghazni, which produced scholars in philosophy, literature and science to serve the people of the region and beyond. The medical treatise, written by Ibn-Sina Balkhi (Avicenna) in the tenth century, was used in European universities until the end of nineteenth century. Abu Rayhan Biruni (tenth century), Hakim Sanai (eleventh centu-ry), Khwaja Abdullah Ansari and Maulana Jalaludin Roumi (thirteenth century), and Kushal Khan Khattak and Rahman Baba (seventeenth century), were Afghan poets and philosophers who enriched human thought and civilization.

Said Jamaludin Afghani, a political philosopher of the nineteenth century who had many disciples, travelled in Asia, Africa and Europe to promote national independence and Islamic solidarity, and to explain the relation between Islam, science and progress. Traditional education for children and young people at different levels was provided at home, in the mosques, in informal schools linked to mosques, in religious centres (madrassa) and in scholar's circles. These institutions were supported by parents, local communities, religious and tribal leaders and private sources. The madrassa provided general knowledge and theological studies for young men, and prepared religious guides and teachers.

Some opportunities for studies in writing, poetry and literature, history, science and traditional medicine, etc., were available through private tutoring and in small informal circles The mosque and related schools served as basic community centres in which pupils could study the Holy Qur'an, learn about Islamic values and ethics, and acquire literacy and numeracy. Traditional education also helped to prepare young people (mainly boys) for work through informal apprenticeship in local arts and crafts, farming and commerce. This was the pattern of education and training prevailing in Afghanistan at the beginning of the twentieth century.

The beginning of modern education (western style) in the

country may be considered to correspond to the establishment of the first secondary school (Habibia) in Kabul in 1903, with the aim of training personnel for the civil service. Afghan and foreign teachers (Indian Muslims) were recruited for this school. In the early years of the 1900s several modern primary schools and a teacher training institution were established. In 1909 the government set up a Board of Education to approve the school curriculum and textbooks, and supervise education, including traditional educational institutions.

Following the independence of Afghanistan in 1919, during the reign of King Amanullah, social and political conditions became favourable for initiating the development of modern education in Afghanistan. The government gave high priority to the development of education and a Minister of Education was appointed for the first time in 1922. During the 1920s, a number of primary and secondary schools (Istiqlal, Amania, Ghazi) including a secondary school for girls and an adult education centre for women as well as several vocational schools (agriculture, art and crafts, and public administration) were established in Kabul. For the first time, a group of young Afghan boys and girls was sent to study abroad. The establishment of diplomatic and cultural relations with foreign countries contributed to the development of modern education. Through bilateral cooperation with countries such as Turkey, France and Germany, foreign teachers and expertise and scholarships for Afghan students were made available to Afghanistan. In January 1929 there was a set-back in the development of education due to the departure of King Amanullah, followed by nine months of civil strife and anarchy (under Habibullah Kalakani) during which the modern schools were closed.

Later that year Nader Shah became king of Afghanistan, schools were reopened and attention was given to the development of education. In 1930 there were 1,590 students and 53 teachers in thirteen primary and secondary schools. In 1931 a new Constitution was promulgated in which reference was made to compulsory primary education for Afghan children with the government responsible for the control and supervision of all educational institutions except those carrying on traditional education. After the assassination of Nader Shah in 1933, and the beginning of the reign of Zaher Shah and the royal family, there was a limited expansion of education, and special attention was given to the development of Pashto as one of the two main national languages of Afghanistan.

During the 1930s, a number of secondary schools were established in the provinces, and several traditional religious schools were modernized and incorporated into the formal education structure. A secondary school for girls was established in Kabul. Two secondary vocational schools (mechanical and agriculture) and a medical school for the training of assistant doctors and pharmacists were established in Kabul. In 1932, the nucleus of a Faculty of Medicine (the first modern institution of higher education) was set up in Kabul with the assistance of Turkish medical advisers and several Afghan doctors who were trained abroad. The Faculty of Medicine graduated the first group of eight intern doctors and twelve pharmacists in 1937. With a view to social and economic development of Afghanistan, and in the absence of facilities for higher education in the country, in 1938, the government sent a group of about twenty-five secondary school graduates to universities in France, Germany and the USA in different fields. During the period of the Second World War (1939-1944), in which Afghanistan maintained its neutrality, the pace of development of education in Afghanistan slowed down owing to economic and technical constraints.

Several foreign experts and teachers left the country. The needed machinery, equipment and teaching materials for schools and training institutions could not be imported. In 1950, there were 95,300 students (including 4,350 girls) and some 3,000 teachers in 368 schools, which consisted of 308 primary schools, twenty-five middle schools, sixteen secondary schools, four vocational schools, one teacher training school and seven formal religious schools (madrassa). There were 456 students including forty female students in five institutions of higher education. The enrolment of children in primary education in 1950 represented six per cent of the corresponding age group (six to twelve years) in an estimated population of eleven million people.

**Systematic Planning**

The systematic planning of education in Afghanistan began in 1956. In the early 1950s, efforts to expand education and improve its quality were initiated. In 1954, under contract with the Unites States Agency for International Development (USAID), a team of specialists from Columbia University, New York came to assist in the qualitative improvement of teacher education.

The first five-year educational development plan (1956-1961) focused on primary education. In view of the country's need for trained manpower, the second plan (1962-1967) placed more emphasis on secondary, technical and higher education. The third five-year development plan (1968-1973), envisaged a balanced expansion of education at all levels with special attention to the qualitative improvement of teacher education. While primary education expanded according to the plan, the growth in secondary education was faster, due to public demand, especially in the provinces. In 1973, following a coup d'etat, Afghanistan was proclaimed a Republic and Mohammad Daoud (a former Prime Minister and a cousin of King Zaher Shah) became the Head of State.

The Republic launched the first seven-year economic and social development plan to accelerate economic growth through industrial development and the modernization of agriculture. The development of human resources including technical and vocational education was a priority in the seven-year plan, which was interrupted in 1978 due to a coup d'etat and a change of regime. The economic development plans were financed from internal resources and external technical assistance funds and loans. In the first five-year development plan, 6.5 per cent of the national budget was devoted to social services including education, in which the share of education was 958 million afghanis (Afs.). During the second development plan (1962-1967), the share of the national budget for social services was increased to 11.2 per cent. However, the resources for capital investment in education (for buildings and equipment) fell short of the expected budget. The resources for education development in the second plan amounted to 1,759 million Afs. The third five year development plan (1968-1973), allocated 16.7 per cent of the total budget to social services in which the share of education was estimated to be over 3,000 million Afs.

The first seven-year socio-economic development plan, which was not completed due to the revolution of 1978 and its consequences, envisaged a total investment of 10.5 billion Afs. in social services, which included 3.5 billion Afs. for education. It should be pointed out that there were a number of factors hindering the development of education in Afghanistan. Like many other developing countries, it had basically an agricultural economy and about eighty-five per cent of the population lived in rural areas; with an estimated population of 12.3 million in 1960, the GDP per capita was US$60. Hence, there were technical and financial constraints for the expansion of education. There were also cultural and linguistic factors affecting educational development. Textbooks and educational materials had to be prepared in the two national languages. In some parts of the country, people were happy with the traditional Islamic education for their children, especially for girls.

**Public Education in Afghanistan**

The concept of modern public education in Afghanistan emerged in the 1920s, following independence. In 1931 a Constitution was promulgated in which primary education was made compulsory for all Afghan children, and the government was responsible for the control and supervision of all schools and educational institutions. A new Constitution was promulgated in 1948, in which primary education was made compulsory for every boy and girl, and the state reserved the right and responsibility for the administration of all education and training from the primary school to the university.

In 1964, a certain democratic reform was introduced in the political system of Afghanistan in the context of a constitutional monarchy. A new Constitution was promulgated, which provided for the separation of the legislative, executive and judicial branches of the government. Article 35 of the Constitution referred to education as the right of every Afghan citizen, which should be provided free by the government. In accordance with the new Constitution, the following Education Law was prepared which provided the basis for education policy during the 1960s and 1970s.

Following the establishment of the Republic of Afghanistan (1973), a new Constitution was promulgated in 1976, whose fundamental objective concerning education was stated as follows: provision of public compulsory primary education; development of free general secondary, vocational and higher education for the training of scientific and technical personnel, with the aim of serving the people. Except for the "loyalty to the Crown", the Republic of Afghanistan followed the provisions of the Education Law, which was prepared in 1964, until the takeover of the government by the communist regime in 1978, and the formation of the Democratic Republic of Afghanistan (DRA).

The Ministry of Education has been responsible for policy formulation, the organization and supervision of education. The administration of education in the provinces was carried out, according to national curricula, standards and regulations, by Directors of Education who were responsible to the ministry of education. The position of the Minister of Education in Afghanistan has always been important and politically sensitive. The Ministers of Education from 1922 to the late 1940s were prominent personalities close to the Crown.

In 1964 a Department for Educational Planning was organized. In 1966 teacher training became a separate department. In the 1960s, the central services for physical education and sport, school health programmes, administration and the employment of personnel were strengthened. In the mid-1960s the organization of the Ministry of Education was fully developed and remained practically unchanged until 1978. The departments of primary, secondary, vocational and teacher education established the curricula and standards. The instructional departments in the Ministry of Education controlled national examinations leading to a certificate. The Department of Compilation developed textbooks for primary and secondary schools. Specialized textbooks and teaching materials for vocational and teacher training institutions were prepared by the relevant instructional departments of the ministry and the Institute of Education.

The department of inspection was responsible for the

administrative inspection of schools in Kabul and the provinces. The provincial Directors of Education were responsible for the application of national curricula and the standards and management of education in the provinces. Educational supervision was carried out by provincial supervisors in coordination with the relevant departments in the Ministry of Education. The school year was organized according to the climate of the region. Generally the schools in the eastern and southern provinces were closed during the summer, whereas schools in other regions, including Kabul, with severe winters had a three-month holiday in the months of December to February.

The administration of higher education was carried out by the respective institutions themselves, under the supervision of the President of the University. The University President was directly responsible to the Minister of Education. The institutions of higher education (faculties) enjoyed academic freedom, and were responsible for their curricula, standards and examinations. In 1968 the government enacted a law for the administration and development of universities. According to the provision of this law, a Board of Trustees was established to "maintain, regulate and coordinate higher education designed to meet the social, economic and cultural needs of the country as determined by the Government".

In 1970 there were 18,060 teachers in the ministry schools, of whom forty-eight per cent had secondary, post-secondary or university education and professional training. The number of administrative and clerical staff in the education system was 4,300, of whom only thirteen per cent had secondary education or higher. The financing of education has been a major constraint for the qualitative and quantitative development of education in Afghanistan.

According to the law, education from primary school to the university was free, and was financed from government sources, which included some international aid. Public participation in educational expenditure was very limited. In addition to human resources, the provision of school buildings and other facilities, such as textbooks and laboratory equipment, were a continuing preoccupation of the Ministry of Education.

The Ministry of Education did not have the resources or the technical capacity to construct new school buildings to meet the expanding needs of the education system. Most schools were operating in double shifts. In 1970, from a total of 3,046 primary and village schools about twenty-five per cent did not have adequate school buildings and were operating in mosques or rented private houses.

At the secondary level, thirty-two per cent of a total of 541 schools did not have properly constructed buildings. It should be mentioned that 971 schools (village, primary and secondary), representing forty-three percent of all school buildings, were constructed with voluntary contributions and the participation of the communities concerned. The problem of school construction was particularly acute in the provinces, due to the inadequacy of funds (budget) and the technical limitations of the public works offices responsible for the construction of schools in the provinces.

The building of physical facilities for vocational and teacher training institutions in Kabul and the provinces, which had relatively higher priority for funding, including international aid, was carried out under the supervision of the construction department of the Ministry of Education.

**Modern Primary Education**

Modern primary education in Afghanistan did not develop until the 1950s and the beginnings of five-year education development plans. According to the studies carried out in the 1960s, it was projected that Afghanistan might achieve universal primary education by the end of the century. However, due to technical and financial constraints the expected rate of growth in primary education could not be attained. In 1975 there were 789,000 boys and girls (thirty per cent) in primary education, which represented twenty-five per cent of the compulsory school age population (7-14 years).

The principal aims of primary education are the development of children's talents and the instilling of desirable skills, values and habits in order to achieve the following objectives:

— Achievement of literacy and the essential general knowledge for living.

- Maintenance of the physical, mental and spiritual health of the pupil.
- Development of a desirable social personality.
- Acquisition of ability for useful and effective participation in the life of the family, the school, the community and the nation.
- Development of the pupil in order to be adherent to Islamic principles. Development of the pupil in order to be faithful to the constitutional monarchy and other positive Afghan traditions and national and universal aims.

From the 1960s there was co-education in some primary schools. Due to the limitation of facilities, most primary schools operated in two shifts. The average class size was about forty. There was an examination at the end of each year (in 1974 automatic promotion was experimented within the first three grades). At the end of the sixth year there was an examination controlled by Directors of Education, leading to a certificate of primary education. Village schools (grades one to three) were first established in 1949; these schools were organized generally in the mosques in thinly populated areas, which were about five kilometres away from the nearest primary school. The availability of a minimum of ten children was required to begin the first class.

The curriculum of the village school was community and work-oriented and consisted of religion, language and arithmetic. Three textbooks were prepared, one for each grade which were supplemented by texts for religious studies; the multi-grade class was taught by one teacher who was a local traditional scholar or imam (Islamic clergyman) in a mosque. Some of the village schools were upgraded to basic primary schools. With the addition of the fourth grade in a village school, a second teacher was appointed.

Children completing village schools, which were not upgraded to a primary school, could enter a primary school or join practical work activities on the farm or in a local craft. The traditional type of private tuition and mosque schools continued to remain as one form of informal educational institution in some areas of the country where formal schooling was not available.

The emphasis in private tuition has been on religious studies, literacy and numeracy. Pupils from these informal schools were accepted, on passing an examination, in an appropriate level of basic primary school, or in one of the formal religious schools.

The department of primary education prescribed the curriculum of primary schools. The syllabus and textbooks were uniform throughout the country, except for the language of instruction which was Pashto in the regions where the majority of inhabitants were Pashto speaking, and Dari in Dari-speaking areas. Schools were allowed to adapt the content of certain subjects such as general knowledge and science to the local and community situation.

**Secondary Education**

Before 1950, there were seventeen secondary schools (lycees) in Afghanistan: six in Kabul including two secondary schools for girls (Malalai and Zerghoona); three in Kandahar including one lycee for girls (Zarghoona Anna); two in Balkh including one lycee for girls (Sultana Razia); one each in Herat, Laghman, Paktia, Parwan, Baghlan and Kunduz. In 1950 the student enrolment in secondary schools was about 3,000. In 1970 there were 133 secondary schools with a total enrolment of 25,910 male and female students in grades ten to twelve. There was a relatively significant expansion of secondary education in the 1960s.

In the context of a new Constitution and a more democratic form of government in the 1960s, there was considerable public demand (through their elected representatives in the parliament) for the expansion of education, particularly at the secondary level, which was the basis for further education and training in the university. The public demand led to the faster development of secondary education. With the rapid expansion of secondary education, the quality of education with regard to the availability of trained teachers, especially in science and mathematics, laboratory equipment and facilities, particularly in the provinces, was affected.

The principle aims of secondary education are stated in the following objectives of pupil's growth:

- Maintenance of the physical, mental and spiritual health of the pupil.
- Development of a desirable social personality.
- Acquisition of ability for useful and effective participation in the life of the family, the school, the community and the nation.
- Acquisition of basic knowledge in sciences and continuation of education at a higher level.
- Development of the pupil in Islamic principles.
- Development of the pupil to be faithful to constitutional monarchy.
- Inculcation of respect for national and universal aims.

Secondary schools were organized in two cycles of grades seven to nine (middle school) and grades ten to twelve (lycee) in separate schools for boys and girls. The reform of education in 1975 had modified the structure of education to basic education (grades one to eight) and secondary education (grades nine to twelve). The admission of students to the middle school and lycee was based on the successful completion of the lower cycle of education and passing the entrance examination of the school concerned.

While the curriculum of middle schools was uniform throughout the country, there was some experimentation in selected schools in the organization of teaching certain subjects such as geography and history as social studies, and chemistry, physics and biology as general science. The curriculum prescribed simple laboratory facilities for demonstration in the middle schools.

However, not all schools were equipped with laboratory facilities for science teaching. A foreign language (mainly English) was prescribed from the beginning of the middle school, and textbooks were developed by the Institute of Education, but there was a shortage of trained teachers. The curriculum of lycees (grades ten to twelve) offered more courses in languages, social studies, science and mathematics with the aim of preparing students for higher education.

Laboratory facilities were generally provided for demonstration and group work. However, not all secondary schools had the necessary facilities and trained teachers. In large secondary schools, departments were organized to coordinate and supervise the teaching of science, social studies, languages, etc. There was no significant difference in the curriculum of boys and girls in secondary education, except for the provision of one to two periods per week of home economics in girls schools.

Examinations were an important part of the school system to measure the achievement of pupils. In addition to teachers, principals and other education authorities were involved in the supervision of secondary school examinations. There was also the possibility of participating in the boys' and girls' scouting activities and the junior Red Crescent societies.

**Technical and Vocational Education**

Modern vocational schools in Afghanistan were developed after the Second World War. In 1975, the enrolment in vocational schools was 6,000 students including 650 girls. Most of the vocational schools made provision for day students as well as residential facilities for boarding students, who were selected from graduates of those schools which were located a certain distance away from the vocational school.

The Afghan Women's Institute offered vocational training for adult women. According to the law, the Ministry of Education was responsible for the approval of the programme and the certification of all vocational schools in the country. Technical and vocational education in Afghanistan was developed with external bilateral and multilateral technical assistance, particularly from Germany, the USA, the USSR and the United Nations.

Vocational training schools did not have the desired social prestige, and attracted those students who could not continue their studies in secondary education. Furthermore, technical and vocational training programmes were generally terminal, and only a small portion of the graduates who had completed, in addition to technical and vocational training, the equivalent of general secondary education, could continue to higher education in their specialized fields.

The initial capital and operating costs of vocational training were high because most of the materials and equipment had to be imported; foreign experts and teachers were needed, who were provided mainly under bilateral technical assistance programmes. While trained Afghans replaced many of the foreign teachers, the machinery and equipment and materials continued to be imported. There was little participation in the training or operating costs of the schools by industry or other employers of the graduates. The use of different systems and expertise, and the lack of teaching materials in the national languages were affecting the standards and efficiency of technical and vocational training programme

**The Curriculum**

The curriculum and organization of training for each type of vocational school was established according to the objectives and level of training and educational background of the trainees. In secondary level training (technicians), consideration was also given in the curriculum to the basic requirements of higher education, to allow a certain percentage of the graduates to continue post-secondary and university education. While the curricula of vocational schools varied, there were some common elements in the core curricula and organization of vocational training. The academic year in vocational schools was organized in two semesters. The average number of weekly periods in vocational schools was forty to forty-five, as compared with thirty-six periods per week in general secondary schools.

Basic science and mathematics were emphasized in the curriculum of technician training programmes. As in general secondary education, a foreign language was required; in some cases the teaching of the foreign language was more intensive in vocational schools, because many of the vocational texts and references were only available in that language. Thus the mechanical and craft schools and the Institute for Industrial Management taught German as a foreign language; the technical secondary school in Kabul (AIT), agricultural schools, the business and administration schools required English; and the two Technicums taught Russian as a foreign language. This arrangement also facilitated the further training of selected graduates of these institutions abroad.

Practical training was organized in one or more of the following ways: training in the school workshop or experimental farm concurrent with class work; block time allocated for training in the workshop or industry, or on an experimental farm; practical training in industries or agricultural extension programmes during school vacations (on-the-job training).

**Teacher Education**

The first teacher training school was set up in Kabul, in which about one hundred young men with the equivalent of primary education were admitted. They graduated four years later as teachers. The school gradually developed in terms of programme and facilities and trained the required teachers. In 1939 a new building with a capacity of one thousand students was constructed in Kabul for the basic teacher training school. With the beginning of the expansion of education in the early 1950s, special attention was given to teacher education as an important prerequisite for the development of education in the country.

In 1954, a team of specialists from the Teachers' College, Columbia University, New York, came to Afghanistan, under a technical assistance programme with the United States, to advise the Ministry of Education on the development of teacher education. A number of seminars were organized to study the problems and issues related to the development of teacher education in the country. The first such national seminar involving provincial Directors of Education and responsible officials of the Ministry of Education was organized in Kandahar, which made important recommendations for the development of teacher education. In 1956, in addition to improvements in the Kabul teacher training school, three new teacher training schools were established in the provinces.

The Institute of Education, that was established in 1955, provided professional support for teacher training programmes. In 1962 the Faculty of Education was established at the University. In the mid-1960s, the national teacher education system was reinforced in terms of new structures and programmes (the Academy for Teacher Educators and the Higher Teachers' College), through a multilateral technical assistance project provided by UNESCO, UNDP and UNICEF.

In 1967 a separate department of teacher education was established in the Ministry of Education to supervise all non-university teacher training institutions and programmes, and conduct in-service training courses for teachers. Teaching was always a respected profession in Afghan society. In villages teachers were expected to set moral and ethical standards, and were treated as community leaders. In general teacher-training institutions attracted students of good educational standards (average or higher). With the expansion of education in the 1950s, the government took a number of measures to promote and encourage the teaching profession. Teachers were civil servants who had job security and other favourable employment conditions.

For the same civil service ranks, teachers had higher salaries (up to twenty-five per cent) compared with other branches of the civil service. As long as a teacher performed satisfactorily, his or her promotion was assured up to the top civil service ranks (no administrative constraints). Teachers could choose to stay in teaching for six years with full salary, in lieu of one or two years of military service (compulsory conscription). To honour the teaching profession, a day was officially designated as Teachers' Day, which was celebrated annually.

Teachers were trained in teacher training institutions, supervised by the Ministry of Education, and at the university mainly for teaching in secondary schools. The admission requirements, duration of study and curriculum, depended on the type and level of the school (village, primary, middle or secondary) and the subject and method of teaching concerned. The standards that were applied, as far as possible, were the following: in village schools one teacher was responsible for grades one to three; in primary schools, there were class teachers for each grade one to three and teachers with focus on language and social studies, arithmetic, science and practical work in grades four to six; in lower secondary or middle level (grades seven to nine), there were teachers for national languages (Pashto and Dari), including a foreign language, science and mathematics, history and geography.

Teachers of upper secondary classes (grades ten to twelve) were subject specialists in national languages and literature, foreign language, science (physics/mathematics or chemistry/ biology), social studies (history/geography), home economics, etc. The faculty of theological studies and a number of secondary level theological schools in Kabul and provinces trained teachers for religion, Arabic and ethics. Teachers for sports were trained at the physical education school. Teachers for post-secondary and higher education were university graduates with advanced education and training in foreign universities in scientific and technological fields, social studies, economics, law, education, etc.

Technical and vocational education teachers were trained at the faculties of engineering and agriculture, Polytechnic Institute, secondary technical teacher training institute and the art school. As most of the technical and vocational institutions were developed with foreign technical assistance, the training of key teaching and supervisory personnel was an important component of these projects. In the field of teacher education, a significant number of teachers, administrators and curriculum specialists received advanced training in foreign universities in the context of the USAID technical assistance, or the United Nations' fellowship programme.

A number of teachers and supervisors of three secondary schools in Kabul (Istiqlal, Malalai and Nejat) were trained through scholarships in France and Germany. The organization of teacher training was adapted to the situation in Afghanistan and evolved with experience as well as the availability of human and material resources.

Teachers for middle schools were trained in a section of the basic teacher training schools until the mid-1960s. In 1964, the Higher Teachers' College (grades thirteen to fourteen) was established in Kabul to train teachers for the middle school. This was a coeducational post-secondary institution which admitted graduates of secondary schools and trained them for two years with specialization in science and mathematics or humanities (languages and social studies). A certain percentage of graduates from primary teacher training institutions could also continue their studies in the Higher Teachers' College. By 1975, in addition to the College in Kabul, four other Higher Teachers' Colleges were established in Kandahar, Balkh, Nangarhar and Herat. These five colleges graduated about four hundred teachers annually for middle schools.

**Kabul University**

The University of Kabul trained teachers for lycees

(grades ten to twelve). The following faculties were primarily concerned with teacher training : Faculty of Science, Faculty of Letters and Humanities, and Faculty of Education. These were co-educational institutions with four year programmes leading to a University Degree equivalent to B.A. or B.Sc.

The Faculty of Science trained teachers with specialization in physics and mathematics or biology and chemistry. The Faculty of Letters trained teachers with a focus on philosophy and languages or history and geography. Until the 1960s the programme of the Faculties of Science and Letters did not include any professional training for teachers. With the establishment of the Faculty of Education, special pedagogical courses were given to the students of other faculties. Teachers for English language, art and home economics and supervisors for different subject areas were trained by the Faculty of Education. With the expansion of teacher training institutions in the 1960s, the provision of qualified staff for these institutions became an important consideration.

For this purpose the Academy for Teacher Educators was established in Kabul to train university graduates with teaching experience for one to two years. This was a co-educational institution that offered studies in the theory and practice of education as well as in the methodology of teacher training. By 1970, the Academy had trained 160 teacher educators, who were assigned to the newly established teacher training institutions. The Faculty of Education also trained teachers for professional subjects in teacher education. The curriculum of the first teacher training school was prescribed by Afghan scholars and teachers, based on the experience of other countries including Turkey.

The Ministry of Education gave high priority to teacher training institutions in terms of the quality of teaching and supervisory staff, as well as physical facilities including laboratories and experimental schools. There was a balance in the curriculum for general education, education theory and professional training including practice teaching.

In view of the cost of higher education (which was free) and the limitation of physical and material resources, special attention was given to adjust the training to the social and economic requirements of the country. Certain faculties such as

Medicine and Law attracted the majority of secondary school graduates. The teacher-training faculties were less popular. It was decided to set enrolment targets for each faculty in the context of the five-year economic development plans. Beginning in 1966 the university introduced an entrance examination.

Admission to the university was regulated by the entrance examination, which took into account the abilities and wishes of the students and the academic requirements and enrolment quota of each faculty. Provision was made for differences in the standards of secondary schools in the provinces. The University of Kabul had full autonomy for its academic affairs. Each faculty established its curriculum and courses for different specializations and the professors were responsible for the content of courses and the evaluation of students. The teaching methods and organization of courses reflected the background and experience of each faculty member. The curriculum and organization of teaching in the Faculties of Medicine, Science, Economics, Engineering, Agriculture, Education and the Polytechnic, which had bilateral technical cooperation with external universities, were influenced by the experience of partner institutions, with adaptation to the needs and situation of the University of Kabul.

Afghan professors lectured mainly in Dari or Pashto. The foreign professors lectured in their own languages which were translated by Afghan counterparts. The students were expected to learn the relevant foreign language in order to benefit from the teaching materials and textbooks. The development of textbooks in Afghan languages, especially in scientific and technological fields, was a principle objective of the university, and a prerequisite for the expansion of higher education in Afghanistan.

# 3

# Social Status

There never has been any reliable demographic statistics on Afghanistan for the past two decades. Of the estimated 16 million Afghans at the end of the 70s, over two million have been killed in the war of resistance against Soviet occupiers and later on in the civil war unleashed by fundamentalist groupings enjoying the support of foreign powers. Another one and half million have been maimed by the war fallout, while nearly five million have been forced into refugee camps in Iran and Pakistan. The majority of the population left inside the country have been internally displaced as a result of the unending war of the past two decades and in particular of the fundamentalist in-fighting of the past eight years. At the best of times the overall literacy rate was less than 20% amongst males and less than 5% amongst females. Against such a backdrop, the country slid into the hands of Islamic fundamentalists in 1992.

With the coming to power of Islamic fundamentalists in 1992, women's right to full participation in social, economic, cultural and political life of the country was drastically curtailed and later on summarily denied them by the Taliban. Under the latter, women were totally deprived of the right to education (all girls' school were closed down), of the right to work (all women were ordered to remain in their houses and employers were threatened with dire consequences for taking up female employees), of the right to travel (no woman could venture out of the house alone and unaccompanied by a prescribed male member of the woman's immediate family), of the right to health (no woman could see a male doctor, family planning was outlawed, women could not be operated upon by a surgical team containing a male member), of the right to legal recourse (a woman's testimony was worth half a man's testimony; a woman could not petition the court directly – this had to be done through a prescribed male member of her immediate family), of the right to recreation (all women's recreational and sporting facilities had been banned, women singers could not sing least their female voices 'corrupt' males, etc.), and of the right to being human (they could not show their faces in public to male strangers, they could not wear bright coloured clothing, they could not wear make up, they could only appear outside their houses clad head to foot in shapeless bags called burqas, they could not wear shoes with heels that click [least the clicking sound of their feet corrupt males], they could not travel in private vehicles with male passengers, they did not have the right to raise their voices when talking in public, they could not laugh loud as it lures males into corruption, etc. etc.)

It is something strange to note that women are looked upon as war booty, their bodies are another battleground for belligerent parties. Atrocities in Bosnia pale when compared to atrocities in Afghanistan, but unfortunately for reason which it may not be appropriate to go into in this context, the world community neither heard nor cared about what goes on in Afghanistan. Beating up of women for 'disciplinary' reasons on the slightest pretext (wearing brightly coloured shoes or thin stockings, having their bare ankles show when they walk, having their voices raised when they speak, having the sound of their laughter reach the ears of men strangers, having their heels click when walking etc.) was a routine phenomenon in Afghanistan under the Taliban. Through such public beatings (which more often than not have resulted in death or disablement of the victim) the Taliban had cowed the civilian population into submission.

With this kind of fundamentalists' war mentality, and fanned by ethnic hatred and religious bigotry, all areas that come under their control are regarded as occupied land and the inhabitants are treated accordingly. Sexual crimes against women, gang raping, lust murders, abductions of young females, blackmail of families with eligible daughters, etc. were commonplace during the rule of the pre-Taliban fundamentalists, who now once again have key positions in the transitional government of Hamid Karzai.

In regarding custodial violence against women, documentation of sexual violence against women during times of conflict and violence against refugee and internally displaced women we would first and foremost like to refer you to Amnesty International's reports such as "AFGHANISTAN: International responsibility for human rights disaster", AI, November 1995, as an eloquent testimony to the situation of women under the fundamentalists. Apart from the above, you can find a number of eyewitness accounts of atrocities by the Taliban and their Jehadi brothers on our web site.

The people of the world should know that though the disgusting, ludicrous and oppressive rule of Taliban was over in our ill-fated Afghanistan, but this never means the end of the horrible miseries of our tortured women. Because contrary to the aspirations of our people and expectations of the world community, the Northern Alliance, these brethren-in-creed of the Taliban and Al-Qaida are again in power and generously supported by the US government.

Afghan people will never forgive them for the crimes they committed along with the so-called older generation of the Alliance, i.e. Dostum, Khalili, Sayyaf, Rabbani, Gulbuddin etc. while in power from 1992 to 1996. Only in Kabul 50,000 were killed during these bloody years. Leaders of the Northern Alliance has no ideological difference with the Taliban. Some of them may talk even about "elections" and "women's rights", but in fact they are as much misogynist as the Taliban.

The war in Afghanistan has removed the Taliban, which so far does appear to be an improvement for women in certain limited parts of the country. In other areas, the incidence of rape and forced marriage is on the rise again, and most women continue to wear the burqa out of fear for their safety. The level of everyday violence in Afghanistan is something we would find it hard to imagine.

"War on terrorism" has removed the Taliban, but it has not removed religious fundamentalism which is the main cause of all our miseries. It will require a very different approach indeed for those evils to be eliminated, which is RAWA's point. And in fact, by reinstalling the warlords in power in Afghanistan, the US is ultimately replacing one fundamentalist regime with another.

**Women at Risk in Afghanistan**

As Afghans Struggle to shape their country's future, US foot-dragging on peacekeeping there threatens to preclude democracy and close off opportunities for women. Unless the United States shifts its security policy in Afghanistan, American commitments to the human rights of Afghan women will amount to little more than rhetoric. Since Sept. 11, the US administration has repeatedly pledged its commitment to Afghan women. President Bush made the case strongly in his June commencement speech at West Point: "A thriving nation will respect the rights of women, because no society can prosper while denying opportunity to half its citizens."

A US- and UN-guided process helped ensure women a place at the table as ministers in the temporary Afghan administration and participants in the emergency grand council, or loya jirga, which met in Kabul in June. During that assembly, women demonstrated why Afghanistan needs them to create democracy. Though a scant 10 percent of those assembled, with no troops or guns at their disposal, female delegates challenged with unparalleled candor the misogynist warrior ethos of both the Taliban and the warlords now in power and said they were looking for a leader who would make human rights a priority.

The lives of women remain vulnerable and there are reports of killings of women by their family members in the name of morality. Despite interventions by local NGOs the authorities have looked away, and have taken no action to investigate such murders. Such gender-based impunity by any State is a clear discrimination of the right to life of women. The female presidential candidate, Massouda Jalal, injected a modicum of democracy into the process, lining up the necessary signatures to run as male candidates fell by the wayside. The women's urgent need for accountable government drew them together in a unity that bridged tribal and ethnic differences.

However, at the end of the day the men with guns had, with apparent US acquiescence, greatly increased their power within the Afghan administration and were escalating the intimidation of "dissenters." During the loya jirga, the Afghan defense minister, Field Marshal Mohammed Fahim, assailed the husband of Massouda Jalal for his wife's temerity in running for president.

Accusations of blasphemy pursued Former Vice-President Sima Samar, who was driven from her post as women's affairs minister. Interim government ministers with civilian rather than military credentials were dismissed, Chief Justice Shinwari, who publicly upbraided Samar and has called for full support of Sharia, or Islamic law, was reappointed; and the majority of the Judicial Commission, responsible for reconciling Islamic principles with other legal traditions, are graduates of religious schools, called *madrassas*, with no further education.

Returning home from the loya jirga, many women faced the threat of violent backlash. Their joy at the promise of freedom and pride in finding a public voice conflicts with the fear of pervasive lawlessness. Taliban-style sexual policing still thrives in a number of places under the aegis of the US Northern Alliance partners as well as in former Taliban strongholds. Taliban pamphlets warn of reprisals for "spreading indecency and vulgarity" by "sending women to offices and daughters to schools." In much of the country outside of Kabul, the crossfire of rival factions has left women immensely vulnerable and victimized anew by a wave of rapes and other forms of sexual violence.

The US failure to support the Afghan administration materially or militarily has blighted early opportunities for women and the rule of law. While spending more than $2 billion a month on its pursuit of Al Qaeda and the Taliban and channeling money and technical assistance to local military leaders, the United States pledged only $2 million this year to help the Afghan administration build a national army.

Rooting out Al Qaeda is an unquestioned American priority, but it falls far short of what we need to achieve in Afghanistan. To lay the groundwork for peace and reconstruction in the aftermath of the loya jirga, the United States must signal its commitment to the rule of law by pushing for the immediate deployment of international security force throughout Afghanistan. We will not measurably increase our security from terrorism unless we keep our promises to help win the peace - and to the participation of women of rebuilding their country.

**Restrictions for Taliban Women in Afghanistan**

Taliban treat women worse than they treat animals. In

fact, even as Taliban declare the keeping of caged birds and animals illegal, they imprison Afghan women within the four walls of their own houses. Women have no importance in Taliban eyes unless they are occupied producing children, satisfying male sexual needs or attending to the drudgery of daily housework. Jehadi fundamentalists such as Gulbaddin, Rabbani, Masood, Sayyaf, Khalili, Akbari, Mazari and their co-criminal Dostum have committed the most treacherous and filthy crimes against Afghan women. And as more areas come under Taliban control, even if the number of rapes and murders perpetrated against women falls, Taliban restrictions -- comparable to those from the middle ages-- will continue to kill the spirit of our people while depriving them of a humane existence. We consider Taliban more treacherous and ignorant than Jehadis.

Taliban restrictions and mistreatment of women include the:

1. Complete ban on women's work outside the home, which also applies to female teachers, engineers and most professionals. Only a few female doctors and nurses are allowed to work in some hospitals in Kabul.
2. Complete ban on women's activity outside the home unless accompanied by a mahram (close male relative such as a father, brother or husband).
3. Ban on women dealing with male shopkeepers.
4. Ban on women being treated by male doctors.
5. Ban on women studying at schools, universities or any other educational institution. (Taliban have converted girls' schools into religious seminaries.)
6. Requirement that women wear a long veil (Burqa), which covers them from head to toe.
7. Whipping, beating and verbal abuse of women not clothed in accordance with Taliban rules, or of women unaccompanied by a mahram.
8. Whipping of women in public for having non-covered ankles.
9. Public stoning of women accused of having sex outside marriage. (A number of lovers are stoned to death under this rule).
10. Ban on the use of cosmetics. (Many women with painted

nails have had fingers cut off).

11. Ban on women talking or shaking hands with non-mahram males.
12. Ban on women laughing loudly. (No stranger should hear a woman's voice).
13. Ban on women wearing high heel shoes, which would produce sound while walking. (A man must not hear a woman's footsteps.)
14. Ban on women riding in a taxi without a mahram.
15. Ban on women's presence in radio, television or public gatherings of any kind.
16. Ban on women playing sports or entering a sport center or club.
17. Ban on women riding bicycles or motorcycles, even with their mahrams.
18. Ban on women's wearing brightly colored clothes. In Taliban terms, these are "sexually attracting colors."
19. Ban on women gathering for festive occasions such as the Eids, or for any recreational purpose.
20. Ban on women washing clothes next to rivers or in a public place.
21. Modification of all place names including the word "women." For example, "women's garden" has been renamed "spring garden".
22. Ban on women appearing on the balconies of their apartments or houses.
23. Compulsory painting of all windows, so women can not be seen from outside their homes.
24. Ban on male tailors taking women's measurements or sewing women's clothes.
25. Ban on female public baths.
26. Ban on males and females traveling on the same bus. Public buses have now been designated "males only" (or "females only").
27. Ban on flared (wide) pant-legs, even under a burqa.
28. Ban on the photographing or filming of women.
29. Ban on women's pictures printed in newspapers and books, or hung on the walls of houses and shops.

Apart from the above restrictions on women, the Taliban has:

- Banned listening to music, not only for women but men as well.
- Banned the watching of movies, television and videos, for everyone.
- Banned celebrating the traditional new year (Nowroz) on March 21. The Taliban has proclaimed the holiday un-Islamic.
- Disavowed Labor Day (May 1st), because it is deemed a "communist" holiday.
- Ordered that all people with non-Islamic names change them to Islamic ones.
- Forced haircuts upon Afghan youth.
- Ordered that men wear Islamic clothes and a cap.
- Ordered that men not shave or trim their beards, which should grow long enough to protrude from a fist clasped at the point of the chin.
- Ordered that all people attend prayers in mosques five times daily.
- Banned the keeping of pigeons and playing with the birds, describing it as un-Islamic. The violators will be imprisoned and the birds shall be killed. The kite flying has also been stopped.
- Ordered all onlookers, while encouraging the sportsmen, to chant Allah-o-Akbar (God is great) and refrain from clapping.
- Ban on certain games including kite flying which is "un-Islamic" according to Taliban.
- Anyone who carries objectionable literature will be executed.
- Anyone who converts from Islam to any other religion will be executed.
- All boy students must wear turbans. They say "No turban, no education".
- Non-Muslim minorities must distinct badge or stitch a yellow cloth onto their dress to be differentiated from the majority Muslim population. Just like what did Nazis with Jews.
- Banned the use of the internet by both ordinary Afghans and foreigners.

In Afghanistan, UN Economic and Social Council

expressed deep concern over the deteriorating economic and social conditions of women and girls in all areas of Afghanistan and condemned the continuing grave violations of their human rights. The Council encouraged the continuing efforts of the United Nations-assisted programmes in Afghanistan to promote the participation of women in those programmes and to ensure that women benefit equally with men from such programmes. In the resolution the Council also urged that all United Nations activities, including humanitarian assistance, be based on the principle of nondiscrimination, incorporate a gender perspective, and actively attempt to promote the participation of both women and men, in conformity with the Strategic Framework for Afghanistan.

The situation of women and girls during armed or other kinds of conflict is increasingly receiving international attention. The special session of the General Assembly on "Women 2000: gender equality, development and peace in the twenty-first century", held from 5 to 9 June 2000, showed a growing appreciation, at the international, regional and national levels, of the different impacts conflict has on women and girls, including an increasing awareness of the need to address their rights and needs in the context of conflict. The role of women in conflict prevention, peacekeeping, peace-building and post-conflict societal reconstruction and building on the critical areas, women and armed conflict, of the Beijing Platform for Action.

The Security Council took a significant decision to incorporate women and girls in all its deliberations, not just as victims of armed conflict, but also as constructive actors in finding peace. The Council affirmed the equal access to and full participation of women in power structures and underscored the importance of promoting an active and visible policy of mainstreaming a gender perspective into all policies and programmes while addressing armed or other conflicts.

The situation in Afghanistan, the Council focused on discriminatory policies against Afghan women, particularly in Taliban-controlled areas. In the statement by the President of the Security Council. The Council condemned grave violations of the human rights of women and girls, including all forms of discrimination against them, particularly in areas under control by the Taliban. It called on all parties, in particular the Taliban, to take measures to end all violations of women's rights. During the debate, the Council requested the Special Adviser on Gender Issues and Advancement of Women to respond to specific questions relating to gender issues.

At the meeting of the Security Council at which it considered "Women, peace and security", held on 24 and 25 October 2000, the Council further underlined the important role of women as equal partners with men in peacemaking and peace-building. Despite international pressure on Afghan parties to the conflict and measures taken by the United Nations and the international community in resolutions and statements of the Security Council, the General Assembly, the Commission on Human Rights and the Commission on the Status of Women and despite the tireless efforts of the assistance community to improve the situation of Afghan women and girls, the overall situation has not shown significant improvement.

The armed conflict between the Taliban movement, which controls 95 per cent of the country, including its capital Kabul, and the United Front continued through the summer and fall of 2000. A significant characteristic of offensives in 1999 and 2000 was the deliberate targeting of civilians. Although the entire Afghan population suffers under armed conflict, women and girls are particularly affected. Afghan women have borne enormous hardships throughout the years of conflict. The population, including women and children have been bombed indiscriminately, deliberately targeted with violence and subjected to a wide range of human rights violations. 76 per cent of women's deaths during the war were due to aerial bombings. A survey conducted by the International Committee of the Red Cross (ICRC) in 1999, replies from Afghan respondents revealed that 83 per cent of the population had been forced to leave their homes due to the war, 53 per cent reported that a member of their immediate family had been killed during conflict, and 16 per cent reported knowing someone who was raped.

Cultural norms and traditions in Afghanistan have been historically conservative and characterized by a strong division of gender roles where political, economic and social decision-making is largely determined by males. Control by the Taliban exacerbated the situation of women. Most members of the Taliban movement appear to hold the belief that the State should preserve the dignity and honour of families and guarantee the personal security of women. The combination of an ultraconservative interpretation of Islam with tribal patriarchal norms of conduct, and institutionalized gender discrimination had been reflected in a series of legislative acts (edicts) affecting women adversely. Despite all the peacemaking efforts undertaken by the international community to end the fighting in 2000, described in four progress reports 8 of the Secretary-General on the situation in Afghanistan, developments in the country give little ground for optimism.

An agreement of 2 November 2000, reached between the Taliban and the United Front, to enter into a process of dialogue under United Nations auspices, without preconditions in order to bring an end to the Afghan conflict by political means, provided a glimmer of hope. However, the recent decision by the Taliban to withdraw from the agreement in protest over the sanctions imposed by the Security Council in its resolution 1333 of 19 December 2000 gave further cause for concern.

The people of Afghanistan continue to suffer from the accumulated effects of war and economic collapse. Some reports have emphasized that the coping capacity of the civilian population has been severely weakened as a result of the war and the erosion of many traditional coping mechanisms including, in particular, the role of extended family networks. The country is also suffering from the worst drought in the region since 1971. The drought has led to increased malnutrition, large livestock losses, the loss of crops, a higher incidence of diseases, and an increase in the overall vulnerability of both rural and urban populations. Two consecutive years of natural emergencies, including droughts, floods and earthquakes, have left millions of people with little access to food. The country faces an acute food crisis in 2000-2001, with the cereal deficit exceeding 2.3 million tons, more than double that of 1999.

The World Food Programme (WFP) Hunger Map, which identifies hunger hot spots, listed Afghanistan as one of the countries facing the greatest problems in 2001. It is estimated that nearly 4 million people are on the brink of starvation. In terms of human development indicators, Afghanistan is ranked among the lowest in the world. It is, for example, estimated that one quarter of all children die before they reach the age of five.

Literacy rates are approximately 35 per cent for the whole population, but only 13 per cent for females in urban areas and 3 to 4 per cent in rural districts. The maternal mortality rates are the second highest in the world, with nearly 1,700 per 100,000 live births. Furthermore, only 12 per cent of women are estimated to have access to even the most basic health care, a situation that has changed little since the Inter-Agency Gender Mission in 1997. The resumption of the conflict in the northeast during the past summer resulted in yet another massive forced displacement of the civilian population.

Almost 130,000 people were displaced in 1999-2000. Large numbers of people have also left their homes due to the drought, in order to search for any available means of livelihood. Currently, some 40,000 people from the severely drought-affected and remote districts of Ghor, Badghis and Faryab provinces, now live in makeshift shelters in Herat, the main urban area in the west. The situation of some 2.6 million Afghan refugees residing in the Islamic Republic of Iran and Pakistan has worsened, owing to both asylum fatigue and donor fatigue.

Despite the harsh economic situation and the ongoing fighting in Afghanistan, many Afghan refugees in Iran and Pakistan have recently decided to return home because their predicament in those countries has become harder. At the end of last September, a total of 170,000 Afghan refugees returned voluntarily with the assistance of the United Nations High Commissioner for Refugees (UNHCR), the WFP and the International Organization for Migration (IOM). However, voluntary repatriation is a durable solution only for those who own productive assets or those who have the means to engage in the limited labour market. Afghanistan is one of the world's most mine-affected areas in the world.

Land mines injure more than 8,000 people each year, including many women and children. It is estimated that over

700 square kilometres of the country are still contaminated by mines. During 1999-2000, the Mine Action Programme in Afghanistan, in close cooperation with United Nations agencies, non-governmental organizations (NGOs) and other entities, cleared over 43.7 square kilometres of high-priority mined areas and 101.2 square kilometres of former battlefield in 20 provinces of Afghanistan. A further 51 square kilometres of mined areas and 103.8 square kilometres of former battlefield were surveyed and marked. Some 28,000 mines and 265,000 unexploded ordnance were destroyed during 1999, with a further 160,574 destroyed in 2000. The Mine Action Programme in Afghanistan also provided mine-awareness training to 332,396 civilians. The severe shortfall of funding for the period September through December 2000 has, however, forced the programme to suspend its staff on two months' leave without pay and to freeze staff salaries and increments. As a further consequence, only 64 per cent of the sites targeted for clearance were completed in 2000. Because of the many years of fighting, almost all institutions of governance have been destroyed.

**Islamic Laws**

Afghanistan does not have an effective government, constitution, rule of law or independent judiciary. The Islamic courts and religious police enforce Taliban's interpretation of Islamic law and punishment. Civil institutions are largely nonexistent and policies and laws vary, depending on the region and the local commanders.

Taliban's edicts are not evenly enforced throughout the areas under its control. For example, projects approved by local officials are not always endorsed by Kandahar officials and vice versa. Many educated Afghans who have had the option to leave the country have done so, either permanently or temporarily, as refugees or migrant labourers in other countries, contributing to a brain drain from Afghanistan. The absence of a central government capable of developing policies and guidelines for the social and economic development of the country has had devastating effects on its population.

The governance environment in Afghanistan today is defined by continuing war. As a result, virtually no domestic resources are marshalled for the purpose of organized relief, rehabilitation or reconstruction. The annual budget, at $70.9

million, is equivalent to approximately 0.9 per cent of gross domestic product (GDP).

**Women and Health**

Following years of conflict, basic infrastructure, including health care, is left in a critical state. This has severely affected the health situation of women and children. The life expectancy for women is only 46 years. Tuberculosis rates for women are among the highest in the world. There are approximately 133,000 cases, 70 per cent of which are females aged 15 to 45.

The drought has, furthermore, aggravated the situation as access to water has been considerably reduced. Water quality has deteriorated in many urban areas and the limited availability of drinking water in both urban and rural areas is now a critical health issue. It is estimated that less than one quarter of the population has access to clean water and that only 12 per cent have access to sanitation. A curable disease such as diarrhoea alone kills an estimated 85,000 children each year.

Moreover, most hospitals, health care centres and medical centres have largely been destroyed by war, and those remaining are mainly located in the urban centres. Currently, there is an average of only one physician for every 50,000 people in Afghanistan.

Combined with the flight of trained personnel and the low capacity to produce new generations of doctors, nurses and health workers the current health care situation remains an area of deep concern to the international community. The health situation of women and girls is further aggravated by the complete segregation in the provision of health services for males and females. This has enormously curtailed women's access to these services, especially when there is only a very small number of female doctors and trained nurses practising under severe restrictions in hospitals.

Basic health indicators reflect the alarming health situation of Afghan women and children, in particular regarding reproductive health where the maternal mortality rate is exceedingly high. An estimated 15,000 Afghan women die every year of pregnancy-related causes. According to WHO, only 12 per cent of deliveries in Afghanistan are attended by trained health workers, mostly traditional birth attendants. The fertility rate in Afghanistan is among the highest in the world, seven births per woman. Approximately 4 per cent of the Afghan population, or some 800,000 people, are disabled as a result of war, landmines, polio and poor basic health care in the country.

A high rate of birth complications, for example, especially in undernourished women with inadequate medical care, gives rise to disabilities such as cerebral palsy. The Comprehensive Disabled Afghans Programme, together with several NGOs and the ICRC, has provided assistance and rehabilitation services to a large number of disabled people in Afghanistan.

The humanitarian challenges involved in assisting the disabled remain enormous. Inadequate referral services mean that minor disabilities that could easily be prevented become complicated and irreversible. Furthermore, many disabled people, because of their lack of employment opportunities, become a socio-economic burden on their families and society. From 1998 onwards there has been a clear, albeit slow, shift in the Taliban's position on the access of women to health services. There are, for example, indications of a relaxation of their ban on employment of females in the health sector.

In 1999, approximately 40 female medical students, who were forced to leave Kabul University before receiving their medical degrees, were allowed to continue their education. In the first quarter of 2000, the authorities in Kandahar agreed, after lengthy negotiations with WFP, WHO and the Office of the Resident Coordinator of the United Nations, to start a nursing school in Kandahar for 50 female and 50 male nurses. A similar school for female nurses is being negotiated for Jalalabad. WHO also implemented two courses of continuing medical education for 48 female doctors, nurses and midwives in 1998-1999. Since 1998, increasing numbers of female nurses, vaccinators and traditional birth attendants are being trained by the assistance community and are currently working in both rural and urban areas. The nursing school in Herat was reopened during the first quarter of 2000 through assistance from WHO and WFP.

Two of the larger women's hospitals - Meerawis Hospital in Kandahar and Rabia Balki hospital in Kabul - have also been rehabilitated jointly with the assistance community.

Furthermore, as reported by the United Nations Children's Fund (UNICEF) and the United Nations Centre for Human Settlements (Habitat), female social mobilizers have played an important role in health education and enhancing awareness about safe water and sanitation, despite very arduous working conditions.

UNICEF, WHO and NGOs, in collaboration with the Afghan Ministry of Health, have developed a Strategy Framework for the Safe Motherhood Initiative with the objective of reducing maternal mortality and morbidity. The Safe Motherhood Initiative was launched in three provinces, Laghman and Logar in 1998, and Farah in 1999, and focuses on awareness raising and has capacity-building and training components. In 1999, the United Nations Populations Fund (UNFPA), UNICEF, WHO and NGOs provided support to over 20 comprehensive obstetric care facilities to support traditional birth attendants and improve the maternal health programme. UNFPA has also developed emergency obstetric and reproductive health kits, which have been distributed in Afghanistan. As reported by UNICEF and UNFPA, despite notable progress in sensitization, efforts in this field are hampered by the scarcity of implementing partners and qualified female staff as well as the various restrictions on the mobility of women.

Progress has been achieved in the area of immunization. UNICEF, WHO and a wide range of NGOs supported the National Immunization Days in May/June and in October/November 2000. During the spring round, approximately 5.3 million children under the age of five, both boys and girls, were vaccinated against polio, providing the highest coverage since 1994. UNICEF data show that there are no significant gender gaps in immunization coverage rates. This is largely a result of the participation of hundreds of Afghan female health staff in the various vaccination efforts, including the National Immunization Days.

In spite of these measures, it is estimated that nearly 1,000 children died during the measles epidemic during the spring of 2000. These deaths could have been prevented if the children had been immunized or had had access to basic health services. Some reports have included information on the problem of the mental health of women in Afghanistan.

Furthermore, despite the lack of statistics on drug use among women, there is strong evidence that the number of drug-addicted females is increasing both in drug-producing provinces and other areas and in refugee camps. Women are using drugs as an alternative to medicine, but also for psychological reasons.

**Warlords Implicated in New Abuses Report Details Threats to Women's Rights, Freedom of Expression**

(New York, July 29, 2003) - Afghan warlords and political strongmen supported by the United States and other nations are engendering a climate of fear in Afghanistan that is threatening efforts to adopt a new constitution and could derail national elections scheduled for mid-2004, Human Rights Watch said in a new report released today.

The report warns that violence, political intimidation, and attacks on women and girls are discouraging political participation and endangering gains made on women's rights in Afghanistan over the last year.

"Human rights abuses in Afghanistan are being committed by gunmen and warlords who were propelled into power by the United States and its coalition partners after the Taliban fell in 2001," said Brad Adams, executive director of the Asia Division of Human Rights Watch. "These men and others have essentially hijacked the country outside of Kabul. With less than a year to go before national elections, Afghanistan's human rights situation appears to be worsening."

The 101-page report, "Killing You Is a Very Easy Thing for Us": Human Rights Abuses in Southeast Afghanistan, documents army and police troops kidnapping Afghans and holding them for ransom in unofficial prisons; breaking into households and robbing families; raping women, girls and boys; and extorting shopkeepers and bus, truck and taxi drivers. The report also describes political organizers, journalists and media editors being threatened with death, arrested and harassed by army, police and intelligence agents. The subject area of the report, the southeast of Afghanistan and Kabul city, is one of the most densely populated areas of Afghanistan.

Because soldiers are targeting women and girls, many are staying indoors, especially in rural areas, making it impossible for them to attend school, go to work, or actively participate in the country's reconstruction. In many places, human rights abuses are driving many Afghan families to keep their girls out of school. The atmosphere of violence, along with resurgent religious fundamentalism in parts of the country, is endangering the most important human rights improvement since the end of the Taliban—the ability of girls to go back to school.

"The fact is that most girls in Afghanistan are still not in school," said Adams. "In many cases, returning refugee families who sent their girls to school in Pakistan or Iran are afraid to do the same in Afghanistan."

The testimony of victims and witnesses implicates soldiers and police under the command of many high-level military and political officials in Afghanistan. These include Mohammad Qasim Fahim, the Minister of Defense; Hazrat Ali, the military leader of the Eastern Region; Younis Qanooni, the Minister of Education; Burhanuddin Rabbani, the former president of Afghanistan; and Abdul Rabb al-Rasul Sayyaf, a powerful former mujahidin leader to whom many of the officials involved in the documented abuses in Kabul city and province remain loyal.

The report urges the Afghan government to sideline and pressure abusive leaders and to seek more international assistance in its efforts.

Human Rights Watch called on the United States, the United Kingdom, Iran, Russia and other external powers to end their support for local strongmen and commanders involved in human rights abuses.

"External support for warlords is destabilizing Afghanistan," said Adams. "The United States and the United Kingdom, in particular, need to decide whether they are with President Karzai and other reformers in Kabul or with the warlords. The longer they wait, the more difficult it will be to loosen the warlords' grip on power."

Human Rights Watch emphasized the need for the Afghan government and the international community to redouble efforts to reform the Afghan Ministry of Defense. The Ministry of Defense in Kabul is currently dominated by the political and military faction "Shura-e Nazar," a loose alliance of former mujahidin parties. Making the ministry more ethnically and politically representative is a vital prerequisite for the disarmament, demobilization and reintegration programmes that could lessen the power of abusive military rulers and their troops.

Human Rights Watch urged NATO to expand the geographic scope of the U.N. authorized security force, the International Security Assistance Force (ISAF), currently stationed only in Kabul, when it takes over ISAF command in August. Human Rights Watch also urged NATO to widen ISAF's mandate to include disarmament and human rights protection. Plans to deploy more international Provincial Reconstruction Teams (PRTs) may be a positive step if they focus on security, but they are not a substitute for an expanded security force.

Human Rights Watch called on the United Nations to increase its human rights monitoring and protection efforts through the deployment of significant numbers of U.N. human rights officers around the country.

"With more U.N. human rights workers on the ground, victims will be better able to seek redress and protection. An increase in monitoring will have the added benefit of giving the Afghan administration and the international community better information about what is happening around the country," said Adams. "This is standard operating procedure in other U.N. missions, but so far the United Nations has refused to take this step."

Human Rights Watch also urged the United Nations to increase its public reporting on the human rights situation and to supply more personnel to work side-by-side with the Afghan Independent Human Rights Commission.

**Afghan Women : Fighting for the Right to Sing**

Although the rule of the Taliban in Afghanistan ended 18 months ago, women in the country are still faced with a huge number of restrictions in their everyday life.

Included among them is a ban on singing in public, on the radio or on television.

"I'm deeply affected by what's going on," singer Najiba

Samin told BBC World Service's Every woman programme.

"I don't understand why we can't record our songs and hear them on radio and on television."

Although Ms Samin is allowed to sing in the Kabul music school, a gunman has to sit at the doorway just in case extremists decide to deliver judgment.

"I think what's happened is that the people who were responsible for the atrocities of the past are in control of this, and they're doing it all over again," she said.

"But I tell myself the fight has to continue, even though there are people determined to stop us."

**'Prisoners in own Homes'**

Ms Samin's situation is indicative of the problems facing women in the new Afghanistan.

Although TV screens around the world were filled with images of women taking off the burqa as the Taliban fell, women's rights agencies are still trying to realise the idea of emancipation in Afghanistan.

They concede there had not been much change. "You can see that there's an obvious increase of women going to school, or having access to higher education, and there are some professional women who have been able to go back to being lawyers or teachers - but I think that is a very, very small step," said Rachel Wareham, who works for the German agency Medica Mondial.

"The majority of women are still more or less prisoners in their own homes.

"The legal system is not functioning in any area or any way that protects them or advances them."

**Trading in Women**

And further out of Kabul and beyond the reach of government, restrictions deteriorate into outright abuse of women's rights.

The province of Shinwari, near the Pakistan boarder, is notorious for opium smuggling - and also for the sale of women.

"I was sold 10 years ago - at the time I'd had three children from my first husband - but when he took a second wife, he sold me," one woman said.

"He and I grew up together, but after I was sold he prevented me from seeing the children.

"My son died. I think his heart broke after I was forced to leave. I'm not allowed to see my daughter.

"When I left my breast used to leak milk. They tore my baby from me."

In Shinwari women are sold for around $3,000 each - either as punishment or purely to earn money for their families or first husbands.

"We are innocent in this - we are just like chickens kept and tied," another told Everywoman.

"Wherever you send us, we go."

**Punishments**

Activist Pawina Heila has tried to raise the issue with local authorities, but said they have done nothing.

"There is no difference between now and when the Taliban were in control," she told Every woman.

One woman she knew of fled the home she had been sold to and returned to her brother's house.

But there she was punished. She was first scalded with hot water, then tied behind a car with a cable, dragged into the desert, and shot.

"These are the lessons women are taught so they go quietly when they're sold," she said.

The women's ministry in Afghanistan is - like the rest of the government—short on authority. The minister Habibi Serabi is under pressure from both international donors and Afghan women themselves to deliver.

"I'm often faced with this problem... people, particularly men, say that it's custom and culture." Ms Serabi acknowledged.

"But this is not impossible. We can change the culture and custom but of course it takes time."

"We have to work very hard, and also not very quickly. We have to take care with each of our steps."

She added that it was not only Afghanistan's women who needed to be made aware of women's rights, but also the country's men.

"Not only women, but we have to educate the men too," she stressed.

"The men should know about the rights of women, about human rights, about everything. After that, maybe they can give women the opportunity to take part in society. "

**Eve Ensler: This is Most Fragile Time for Afghanistan**

After her most recent trip to Afghanistan, playwright and women's activist Eve Ensler pleads for the U.S. to keep its promises to stabilize the country, which she likens to a patient at a dangerous point of recovery.

(WOMENSENEWS)--l have just returned from Afghanistan. This was my third trip. I write now because the situation is urgent. I would say this is the most fragile time in Afghanistan I have experienced. Afghanistan today reminds me of a person who has been seriously ill. She is just beginning to recover. The fever has broken and there are those early moments where she suddenly feels alive.

We know this is the most dangerous time. The energy is still part of the fever itself, a kind of delirium. Now the patient, thrilled with the possibility of living, if not protected, can go wild with activity. This exertion can have deadly consequences. In the case of Afghanistan this somewhat frenzied, disorganized activity comes not just from a momentary recovery—a ceasing of bombs falling—but from a deep panic that the recovery is short lived and not guaranteed and so everything must be done now or it will disappear forever.

Women's Minister Cannot Travel without Bodyguards Under the Taliban, Afghanistan was a tortured, ruinously oppressed country, but women in particular knew what to prepare for. They knew how to defend themselves against the madness. They could identify their enemies. They were braced for violence. They had learned how to manoeuver in clandestine ways. Now the situation is less clear. There is the pretense of liberation while the ongoing threat of violence can be felt.

For example, at our recent women's leadership training conference, women who were visionary about the future, felt compelled to still wear *burqas*. On March 8, there were huge events celebrating International Women's Day. One event at the Afghan Women's Union unveiled a statue symbolizing women's freedom and power. Hundreds attended. A day later the statue was stolen. The Women's Minister, who in theory is the symbolic representative of Afghan women, cannot move anywhere in the country without bodyguards. Although women are now working to create new businesses, build schools, open hospitals, the majority of the people in Afghanistan still live without heat, electricity or running water.

Having spent time in recent months with Afghan women in Kabul—as well as women and men in Amman, Jordan; Cairo, Egypt; the West Bank town of Ramallah; Islamabad, Pakistan and Peshawar, Pakistan I can say that the Muslim world is highly suspect of the intentions of the U.S. government. It is watching Afghanistan as a test case. If the U.S. does not deliver security, substantial aid and reconstruction, we may never recover the trust of the Muslim world. If we turn our backs on Afghanistan, if we do not fulfill our promises, there is a good chance that the patient will never recover. Nor will she fulfill her dream of a free, safe and prospering Afghanistan. Terrorists are born in the cracks of broken promises.

Play Wright Eve Ensler, author of *The Vagina Monologues,* is the Founder and artistic director of V-Day, a global movement to end violence against women and girls.

**Education for Women**

Women's equal access to education is key to improving the health, nutrition and education of the family as a whole, as well as to empowering women to participate more fully in the rehabilitation and development process. In Afghanistan, the education sector is characterized by limited human and financial resources, the absence of a national education policy and curricula at pre-university levels, and by the lack of resources and political will to rehabilitate school buildings and facilities destroyed by war.

Home- and community-based schools in both rural and urban areas function more as literacy centres than formal schools. The Badakhshan Province, controlled by the United Front, is currently the only location in the whole country where girls are studying up to the twelfth grade. NGOs such as the Swedish Committee for Afghanistan, Save the Children-USA and Care International, provide the majority of education services, in coordination with UNICEF and WFP.

The principled position of the United Nations system on

equality of access of girls and boys to education has been the guiding principle in United Nations negotiations at all levels with the Taliban authorities. However, despite strenuous efforts led by UNICEF, no significant progress in improving girls' access to equality in formal education has yet been achieved. In Islamabad in November 1999, the World Bank organized a workshop on education in Afghanistan which was attended by a wide spectrum of assistance actors.

Participants concluded that even within the current restrictive environment, opportunities existed for expanding the education base for Afghan children. However, medium- and longer-term investment in human and financial resources is urgently needed to address the enormous problems faced by the education sector. According to UNHCR data, only 30 per cent of primary school age children in the refugee camps are attending schools. Education in refugee camps is more formalized and girls of school age have more access to education at all levels.

In cooperation with international NGOs such as the Swedish Afghanistan Committee for Afghanistan, Save the Children-USA, Care International mentioned above and others, UNICEF and UNDP provide literacy skills and education to girls and have, as noted above, achieved some progress in the provision of alternatives to formal education in some Taliban-controlled areas. It is estimated that 300,000 children receive informal education.

Moreover, community-based schools for girls are on the increase in urban areas. In November 1999, 9 community girls' schools were established in Kandahar Province and 13 girls' schools were established in Kabul; all of these were financed by local communities in agreement with the Taliban authorities.

The number of privately organized home-based schools also increased in the urban areas. Furthermore, the British Broadcasting Corporation has developed an education programme through radio (BBC Reach) as an innovative attempt to increase access to education in the country. The brain drain from Afghanistan, combined with the collapse of the education system, constitutes one of the great challenges for the future rehabilitation of the country. The war has destroyed the formal economic sectors in the country. According to the

1997 World Bank report, the Afghan economy is currently reliant on subsistence agriculture, unofficial transit trade, war-related financial flows, drug income and international assistance. For women, agriculture, animal husbandry and small home-based crafts such as carpet weaving, tailoring, embroidery, soap making, candle making, poultry raising, honey production and bakery activities have provided the only opportunities for employment.

**Role of UN**

The United Nations and the assistance community have been involved in projects creating this type of employment to provide women and their families with a subsistence income. However, these types of employment have only a limited impact on the status of women, as they require basic skills and are poorly paid.

Women have no access to markets, due to the Taliban's imposed restriction on their movement. This leads in many cases to women's exploitation by male middlemen, except where NGOs take the responsibility for the final marketing of their products.

Women are employed as doctors, midwives, social mobilizers and community mobilizers. A number of female teachers have also been employed at community-based schools for girls. These types of employment were facilitated by indications that the Mahram Edict, issued by the Taliban in March 1998, banning women from travelling inside Afghanistan without being accompanied by a male relative, was being relaxed. A major setback to the achieved improvements in women's employment came on 6 July 2000 when the Taliban's Council of Ministers banned Afghan women from working in "foreign organizations and NGOs".

On 16 August, the Taliban authorities forced WFP to close its 24 women's bakeries in Kabul. The bakeries were run by 360 women workers providing subsidized bread to 7,200 families, comprising over 42,000 people, predominantly women and children. The women and children benefiting from the programme were amongst the poorest and most vulnerable people in Afghanistan. Further complicating the difficulties faced by United Nations agencies was the issuance of a revised "Statute on the Activities of the United Nations in Afghanistan" of 14 August 2000. These measures indicated that the authorities felt a strong need to exercise more monitoring and control over the assistance community's programmes, especially those where women were involved. Reacting to the laws, the assistance community joined me in expressing deep concern regarding the ban against women's employment with the assistance community, which exacerbated the discrimination and suffering of Afghan women and children and constituted a gross violation of the rights of Afghan women.

Lasting more than 20 years, the conflict in Afghanistan has created a large number of widows. Currently, there are about 2 million war widows living inside Afghanistan who are the sole providers for their families. The majority of these widows are unemployed, unskilled and live well below poverty levels. In 1999, the Taliban authorities issued an edict allowing needy widows with no other means of support to seek employment in the health and social service sectors.

However, the opportunities in these sectors are extremely limited and many recent reports have noted an increase in impoverished women who are reduced to begging to help them survive. The plight of widows who cannot support themselves because they are not permitted to work or benefit from humanitarian assistance is cause for particularly deep concern within the assistance community. Unemployment rates are extremely high in Afghanistan and the need to create income-generating employment cannot be exaggerated. This applies to all parts of the country, but is especially severe in urban areas.

Unemployment in Kabul alone has reached serious proportions, with approximately one quarter of all families surviving on United Nations-subsidized bread and many others on remittances from abroad. Several central ministries have been downsized - the Ministry of Higher Education by 6,000 employees and the Ministry of Education by 12,000. Female teachers who were no longer allowed to work but were still on the payroll have now lost their incomes.

**Women's Rights**

The Inter-Agency Gender Mission to Afghanistan in 1997 found that women in Afghanistan were unable to enjoy even the most basic rights under the 16 main articles of the Convention on the Elimination of All Forms of Discrimination against Women, to which Afghanistan is a signatory. Since then the situation has not improved.

The Taliban authorities do not recognize the commitments made by previous Afghan regimes to the Charter of the United Nations, the Universal Declaration of Human Rights and other human rights instruments. The restrictions by the Taliban have severely affected women's civil and political rights, freedom of movement, and freedom of assembly, as Afghan women are confined to the home.

The right to personal security has been violated as a result of the civil war, but also by the arbitrary and summary beatings of women by members of the Department for the Promotion of Virtue and Prevention of Vice. There is, as expressed by the Special Adviser on Gender Issues and Advancement of Women at a briefing for the Security Council on 7 April 2000, a need to continue to press for the full enjoyment of the rights of women and children, not only for education, health and employment, but in all other areas. War still continues to be the most significant factor preventing the enjoyment of human rights in Afghanistan.

The right of civilians to be treated as noncombatants continues to be ignored, resulting in significant loss of life and human suffering. Summary executions and arbitrary detentions are known features of the conflict and still continue. The socio-economic conditions which are both an outcome of the war and a contributing factor to it, constitute the biggest threat to the lives of Afghan children, women and men. Gender differences and inequalities in Afghanistan's patriarchal society are deep-rooted and multifaceted. During previous years of conflict, prior to the arrival of the Taliban, the rights of Afghan women were also largely ignored. The debate following the Taliban takeover in 1996 and the imposition of a number of edicts restricting the rights of both women and men in Afghanistan has led to an increased awareness about the need for the Afghan people fully to enjoy fundamental rights and freedoms. Aid organizations report that work in non-Taliban areas is not much easier despite the greater official openness of the authorities.

To respond to the continued restrictions on women's human rights in Afghanistan a set of policy recommendations for a principle-centred approach to these violations was developed by the Executive Committee on Humanitarian Affairs of the United Nations in 1997. This approach was intended to enable continuation of life-sustaining assistance, that is, immediate survival and other humanitarian activities, while recognizing that selective disengagement of some United Nations agencies from some institutional assistance programmes may be required.

The Inter-Agency Gender Mission translated these policy recommendations into practical operational guidelines and provided recommendations on their interpretation, taking into account the complex and quickly changing Afghan context. The policy recommendations and the findings of the Inter-Agency Gender Mission provided the basis for the Strategic Framework for Afghanistan established in 1998. The principles set forth in the Strategic Framework have since then guided the United Nations and its assistance partners in their activities.

By applying the principled approach as far as possible combining gender equality, human rights and humanitarian aspects, during 1999 and the first half of 2000, the United Nations and the NGO assistance community have been able to bring about a number of positive developments in the areas of health, employment and education.

This brought some hope for Afghan women's future, despite the bleak overall picture of the reality. This shift was also due to increased demand from local communities for health and education for girls and women and for income-generating employment for women, especially for war widows heading households. The United Nations and the assistance community have been instrumental in preparing the ground for this shift, through continued advocacy, principled engagement, and constructive dialogue and negotiation with the authorities. The work of the Gender Adviser and the Human Rights Adviser, whose posts were recommended by the 1997 Gender Mission has been central in enhancing knowledge and awareness in this respect. They interact regularly with programme staff of United Nations agencies and NGOs and help to deepen understanding of how human rights and gender perspectives can be integrated in the programming process.

Today, there are well-structured mechanisms such as

thematic and working groups, including a Thematic Group on human rights, and Regional Coordinating Offices which facilitated the efforts of assistance actors to give concrete effect to the principle of non-discrimination. Furthermore, Regional Coordinating Bodies with the support of the Regional Coordinating Offices facilitate common programming initiatives at the regional level. With the assistance of the Regional Coordinating Offices, coordination arrangements are becoming more established and the limitations of access and capacity, constraints experienced through much of 1999, are being overcome. The Principled Common Programme for provision of assistance has, furthermore, facilitated the coordination of the activities of the United Nations and international and national NGOs. This programme addresses the priority needs required (a) to alleviate human suffering, (b) to protect and advance human rights, with special focus on women, (c) to provide minimum basic social services on a nondiscriminatory basis, and (e) to ensure the return of refugees.

The United Nations system in Afghanistan has furthermore established a number of monitoring mechanisms in order to review compliance with principles and guidelines, such as the Strategic Monitoring Unit, the weekly inter-agency senior staff meetings and the Gender Forum. Furthermore, the Memorandum of Understanding between the United Nations and the Taliban authorities established the Joint Consultative Committee to discuss United Nations standards on human rights and gender equality and the right to health, education and women's employment opportunities. The Joint Consultative Committee discussions have, however, not proved highly effective in solving policy and programming problems, in part owing to a low level of representation by the Taliban and frequent shifts in the Taliban's positions and organization.

The United Nations has followed a policy of constructive engagement consistent with agreed principles. Dialogue with the Taliban and the United Front authorities on the Universal Declaration of Human Rights, with a special focus on the rights of women, is an ongoing process. Individual agencies are actively engaged in advocacy and dissemination of information at the local and central levels on issues such as the rights of the disabled, children and women. UNICEF has, for example, held successful negotiations with the clergy to convince them of the importance of the Safe Motherhood Initiative. The field visits by the Gender Adviser and her regular meetings with Taliban political leaders and heads of technical departments have been very helpful in establishing contacts with the Afghan authorities.

A few women professionals are now also on the staff of the United Nations Special Mission to Afghanistan. The former United Nations High Commissioner for Refugees, Sadako Ogata, on her mission to Afghanistan in October 2000 emphasized the issue of suppression of women's rights as a serious concern to the international community and a hindrance to the return of female refugees driven from the country by years of civil war.

The Task Force concluded that it was particularly important that the international community find a way to respond to humanitarian needs while simultaneously pursuing an approach that gives concrete effect to principles. It is equally important that the aid community take a proactive and collaborative approach and speak with one voice on issues of principle. The concluding comments of the Task Force were made available to the Executive Committee on Humanitarian Affairs.

A wide range of NGOs, both national and international, as well as individual women and men, organized a series of advocacy campaigns expressing concerns about the denial of human rights of women and girls under the Taliban regime. Although under the Taliban's laws women and men cannot always undertake the same activities, wherever possible men's activities are complemented by parallel women's projects, ensuring equal benefits in participation and results.

In Kandahar, UNCHS engages men in solid-waste collection and women in a complementary sanitation education campaign. UNDP has developed the P.E.A.C.E programme (Poverty Eradication and Community Empowerment) which addresses poverty, food insecurity, lack of basic social and economic infrastructures, environmental devastation and governance problems.

Women are specifically targeted in all aspects of the P.E.A.C.E programme and efforts continue among the United

Nations agencies and NGOs implementing the UNDP-funded projects to engage more women. However, there is still a great deal of resistance, both cultural and political, to involving Afghan women at the different levels of the programme cycle. The P.E.A.C.E programme has shown that stable rural communities have more potential to demand services from the authorities, including girls' education than in the past. The United Nations Office for Project Services (UNOPS)/ Afghanistan Rural Rehabilitation programme (ARRP) aims at fostering community participation, improving living conditions and human welfare for rural community members, in particular women, and promoting greater access to productive assets and income-earning opportunities.

The programme is implemented through skills development and community-managed micro-credit schemes. Whenever possible, UNOPS/ARRP aims at organizing separate women's development committees, in an attempt to ensure that women are involved in planning and implementation of infrastructure projects. UNOPS/ ARRP interventions under rural credit and income-generation activities have mostly targeted women. Under its community development programme, Habitat is developing "Community Forums" across urban Afghanistan, emphasizing a participatory decision-making process. FAO has also specifically addressed the needs of women, for example, through its livestock initiators programme. Activities within this programme have included the training of 302 women in different animal health and animal husbandry packages, and the provision of veterinary services to village women through four veterinary sub-clinics. A three-week refresher training course was held for livestock initiators in Peshawar. Participation in the training programmes was facilitated through culturally acceptable resource persons. UNICEF has provided support to internally displaced persons that is specifically targeted to children and women.

In Panjshir in 1999, UNICEF encouraged the involvement of female internally displaced persons in planning and implementation of projects. UNICEF staff have made regular field visits, insisting on meeting with women and visiting projects for girls and women, and have made relevant recommendations. UNICEF has also insisted that drought relief assistance reach women, girls and boys. Under the umbrella of its parallel programmes Protracted Relief and Recovery Operations and Emergency Operation for Drought Victims, WFP's food assistance has reached a total of 2,650,122 of Afghanistan's most vulnerable people. Of this number, 826,838 are women and 1,060,048 are children, which represents 72 per cent of the total number of vulnerable beneficiaries reached by WFP.

Women food aid monitors have carried out intensive monitoring of some of the WFP food assisted projects in urban areas in order to ensure that women and children have access to and benefit from WFP food supplies. Furthermore, to the extent possible, WFP seeks to build mother and child health clinics, girl's schools and maternity wards, which largely or exclusively benefit females. In July and November 2000, WFP organized two workshops for its gender focal points in order to elaborate on a strategy to reach more female beneficiaries.

The involvement of women in programme activities offered by the United Nations and the assistance community has been severely limited by the Taliban's restrictions on women's employment and mobility.

**Training Courses**

United Nations agencies and NGOs conduct training courses on the rights of children, women and refugees. UNICEF has, for example, trained over 3,000 persons on the Convention on the Rights of the Child in six regions of Afghanistan, both Taliban and non-Taliban controlled, and supported awareness-raising activities on the Convention on the Elimination of All Forms of Discrimination against Women.

Internal capacity-building on the rights-based approach to programming has also continued and additional gender training for staff is being planned. UNICEF plans to carry out training on children's and women's development issues for journalists and provide support to the only remaining television network in the country in Badakhshan. UNFPA, in cooperation with the BBC Afghan Education Project, contributes to the increased understanding of women's reproductive rights and dissemination of health information.

A comprehensive human rights training programme for aid workers covered by both the Committee on the Elimination of Discrimination against Women and the Convention on the Rights of the Child, has been developed and launched in May 2000. Although the related funds have now been received, slow availability and disbursement of funds delayed the pace of the training.

The Gender Adviser has also initiated a series of gender training workshops for United Nations staff. Gender training workshops for UNDCP and WFP programming staff were, for example, implemented during June and July 1999. The observation of special days, such as International Women's Day and International Day for Disabled Children have contributed greatly to raising awareness of women's human rights. On 8 March 2000, for the very first time during the Taliban rule, a formal public celebration of International Women's Day was held in Kabul.

Seven hundred women of all ages, including former university professors, engineers, teachers, doctors, nurses and school principals attended the celebration. Ten of them were honoured with prizes from the organizers of the celebration, namely the United Nations system working in close collaboration with the Taliban authorities. A representative of the supreme leader of the Taliban, Mullah Mohammad Omar, made a statement at the celebration. Radio Shariah, the official Taliban radio station, covered the event and permission was granted to a wide cross-section of international media to attend the event and conduct random interviews with the women present. At the end of the celebration, it was announced that six women prisoners would be released in celebration of the Day.

Security concerns continue to be a major cause of constraint in the provision of humanitarian assistance and in accessing Afghan women. The unstable political environment and ongoing conflict make delivery of assistance very difficult and sometimes dangerous. The murder of seven Afghan workers from the United Nations-supported mine awareness programme by an unidentified armed band in western Afghanistan earlier last year illustrates the everyday risks taken by humanitarian personnel. Moreover, in an environment where only female employees have access to Afghan women, the importance of the full removal of all restrictions on female employment and freedom of movement cannot be understated.

The question of free and unhindered access for United Nations programmes and personnel to all populations in need, including the most vulnerable, such as female-headed households, the elderly, disabled individuals, children, marginalized groups and minorities, including refugees, has been one of the priority areas in discussions with the authorities during 1999-2000. All United Nations agencies strongly advocate the safety and mobility of female staff. Although the supplementary protocol on security concluded with the Taliban in March 1999 still remains as the framework for ensuring that agencies are allowed to work effectively in full security, problems remain with its implementation.

**Recruitment of Women**

The rigid division of gender roles in Afghanistan creates a situation where access to Afghan women can be achieved only through female international and national staff. Employment of women by United Nations agencies is therefore a necessary prerequisite for the functioning of all programmes addressing the needs of the female population. Although some agencies, such as WFP and UNICEF, have made strong efforts to improve the gender balance of both their international and national professional staff, the goal of 50/50 gender distribution was not achieved. Furthermore, all incumbents heading United Nations agencies in Afghanistan are still occupied by male professionals, as was the case in 1997.

The Secretary-General noted that the significant lack of resources often means that humanitarian agencies cannot respond to "brutal, life-threatening needs", and he appealed to donors "to respond generously to requests for support".

Of the $221 million requested at the beginning of 2000, donors have contributed $107 million, or 48 per cent. Reports of diminishing international assistance due to donor fatigue are therefore alarming, e.g., for refugees, mine-clearance and drug programmes. The assistance community has been providing Afghanistan with approximately $200 million annually in the last decade.

Most of this assistance has been allocated to short-term humanitarian and emergency programmes. As a result, international assistance addresses human suffering and provides deterrents to major humanitarian disasters, but it does not allow for sustainable medium-term interventions that create an enabling environment for the rehabilitation of the country's social and production sectors, thereby improving the situation of women.

UNICEF has pointed out that there is the need for an assessment of the gender aspects of the drought affecting the country. There is also a need for United Nations agency-specific training plans to strengthen the monitoring, evaluation and impact assessment competencies in programming, including gender-related monitoring and impact assessment competencies. The establishment of an independent Strategic Monitoring Unit to provide indicators and baseline data against which to measure progress on issues of principle, including the assistance community's capacity to address the needs of the most vulnerable, is therefore a welcome development.

**Health Crisis in Afghanistan : Women and Children**

I want to thank congresswoman Maloney, her office staff, and other organiser for this opportunity. Congresswoman Maloney has been a great friend of the Afghan women and has been a strong voice for the cause of the Afghan women since 1996. Congresswoman Maloney, thank you for your care, concern and friendship.

I remember well when President George Bush during his January, 2002 state of the union speech, introduced Afghan cabinet minister Dr. Sima Samar and stated "Today, women are free. "The Afghan women and girls were promised of full restoration of their rights. The Afghan people were promised of peace, security, and a democratic government that represented all the people of Afghanistan, and many other promises.

The bitter truth is that over one and half year after the demise of the Taliban, the warlords are still in power, in most of Afghanistan women and girls still do not have any rights. Women and girls are still suffering severe abuse, harassment and repression at the hands of some of Afghanistan's post-Taliban leaders. Women are still harassed by the religious police. Even in Kabul a team of 90 women from the Ministry of Religious Affairs abuse women in the streets for "un-Islamic behaviour." And Dr. Sima Samar was forced out of government by extremists' six months after the president State of Union Speech.

In sum, the United States government as well as the world's community made many wonderful promises to the Afghan people. The horrible condition of the Afghan women and children's health is an example of many promises unfulfilled.

At meetings in Washington in December 2002, Ferozudeen Feroz, Afghanistan's deputy public health minister stated that 70 per cent of Afghanistan's primary health care clinics could not provide even basic maternal and child services. And that 90 per cent of hospitals lacked equipment to perform caesarian sections. More than 25 per cent of children die before their fifth birthday, and 40 per cent of children deaths are due to such preventable causes as diarrhea and respiratory infections (*The New York Times,* January 2003.)

The Afghan health care system's infrastructure is in ruins. It is reported that about two-thirds of the facilities have toilets, but a majority of these are pit latrines which pose health hazards. Only one-fourth of health care facilities has electricity and about half of them depend on generators. There is no adequate transport system for the patients. Some health facilities use bicycles as the means of transporting patients. In some remote areas where roads do not exist horses are used to transport patients. (Boston-based Management Sciences for Health Survey, 2002).

Afghanistan's health problems include polio, scurvy, malnutrition, anemia, tuberculosis, whooping cough and a high maternal mortality rate. A recent report by the United Nations Assistance Mission in Afghanistan describes the country's maternal mortality as "one of the highest in the world, with two to three women dying every hour." More than half of all Afghan children is suffering from iodine deficiency (BBC, February 2003).

According to Dr. Yon Fleerackers of World Health Organisation, the rate of infant mortality is extremely high. Of every 100 babies born in Afghanistan, 14 are likely to die before reaching the age of five. Those more fortunate can look forward to a life lasting an average of 46 years (BBC, February 2003).

The lack of female health care workers has brought about

the worst health crisis for the Afghani women. The sociocultural restrictions do not allow women to seek care from male health care workers. Almost all of the pregnant women in rural areas and most women in many cities in Afghanistan do not have access to trained female health care professionals for prenatal, childbirth and postnatal care. This combined with war, poverty, and many other factors have led Afghanistan to have the world's highest maternal mortality rate. There are 1,600 deaths per 100,000 births, (Boston-based Management Sciences for Health survey, 2002).

According a joint study by UNICEF and the Atlanta-based Centres for Disease Control and Prevention report (2002) in the remote northeast province of Badakshan, for every 100,000 birth there are 6,500 maternal deaths. The report states that at least 30 per cent the deaths were caused by hemorrhaging and 23 per cent of deaths were caused by obstructed labour. The deaths are preventable if there is proper medical care to stop bleeding or if the babies are delivered Caesarian section. Three-quarters of the babies born to mothers who die in childbirth die themselves within the first year of life, mostly from malnutrition due to lack of breast milk. (UNICEF and CDC Report 2002).

Another disease that kills in Afghanistan, is tuberculosis. The majority of patients infected by the disease are women, that is, 70 per cent of the cases are female patients. The World Health Organization does not have a clear explanation for the phenomenon. However, it believes that some of the social reasons may be relevant to the spread of disease among women. For example, confinement of women to the house, frequent child births, undernourishment, and living in close quarters (WHO Report Cited in IRIN, March 2003).

Mental health care system is almost nonexistent in Afghanistan. Afghanistan's only mental health hospital in Kabul is in ruins and is ill equipped. Some patients are permanently chained to the beds. Violent and schizophrenia patients are confined to darkened cells (WHO report Cited in IRIN, March 2003).

World Health Organisation reports that about four million people, that is, about 20 per cent of the population, suffer from various forms of mental health problems that include depression. Depression is particularly widespread among women. Moreover, thousands of children demonstrate learning or behavioural problems that is the result of war-related trauma. About 95 per cent of the population are affected psychologically by over two decades of war, and yet there is only one mental health hospital for the entire nation (WHO report Cited in IRIN, March 2003).

Added to this horrendous picture of the Afghan health crisis, are the victims of landmines who try to cope without much assistance and the spread of HIV AIDS disease because of drug addiction and sharing of dirty needles.

The state of Afghan women and children health is an example of other state of affairs in Afghanistan. It is not only disappointing it is unsettling. How could the people of Afghanistan (or other areas of conflicts in the world) trust the credibility of promises made by the United States and the rest of the international community? The painful question in the Afghan mind is: are we going to be abandoned again?

We urged the Administration and the international community to keep their promises to the Afghan people. We call on the United States Congress to bring the Afghan women, men and children's miserable condition to attention of the Administration and the international community.

This page is dedicated to the plight of the Afghan Woman. Currently, there are thousands of widows in the capital of Afghanistan. Women are forced to cover themselves from head to toe, denied access to education and proper health care, forbidden to work in order to support their families, and face brutal beatings if they do not comply with the rules set forth for them by their oppressors. The world needs to know about this tragedy; our hope is that this page will become a good source of recent news and information pertaining to the current struggle women in Afghanistan are facing.

### Muslim Women's Perspective on Women's Plight in Afghanistan

The Taliban have forced Women to cover themselves from head to toe. Even the face is covered; this is in direct contradiction to Islamic Law!

Today , in Afghanistan woman's basic right to vote, to pursue an education, and to join the job force, is threatened by

Taliban, a political group that has recently gained control of the country. Taliban's insistence on secluding women from public life is a political manoeuvre disguised as "Islamic" law. Before seizing power, Taliban manipulated and used the rights of women as tools to gain control of the country. To secure financial and political support, Taliban emulated authoritarian methods typical of many Middle Eastern countries.

Taliban's stand on the seclusion of women is not derived from Islam, but, rather, from a cultural bias found in suppressive movements throughout the region.

Once Taliban seized power, a classical pattern tnat has been observed in some Muslim countries repeated itself. In this scenario, political instability coexists with an extreme and oppressive ideology regarding women. Some members of Taliban have been quoted as saying that these actions are temporary and that women's rights will be restored once the government is more stable. One must bear in mind that, as history has amply demonstrated, other Muslim countries have committed the same atrocities and the result is that women within their boundaries continue to be oppressed, politically and otherwise. To maintain control over the people, radical groups such as Taliban divert attention away from political and economic crises by oppressing half of the population.

Such a view has no basis in the Qur'an, yet it has been promoted by Taliban as "Islamic." This situation is very distressing considering that women were given rights in the Qur'an to contribute to the economy by owning and selling property 1400 years ago:

*Men shall have a benefit from what they earn, and women shall have a benefit from what they earn. (4:32)*

This verse emphasizes the equality of men and women in the economic growth of a society. In the earliest Muslim community, women carried out business transactions and participated in battles without restriction. The Qur'an and the examples of the first Muslim society give the Muslim Women's League a voice to state that the current manipulation of women to serve geo-political interests, in Afghanistan or elsewhere, is both unIslamic and inhumane.

**Women's Position, Role, and Rights in Islam**

In this paper I argue that the position of women in Islam

in theory, that is, according to the Qur'an and Hadiths (tradition) of the Prophet, differs vastly from Islam in practice. It is not the Islamic ideologies that determine the position of women in the Islamic societies, it is rather the pre-Islamic patriarchal ideologies existing in a particular society, combined with the lack of education and ignorance, that construct the Muslim women's position.

**Women's Position in Islam in the Idea of Creation**

Islam in theory, has given men and women equal rights in every aspects of life. Islam gives men and women equality in the idea of Creation of human beings. Concerning the idea of Creation the Qur'an in Sura 4, Verse 1 states:

O mankind! reverence your Guardian-Lord Who created you from a single Person, Created, of like nature, His mate, and from them twain Scattered (like seeds) Countless men and women-Fear Allah, through Whom ye demand your mutual (rights) and (reverence) the wombs (that bore you): For Allah Ever watches over you.

In Sura 7, Verse 189 the Qur'an States:

It is He Who created you from a single person, and made his mate of like nature, in order that he might dwell with her (in love)...

Sura 42, Verse 11 states:

(He is) the Creator of Heaven and the Earth: He has made for you pai from among yourselves...

Sura 49, Verse 13 states:

O mankind! We created you from a single (pair) of male and female, and made you into nations and tribes, that you may know each other (not that you despise each other)...

And Sura 16, Verse 72 States: And Allah has made for you mates (and Companions) of your own nature...

**Women's Spiritual Status in Islam**

Not only in the idea of creation Islam has granted equality to men and women, but also women are given the same spiritual status as men. For example Qur'an Sura 33 Verse 35 states: For Muslim men and women-For believing men and women. For devoted men and women, for true men and women, for men and women who are patient and constant, for men and women who humble themselves, for men and women who give in charity, for men and women who fast (and deny themselves), for men and women who guard their chastity, and for men and women who engage much in Allah praise—for them has Allah prepared forgiveness and great reward.

In Sura 74, Verse 38 the Qur'an states:

Every soul will be (held) in pledge for its deeds. In Sura 16, Verse 97 the Qur'an states: Whoever works righteousness, man or woman, and has Faith, Verily, to him will We give new Life, and life that is good and pure, and We will bestow on such their reward according to the best of their actions. In Sura 4, Verse 124 the Qur'an states: If any do deeds of righteousness-be they male or female and have faith, they will enter Heaven, and not the least injustice will be done to them.

In the above verses a woman's obligations to the Islamic principles and practices are the same as those of a man. Women are not exempted from any of these obligations because of their gender. However, under special circumstances a woman may not be required to fast, examples would be when she is pregnant, or is nursing a child—if fasting threatens her life or her child's life. A man or a woman is exempt from fasting if he/she is sick or traveling. But he/she must make up for days he/she has missed in fasting at a more convenient time. A woman may not fast or participate in the performance of prayers during her menstrual periods and after child birth as long as she is bleeding. But again, she must make up for the days she has missed fasting.

**Women Rights in Islam Regarding Education**

The Qur'an and Hadiths of the Prophet both obligate Muslim men and women to acquire knowledge and education. It is a duty for every Muslim. For example, concerning knowledge and education the Qur'an Sura 35 Verse 28 states:

Those truly fear Allah, among His Servants, who have knowledge. Prophet's Hadiths repeatedly emphasizes the acquirement of education and knowledge for every Muslim male and female. For example, one Hadith states that, "Seeking knowledge is a duty of every Muslim, man or woman." (Ayisha Lemu 1978: 25). Another Hadith states, "Seek knowledge from the cradle to grave." (1978:25). Another Hadith states that, "The Father, if he educates his daughter well, will enter Paradise." (The World Bank Report July 9, 1993: 25). Yet another Hadith states that, " A mother is a school. If she is educated, then a whole people are educated" (1993: 25).

In early of Islamic history there were many women scholars who had very significant roles in the Islamic world. For example, Ayisha, the Prophet's wife was one of the most famous Muslim scholars. Not only was she very intelligent, she had an exceptional memory. That is why she was considered one of the most important sources of Hadith. It has been stated in some Islamic reports that the Prophet told the Muslims to go to Ayisha for guidance and learning of religious duties. The Prophet also told the Muslims to trust Ayisha's teaching and guidance (Lemu 1978:: 251). In the Islamic world, at the beginning of Islam, there were no restrictions or prohibitions toward women to seek knowledge and education. There were many women scholars in the fields of religion, literature, music, education, and medicine. For example, a woman named Nafisa who was related to Ali, the fourth Khalif, had a vast knowledge of and was an expert on the Hadiths of the Prophet. Many famous Muslim scholars of the time, such as Imam Shafiai would participate in Nafisa's scholarly discourse and learn from her (1978: 251-253).

**Women's Social Position in Islam**

In the pre-Islamic era, in the Arab societies, the women were deprived of the most basic human rights that is required for human existence. The practice of female infanticide was widely practiced among some of the Arab tribes. The first and foremost contribution that Islam made to elevating the social status of the Arab women was to give them the right to live. Islam forbade this inhuman practice and was highly critical of the attitudes allowing parents to reject their female children. Islam viewed the practice as a crime and murder.

Concerning the birth of a girl child and the patriarchal Arab society's attitudes toward it, the Qur'an Sura 16, Verse 58 states:

When news is brought to one of them, of (the birth of) a female (child), his face darkens, and he is filled with inward grief!

The issue is continued in the Verse 59 in the same Sura : With shame does he hide himself from his people, because of the bad news he had! On (sufferance and) contempt, or bury it in dust? Ah! what an evil (choice) they decide on?

In Sura 81 Verses 8 and 9 the Qur'an states:

When the female (infant) buried alive, is questioned-For what crime she was killed; Thus, the Qur'an viewed both the attitude of contempt and shame concerning the birth of a female child and the act of infanticide as equally evil. Along with saving the lives of women, Islam made sure they were treated with respect, kindness and justice. Women's Rights Concerning Marriage.

The equality of men and women is recognized by Islam in marriage. The Qur'an views the marriage of a man and a woman as sharing of the two halves of society. The objective of marriage, aside from human reproduction, are love, mercy, mutual respect, justice, emotional well being and spiritual harmony. Concerning this subject, the Qur'an Sura 30, Verse 21 states:

Among His Signs is this, that He created for you mates from among yourselves, that ye may dwell in tranquillity with them, and He has put love and mercy between your (hearts): Verily in that are Signs for those who reflect. This verses is central because it defines the relationship between the husband and the wife. Their relation is not just sexual, but also it involves love, mutual care, consideration and respect.

The Qur'an strongly emphasizes regulations governing behaviour, conduct and human relation, for the purpose of preserving the family. The woman's role within the family is a crucial one, because it is in the family that the next generation of Muslims are raised. The woman as the mother has the crucial role as the early socializer and educators of the children. This role has a long lasting effect on the behaviour, character and attitudes of the future generation of Muslims.

Islamic Law forbids the marriage of a woman by force. The girl's and the boy's consent is necessary. Although the parents play a major role in deciding a girl's or a boy's choice of mates, the final decision is up to the girl and the boy. For example, according to Ibn Abbas, a girl came to the Prophet and said that her father had forced her into marriage without her consent. The Prophet gave her the choice of either continuing the marriage, or invalidating it (Badawi 1976: 139).

There are verses in the Qur'an concerning men and

women that are controversial and have been the topic of discussion by various scholars throughout the Islamic history. These verses have been used by different individuals in order to discredit Islam. For example, in Sura 2, Verse 228 the Qur'an states:

And women shall have rights similar to rights against them, according to what is equitable. But men have a degree (of advantage) over them. And Allah is Exalted in Power, Wise.

This verse has been interpreted in different ways. Some see it as a degree in intelligence, other view it as a degree in superiority. However, many Muslim scholars argue that the degree is related to qiwama, that is, maintenance of the family. A man is legally obligated for this responsibility. Therefore, this "degree above them" has an economic base and has nothing to do with intelligence or superiority of men over women (1976 : 138-139).

Another controversial verse deals with the marriage of a men to two, three or four women. In Sura 4, Verse 3 the Qur'an states:

If ye fear that ye shall not be able to deal justly with orphans, marry women of your choice, two, or three, or four; But ye fear that ye shall not be able to deal justly (with them), Then only one..

This verse first sets the conditional clause of the orphans, that introduces the rules for marriage. This verse comes after the war of Uhud when the Muslim community had to deal with many orphans and widows. The Qur'an allows marriage of a man to up to four women, so that the war widows and their children are protected from destitution. The Qur'an also orders the Muslims to treat the orphans and widows with justice and equality (Qur'an note 508, page: 184).

However, in Sura 4, Verse 129 the Qur'an states:

Ye are never able to be fair and just as between women, even if it is your ardent desire: but turn not away (from a woman) altogether, so as to leave her (as it were) hanging (in the air). If ye come to a friendly understanding, and practice self-restraint, Allah is Oft-Forgiving, Most Merciful.

Although the Qur'an allows a man to marry up to four women, it also sets conditions to this rule, that is, the husband must treat his wives with equality and justice in every aspect, that is, love, maintenance and so on. Moreover, in the verse 129 that the Qur'an states that a man is never capable of treating all his wives equally and justly in every aspect of life. Thus, in truth, Islam encourages marriage with only one woman.

From the Islamic point of view, all family decisions should be done with mutual agreement of husband and wife, even if it is only weaning of a child from nursing.. For example, in Sura 2, Verse 233 the Qur'an states: ... If they [husband and wife] both decide on weaning, by mutual consent, and after due consultation, there is no blame on them.

The Qur'an and Hadiths both emphasizes the treatment of women with respect, justice and kindness. For example, one Hadith states "Fear God and respect women," another states "the best person amongst you is the one who has the best attitude toward women".

In pre-Islamic Arab societies, women were bought and sold as commodity. Islam by giving women the right to decide who to marry, and have a part in the marriage contract, elevated her status from that of a commodity to that of an equal partner in the marriage institution.

The Qur'an also gave women the right to own her own *mahr*. The *mahr* is a payment that the husband makes to the wife and is an important part of the marriage contract. It provides a woman with some kind of economic means in case of divorce and it also gives the woman the means of controlling the man's power of divorce (Esposito 1982: 17, 24-26).

The rights of women concerning divorce are also recognized by Islam. Women have the same rights as those of men. However, due to the importance placed on the family in Islam, for its protection and maintenance, certain procedures must be followed by both men and women. For example, after the divorce both a man and a woman must wait a period of three months, called *iddah*. During this period of time the husband is responsible for the wife's maintenance. This waiting period has two functions: (1) to clarify whether the woman is pregnant or not. If she is pregnant, the husband is responsible for the wife's maintenance until the child is born. Furthermore, if the woman who is divorced has a young child, she can nurse the child for up two years and the father must maintain both the woman and her child. (2) Iddah also function as a cooling-off period during which the relatives and the community will try to help reconcile the couple (Lemu 1978: 257-258).

**The Economic and Political Position of Women in Islam**

Islam has given women the rights to work, to own property and to have wealth. Women can seek employment and work in profession such as medical care, teaching, civil and justice professions. These rights remains the same before and after marriage.

Regarding the right to work, the Qur'an Sura 4, Verse 32 states:

And in no wise covet those things in which Allah hath bestowed His gifts more freely on some of you than on others: to men is allotted what they earn, and to women what they earn: But ask Allah of his bounty. For Allah hath full knowledge of all things.

In the Islamic history there were no restrictions in women's full participation in the economic, political and social spheres of their society. For example, Khadija, the Prophet's first wife was one of the most important merchants of the time, and the Prophet himself was her employee. Ayisha, the Prophet's other wife was one of his most important advisers and consultants. In the early Islamic history women not only participated in various aspects of their society's public sphere, they also had the right to be elected to political offices. For example, Omar the second Khalif appointed a woman to oversee the affairs of the marketplace. The women also participated in wars and fought in the battles.

Islam give women the right to inheritance. Neither her father nor her husband can lay any claim to her share of inheritance. Regarding this issue the Qur'an, Sura 4, Verse 7 states:

From what is left by parents, and those nearest related there is a share for men and a share for women, whether the property be small or large—a determinate share.

In Sura 4, Verse 11 the Qur'an states:

Allah (thus) directs you as regards your children's (inheritance): to the male, a portion equal to that of two females... This Verse also has been the centre of controversy. Many individuals believe that this decision does not benefit women economically. Others argue that the decision is fair because a man is legally obligated to maintain his wife, children, parents and other relatives who are in need of assistance. Whereas a woman is exempt from these legal obligations. Her share is hers alone, she does not have to contribute to the family's maintenance if she does not want to do so.

The above brief discussion shows the equal status of men and women in Islam. However, in practice, these rights have been violated and the position of Muslim women has undergone dramatic changes for the worst since early Islamic era. Upon the death of the Prophet, the restriction of women's rights began to increase with the course of history. The pre-Islamic societies of Arab, Persian, Indians and others were patriarchal societies. They had their own cultures, customs, and belief systems.

The rapid expansion of Islam did not leave the new converts enough time to obtain sufficient Islamic education. This lead to disagreements between the new converts and the process of Islamization, that is, Islamic education and acculturation. These factors, in conjunction with growing wealth, leisure activities, sensuality combined with the corrupt morality of royals that influenced the upper class, stirred fear in all classes of urban groups for the chastity of their women. The socio-historical causes which led to the deterioration in the position, status, and role of Muslim women are many the effect of these causes on the position of women was grave and led to their severe oppression. Her social, economic and political rights were violated. To make matters worse, her face, public presence, and voice became Awarah, that is, the subject of concealment (Alyamoni unpublished Dissertation, University of Illinois at Urbana-Campaign 1985: 48-50).

**UN Report Flays Taliban Rights Violations Against Women in Afghanistan**

A UN report accused the radical Islamic regime in Afghanistan Thursday of violating women's rights with "unabated severity," including mass abductions and forced prostitution.

The report cited testimony from refugees about the large-scale abduction of women and girls by militia of the ruling Taliban movement during fighting last year in the northern and central parts of the country.

UN rapporteur Kamal Hossain provided testimony about ethnic Hazara and Tajik women being rounded up in trucks and taken from the regions of Mazar-e-Sharif, Pol-e-Khomri and Shamali to neighbouring Pakistan and the Taliban stronghold of Kandahar.

"Many suspect that women and girls end up forced into prostitution," his report said, adding that "women have been killed and maimed trying to escape from these trucks."

Women from the Kabul, Mazar-e-Sharif and Shamali regions also gave accounts of forced marriages to Taliban members, it said.

"When families refuse they take the women and girls away by force," it said, adding that many families in Shamali had sent their daughters away to avoid such a fate.

The Taliban militia, committed to a radical fundamentalist form of Islam, swept to power nearly four years ago and now controls most of Afghanistan, although fighting against rival movements continues in parts of the country.

Since coming to power, the Taliban has barred women from attending schools or working outside the home. Women can only appear in public hidden in head-to-toe robes.

Routinely targetted by the world community for abusing women's rights, the Taliban on Wednesday marked International Women's Day for the first time, bringing around 700 women to a Kabul women's hospital in buses with dark curtains drawn.

But the UN report insisted the Taliban continued to enforce its severe edicts against women's participation in public life "with unabated severity."

It said the regime continued to deny women access to education, health and employment and quoted refugees relating stories "of the abduction of women, rape, infliction of the punishment of stoning, lashing and other forms of inhuman punishment."

The report by Hossain, who conducted several visits to Afghanistan and Pakistan, was based on a survey of internally displaced Afghans and refugees who left the country between the end of 1998 and third quarter of 1999.

The report was compiled in January and will be presented to the UN Commission on Human Rights during meetings beginning on March 20.

Hossain gave evidence that non-Afghans, including Pakistanis and Arabs, who are fighting alongside the Taliban, are also involved in the rights violations against women and ethnic minorities.

Fighting in Afghanistan intensified last year in the central highlands particularly in Bamyan and in the Shamali Plains north of Kabul.

Hossain related evidence of summary executions of non-combatants by Taliban forces, arbitrary detentions and forced labour.

"All these practices constitute grave human rights violations," he said.

"The actions, reportedly carried out by Taliban forces who were engaged in military operations, ran directly counter to assurances publicly given by the Taliban leadership with regard to the rights of the civilian populations," the report said.

**Taliban Reject UN Report on Violation of Women's Rights**

Afghanistan Foreign Minister Mulla Wakil Ahmad Mutawwakil on Sunday rejected a United Nations (UN) report that accused Afghanistan's ruling Taliban of violating women's rights with unabated severity. Speaking from Kandahar, southwestern Afghanistan, he questioned the methods used to arrive at such conclusions. He described the UN rapporteur Kamal Hossain, who compiled the report, as "an ignorant and incompetent man who is working solely for money."

Mutawwakil said human rights issue had been turned into a business by the people like Kamal Hossain. "This man hasn't taken the trouble to verify facts, seek Taliban version regarding allegations against them, and check his information before making his report public," alleged the Afghan foreign minister.

Mutawwakil claimed Kamal Hossain was biased toward Taliban. "He lacks experience to tackle human rights issues and has fallen prey to propaganda against the Taliban by their opponents. Where is the proof that Taliban have abducted women or forced them into prostitution. It is an irresponsible statement and the UN has lost all credibility by publicising such baseless reports."

Kamal Hossain, a former foreign minister of Bangladesh, compiled his report following visits to Pakistan and

Afghanistan. The report is based on a survey of internally displaced Afghans and refugees who left the country during 1998-99.

**Afghan Women Remain Victims of Hope Unfulfilled**

It's a small but deadly undertow in Afghanistan's tide of rising expectations.

Under the religio-psychotic Taliban, Afghan women inhabited a unique and living hell. Now the Taliban are forgotten, though not entirely gone. And yet, girls and young women in Herat, on Afghanistan's southwestern border with Iran, are drenching themselves in gasoline and setting lit matches to their clothes.

George Bush vowed a year ago to wreak vengeance on Osama bin Laden, destroy the Al-Queda network, rebuild Afghanistan so that it would never again serve as a hatchery for insane mass murderers—and, by George, to liberate the women. (Women's liberation has had many cynical and insincere allies, but George and Laura Bush must trump them all).

Despite all this, nine young women in Herat have, within the last year, tried to immolate themselves to escape from forced marriages. Four have died.

A 19 year old had time to explain, before she died of burns to 92 per cent of her body, that her family had sold her for $10,000 as a second wife to a 28 year old man. A 14 year old girl died the same way after being married off to a 60 year old man. Local authorities say they are baffled by the sudden storm of self-immolations. Why now? Under the vile Taliban, this didn't happen. Why despair now that there's hope? they ask. I think I know why: precisely because the hope has been so illusory. If Bush carries out his war on Iraq, we had better pray that he doesn't bungle the job as disastrously as he has in Afghanistan, where Osama bin Laden is still undiscovered, the Al-Queda network is said to be shipping vast amounts of gold to new hiding places, the country remains in ruins, the people face mass starvation, known criminals among the Northern Alliance are ensconced in government, and the situation of women has changed only marginally. One of the two women in cabinet, Dr. Sima Samar, has already been hounded from office by Islamic conservatives. The problem is that the Americans have never delivered on their promises. Last January, the U.S. promised a paltry $296 million in aid for the year—but only $50 million of that was actually new money. The rest had already been pledged to ongoing projects. (Meanwhile, the U.S. spends $1 billion a month on 'Operation Enduring Freedom').

"You can't rebuild a country without roads, water, electricity, housing," said author and activist Sally Armstrong. Her recent book *Veiled Threat,* offers a vivid picture of Afghan women's struggles, based in part on Armstrong's frequent and daring visits to the country. "No government can possibly achieve stability without doing something for its people. The conservatives in government are constantly pressuring President Karzai. The chief justice himself is a fundamentalist, and just last month the court ordered that women's voices not be played on the radio," Armstrong said in an interview.

The media feasted on pictures of Afghan women in Kabul throwing off their burqas, and on the photogenic little girls grinning rapturously on their first day back at school. We all had a pleasant snapshot of triumphant liberation before our attention drifted elsewhere.

Meanwhile, the life expectancy for Afghan women is 40 to 45 years; maternal mortality is probably the highest in the world. The U.N. says 70 per cent of Afghans suffer from malnutrition. Although almost half the girls in Kabul are attending school (and let me not minimize that wonderful victory), outside the capital the numbers fall to a puny 9 per cent. In a town west of Kabul, the local Taliban has just blown up a girls' school and vowed to kill any woman who goes to school or work.

It will take Daryas of money and years of education to scrub away the toxic legacy of male domination in the Afghan culture. "Even now, you can hear five year old boys talking so horribly to their mothers, ordering them to be silent, to hide themselves, fetch this, do that," Armstrong said. The women barely have time or energy to resent such injustices (the swimming pool in Kabul, for example, recently re-opened for boys and men only) when merely keeping themselves and their children alive is an exhausting struggle.

The most remarkable thing I've learned about these women, from Armstrong and from dozens of international news accounts, is their gritty resolve to go to school. In story after story, I read of women who have never had so much as the freedom to leave their houses without male permission - and yet, in the teeth of continuing opposition from fathers, husbands, sons and mullahs, they are determined to get an education.

Because so many continue to wear the burqa (in self-protection from armed and fanatical men), it has been easy for outside observers to conclude that the Afghan women consented to their own subjugation. But the opposite is true. In self-preservation, they are grimly biding their time.

"I had to wait until my husband died before I was able to come to school," a 79 year old woman told a reporter as she clutched a grade one primer.

It's not so hard to imagine the despair of those young women in Herat, also facing decades of marital slavery. Death in the flames could seem preferrable to the bitterness of hope held out, and then snatched away.

It seems to me that this despair of the Afghans is a storm warning to Americans and their "enduring freedom".

**Of Afghanistan**

The students are crammed on to the benches in the cavernous lecture hall of Kabul University's science faculty. Four hundred eager faces stare down at us, and 150 of them are female. A few rows from the front sits a young woman wearing a white lace scarf tucked tightly around her rosy face. Her name is Zohal Faiz Mohammed. She shakes her head, smiling, when I ask how she feels to be back at university after five years' absence. "I can't say my feelings - you can see. For the first time we can experience the university, this atmosphere. We can all study, boys and girls together."

That evening, Zohal invites us to have supper with her and her parents. They live in what is, by Kabul's standards, a comfortable neighbourhood, but that still means a chaotic stretch of apartment blocks with blown-out windows and walls riddled with bullet holes. While Zohal prepares the meal, we sit on cushions on the floor of the pink sitting room, talking to her parents. Suddenly Zohal rushes in, worried that we are bored, and shows off one of her most precious possessions, a video of songs from Indian films. "My father and I love these," she says eagerly.

She watches the gorgeous Aishwarya Rai dancing in a Technicolor field of dreams. "Isn't she beautiful?" As she watches the video, Zohal, in jeans and a white shirt with the sleeves rolled up, her thick black hair in a ponytail, looks younger than her 22 years.

She is determined to be young, determined to be happy, determined not to talk about politics instead, we talk about her errant fiance and her plans for the future. After dinner, she, her mother and her cousin squabble over the arrangements for the photographs. "Don't fight!" Zohal says. "All right, do fight." "I'll be Rabbani and you can be Hekmatyar," says the photographer. Peals of laughter ring out. Those are the names of the men whose armies laid Kabul waste in the 1990s. "All you can do sometimes is laugh," says her mother, wiping her eyes with a corner of her scarf.

As we talk over dinner, I can't help thinking that Zohal's happiness feels like the uncomplicated optimism of any young woman at the start of her life. But Afghan women are not like other women, and when they sound optimistic, this is an act of determined bravery. On another day, when Zohal and I meet for tea, she talks about the past. Her face changes, loses its pink glow, and she fumbles with her fingers.

Her comfortable childhood came under siege in 1992, after the Soviet - backed regime fell and mujaheddin armies - armed by the west - battled for control of Kabul, street by street. "I remember every night, sitting in the corner of the room, listening to the rockets and the bombs," says Zohal in a dull tone very different from her earlier quick chatter. "And every morning we would go out and help to collect the dead bodies. There was nothing to think about. We were just waiting for our death. We had no hope for the future, not even for our lives."

Zohal's family were forced out of their home more than once when the fighting concentrated around their area. They became refugees again when they fled from the extreme oppression of the Taliban, and spent two years in Pakistan, but the destitution that faced so many Afghans there forced them back to Kabul last year. They went on the move again to the

Pakistani border during the US bombing last winter. Refugees three times - from the mujaheddin, the Taliban and the Americans - Zohal's family are now starting over, trying to put their lives back together out of the fragments they have left.

But Zohal's face is set towards the future. She wants to be an engineer, studies at the university in the morning, and takes English and computing classes in the afternoon. Since today is a holiday, we visit one of Kabul's newly opened beauty saloons. Marya saloon sits next to a restaurant where lamb kebabs are seared over open barbecues, and beside a music stall that is stacked with colourful Indian and Iranian cassettes. But even here, in this reawakened part of Kabul, if you stop on the street for a moment, the beggars, women and children, tug at your arms and hands.

Inside the saloon, the air is thick with hairspray and scent, and Fazila, the owner, a stout woman in a black dress with neatly styled auburn hair, is getting through one client after another with astonishing speed. She and her two young daughters work like an assembly line. Curlers are whipped out and in, tweezers tug at eyebrows, kohl is rubbed on to eyelids. Shaima and Suheila, two sisters, both doctors, are waiting on Fazila's couches. Both have their hair pinned up under hairnets. Tomorrow is Shaima's wedding day and they are determined to do it in high Afghan style, all glittery dresses and curled hair and hennaed hands.

"When she had her engagement ceremony," Suheila explains, "we couldn't take photographs though we did, secretly. We couldn't even have musicians." What would the Taliban have done if you had invited musicians? Suheila draws a finger across her throat. "But I played a cassette, quietly, and I danced - I was determined to dance." She is about to tell me more when a little boy runs in. The girls at home need more curlers. Suheila springs to her feet and picks up her burka. "Don't you want to know why I still wear this?" she asks. She stands silhouetted in the bright doorway, holding the swathe of blue nylon above her face.

The western press has made so much of the idea that, as the Taliban left Kabul, the liberated women threw off their blue shrouds. But in Kabul, almost all the young women are still wearing the burka. This is not through force of tradition. There was a custom of wearing the burka among some ethnic groups in Afghanistan, but not among educated women in the cities. I asked 20 or 30 women why they were still wearing it, and all gave the same answer. Fear.

"We aren't safe yet," says Suheila succinctly. This sense of insecurity is understandable. The mujaheddin and the Taliban weren't just a few maniacs who have now disappeared, but hundreds and thousands of "willing executioners" - men who gang-raped women as part of their wars, as the mujaheddin did, or who beat women savagely for showing their faces, as the Taliban did. These men have not gone away, and although in Kabul they are kept quiet by the presence of the international security force, if that departs, many women fear that the violence will start again.

"Of course, the burka was not the worst thing about the Taliban time," Suheila emphasises. "But until we are safe, we can't take it off." Even now, reports of politically and religiously motivated violence against women continue. Human Rights Watch has documented rapes and assaults against certain ethnic groups in northern Afghanistan. Female aid workers have even been withdrawn from Mazar-i-Sharif after one was gang-raped. In Kabul a month ago, two women wearing scarves instead of *burkas* had acid sprayed in their faces. So, for the women of Afghanistan, the anonymity of the burka still gives them a sense of protection. Zohal, who also wears the burka when she goes out, agrees with Suheila.

"Of course we would like to take it off," she says, "but it just isn't possible yet."

Some of the women who have taken off the burka are those now moving into politics. My visit coincides with the start of the loya jirga, the gathering of a council of 1,500 delegates who are to decide the structure of the future government. Nearly 200 are women. I visit the council offices, where dozens of Afghan men circle the courtyard, talking eagerly. Out on the parched A grass is a tent, and inside the stifling tent sit 15 women, newly arrived delegates from western provinces of the country.

A woman in her early 30s, also called Zohal, talks enthusiastically about what this means to her. Her two-year-old daughter, silently playing with a wilted pink rose, sits on her lap as she talks. "The doors of everything have been closed to women for so long," she says. "Now we hope that the doors are swinging open. This loya jirga is only a first step, but in the future parliament there must be equal representation for women and for men."

Mindful that even in western countries women haven't achieved such representation, I ask the other women in the tent if they feel the same. There is an eruption of noise. "Yes, they all agree," my translator says solemnly. "They say that women make up more than half of the population of Afghanistan and that they have been the first victims of war. They must now be allowed their rights."

Sitting next to Zohal is Bibi Kur, a woman with a look of the younger Doris Lessing. She comes from Herat. "There, our leaders did not want a single woman to go to the loya jirga," she says scornfully. "But people from Kabul came and insisted, so they said there could be one woman from each province, one out of eight delegates." Is she scared to be a delegate when the warlords are so against women's involvement? "I am afraid," she says. "I know these men. But I've survived 23 years of war. I have been injured.

My husband has been injured. Now I am happy that I am here and that I can defend women's rights."

It is easy to be delighted by the energy and determination of these women who are moving back into politics. But in the weeks that follow, as the loya jilrga progresses, the idealistic women are sidelined. The power is still held by men who control the guns and the money, former mujaheddin who gained their influence through bloody fighting and terrorising civilians; men such as Abdul Rashid Dostum, Ismail Khan and Burhanuddin Rabbani, all of whom retain power over areas of Afghanistan and who pack the loya jirga with their supporters. Although we in the west see such men as useful allies, the women I spoke to have not forgotten their crimes. Indeed, on the first day of the loya jirga, some female delegates, among them Tajwah Kakur, confront Rabbani. "Why did your armies kill and rape so many women?" Kakur asks. "Why are there so many widows in our country?" He is silent.

I spend an afternoon talking to Kakur at her office in the women's ministry, set up last year by the interim administration. Kakur, the deputy women's minister, sits still as a monument behind her glass-topped desk, her silver hair piled up under a grey voile scarf. She is unusual among the new women in Afghan politics, because she was even tolerated by - and herself accepted - the Taliban regime, and ran a boys' school in Kabul during their rule. Even so, she says her dreams have now come true: "I am so happy looking at women going back to work and school. I think, is this a dream? Or is it real life?"

But for all her optimistic talk, Kakur is angry about the current situation and the men who are moving back into power. "All Afghan women know who I am talking about. These men kidnapped and raped the women of Afghanistan. Until the guns are taken away from them, women will not have security. Yes, now we are told that these men are heroes. But who broke all the buildings and kidnapped the women? They are not heroes. They are zeroes."

But women in Afghanistan are not only struggling against the men who rule them. Many are simply struggling to survive. As we leave Kakur's office, we walk through a corridor where dozens of women with their *burkas* pushed back from their faces are squatting outside the offices. A female official shoos them away into a courtyard. We follow them into the blinding glare of the midday sun, and ask who they are and why they are here. As they speak, I catch a glimpse of another Afghanistan, the one where so many women, especially those whose husbands and brothers were killed in the decades of fighting, now live.

One of these women, Khandijal, is five months pregnant, although her bump hardly shows on her skeletal frame, wrapped in its blue burka. Five months go, a US bomb killed her husband and injured her leg. "For four months I have been coming here every day to beg for work," she says. "There is no work for us." Khandijal has five daughters, all younger than 12. "Every day I go back home and my children cry out, 'Where is the money, where is the food I have nothing for them. My children are starving and nobody here will do anything for me."

"Life for me was better under the Taliban," Hanifa, a tiny, skinny woman, says defiantly. Her husband was killed three years ago, and she has seven children. "The UN gave the widows in Kabul a card to take to a centre to get food free. We got five naan bread a day. So our children ate lunch and dinner. Now we have nothing. At first, when the Americans came, I was happy. I thought, our lives will get better. But there is nothing for us. The Americans never asked about us."

"Will you help us?" all the women ask, one by one. "Will you help to find us work?" When we explain that we don't work for the UN or an aid organisation, they look puzzled. I go on asking questions, which they answer eagerly, perhaps hoping that we will give them something in return. We have all seen and read tales of such desperation a thousand times, but looking at desperation is very different from having desperation look back at you, hungrily.

If you listen to the talk of the amount of money that has been promised to Afghanistan, it is easy to feel complacent about the way the international community is stepping in to reconstruct the country. Certainly, for many people life has improved - despite what Hanifa says, for instance, the UN World Food Programme tells me that it is now reaching about three times as many destitute people as it could under the Taliban regime. But although more aid is coming in now, far more has been promised than is reaching the country, as donors hold back in case the fragile peace collapses. And what has arrived - around $800 m in the first half of the year - is not enough to stop the immediate suffering of millions of ordinary people. Afghan women are thought to have the highest maternal mortality rates of women in any country, at around 1,700 per 100,000; life expectancy is about 46 years, and around 50 per cent of children are stunted through malnutrition - yet donor fatigue is already a real danger. Dr Lynn Amowitz of Harvard Medical School, who is leading a new matemal mortality survey in Afghanistan, said recently,

"Afghanistan is falling off people's radar screen and funding is becoming harder to find."

One of the women standing with the widows is younger than they are, and her face still has the sleekness of a girl who eats every day. Akala is only 19.

"I started school again last month," she says. "But every afternoon I come here and ask for work. There are 10 of us brothers and sisters, and my father is too old to work. For us, life is becoming worse day by day." Has she seen anything get better? "Yes, of course, we are free to go outside," she says quickly, "and now I can go to school. But what can I say about my future? Unless I find work, I will I have to leave school. I can't pay for paper and pencils. And I can't go to school if my brothers and sisters are starving."

As we drive away from the government buildings, clouds of dust rise from the roads and even the men walking on the streets pull scarves over their faces to protect their eyes and mouths. This is the regular Kabul dust-storm that rises up every afternoon. One returning Afghan told me that in his childhood, before the wars, they never used to have this weather, these clouds of dust blocking out the sunlight and surrounding the mountains with what looks like drifting smoke. He was probably right, since this drought started only a few years ago, but his statement sounded metaphorical - as if the very earth had begun to choke on its burden of misery.

The idea that Afghanistan was destroyed by war was only an image to me until I actually saw Kabul, with the rubble and ruins stretching for mile after mile into the bleak mountains, like a film set designer's vision of a city after a nuclear war. I had to keep reminding myself that Kabul was not always a dystopian city - that once, in the 1970s and 1980s, it was cosmopolitan, with women walking down the streets in miniskirts, crowded jazz clubs and colourful parks. It's also important to remember that Afghan women were not always victims. In the 80s, 40 per cent of doctors and 50 per cent of university students in Kabul were women - and though such liberation did not extend throughout Afghanistan, many urban, educated women lived lives of relative freedom.

But one thing that astounded me was that even those women who have lived all their lives in the most traditional sections of society can still speak a language of resistance. One day, for instance, I visited Sarasia, a bleak little village west of Kabul. Women here live close to the edge; even the village well, after three years of drought, is no longer working, so the women and children traipse across the fields to the neighbouring village every day to collect water. In one of the stark white houses, a literacy class is in progress. The women in this class couldn't be further from the educated elite. Soraya, for instance, is a widow of 50 and has been illiterate all her life. "If you are illiterate, it is as if you are blind," she says. Her eldest son doesn't want her to learn to read, but she has finally won his permission because this class is run by women for women in their own village.

In this village, all the women wear *burkas;* they always have. None can leave the village without the permission of the men in her family, and none of the women in the room has had any formal education. And yet, somehow, they have kept alive the idea of a different society. Aisha, a middle-aged woman whose husband is too old to work, says, "Because we are uneducated, we can't speak out and defend our rights. We don't want that for our daughters. We want them to know how to speak up in front of outsiders." Again and again, I ask if all the women they know, even in the most traditional families, feel the same. They almost get angry trying to convince me, and the hot little room seems to get hotter as they all speak at once. "Of course we want more freedom," says Soraya. "Even women who are not allowed to come to this class want that. But our husbands and brothers and fathers don't want it. The mullahs keep saying freedom is not good for us."

The literacy course in Sarasia is funded by the Revolutionary Association of the Women of Afghanistan. This extraordinary organisation has been going since 1977 and is a testament to the determined resilience of Afghan women. The thousands of RAWA members have worked underground and in exile for nearly 30 years-against the Soviet regime, the mujaheddin, the Taliban - and they are now stronger than ever. But although RAWA is beginning to operate more openly, most of its work is still anonymous and underground. Oddly, despite the west's much-touted support for a more liberal society, RAWA has never received support from any government.

But RAWA's members are still agitating for women's equality and a secular government, and they are also passionately involved in rebuilding civil society. In contrast to some of the rather chaotic government and non-governmental projects, the couple of RAWA schemes I see, in Sarasia and Kabul, are models of good organisation and sustainability. One day, I visit one of their schools in Kabul, which operates in the family home of a former radio broadcaster from Mazar-i-Sharif, who prefers to remain anonymous.

On the street outside, it is the usual Kabul scene: heaps of rubbish, a blinding glare, dust-filled air. Then you push open a large blue door to a courtyard. Here, somebody is growing herbs and vegetables, and two white and-yellow butterflies dip their wings over the thick green fronds of radish plants. Under awnings on the sides of the courtyard, one group of women is spelling out its Persian lesson and another is cutting bright cloth, learning to make shirts.

One of the teachers here is Zahmina Nyamati. She is 42, with a weather beaten, sensible face. Twenty years ago, Zahmina was like Zohal Faiz Mohammed, an optimistic science graduate from Kabul University. She married a civil servant and had five children. But after her husband died seven years ago, she took her family to live in a refugee camp in Pakistan. She became a servant for Pakistani families all day and sewed all night, trying to earn enough money to keep her children in school. As she speaks, the tears run down her face. She doesn't try to wipe them away.

"I have good memories in my life, from my childhood, and when I was first married. But then everything was lost. I worked in houses where I was dirt, and I was allowed as a great favour to collect the food they were going to throw out to take to my children.

"When I got married, I thought at least we will live in peace. At least we will have a simple house, where we can say, 'It's my room'; at least when my children go to school, they can say, 'These are my shoes, this is my pencil.' But my children sit alone. They never play with other children. When I come home, they say, 'What have you brought us' And I can't say anything. My life is over. But I want a better life for them. This is why I work all day and all night. I must be strong. I pray every day, 'God make me strong.'"

After her class is over, Zahmina takes me to her home. This neighbourhood is what most of Kabul looks like - a slum, where the sewers drain into the street, and the street is just packed dust. She lives in one room with her four children, one of whom is handicapped and lies on the floor, unable to walk or crawl. There is no furniture except for one bed heaped with scraps of clothes and blankets. After the Taliban fell, like hundreds of thousands of others, Zahmina returned to Kabul with the help of the UN refugee agency, which gives returning refugees $10-$30 per person. Zahmina's family also received two plastic sheets, two blankets and three bags of flour. First, they went to live in Chehl Sutoon, a ruined area where there is no running water, no roofs, no windows. Now they feel lucky to have found one room with a roof. If it wasn't for RAWA, she might soon be begging like the other women whose claw-like hands grab at you on the streets.

As we talk about the past, she asks her daughter, a fresh-faced girl of 12, to get out the photographs. Alya pulls the box from under the bed. The few family snaps show a big, happy family at birthday parties, sitting around with the children on their parents' laps, a cake and watermelon and biscuits on a table, ballons in children's hands. Alya and her brothers handle the pictures reverently, dreaming over them.

I ask Zahmina if she has any hopes for the future. She doesn't hesitate. " I hope, it is my only wish, that the international organisations that have promised to help Afghanistan will fulfil their promises, especially for women. And I have heard our politician talk about women's rights. I hope Afghan women will achieve these. We have known such suffering for these 23 years. We just want to give our children what they need, so they can grow up to fulfil their dreams. "I am struck once again, struck with an almost physical shock, by the way in which Afghan women are facing the future with such stony determination.

Alya listens to us talk. The little girl, who has grown up in a refugee camp, then moved to a ruin and then to a slum, is slender and bright-eyed in green shalwar kameez. I ask what she thinks she will do in the future. "I will be a doctor!" She says determinedly.

# 4

# Discrimination Against Women

After so many years on the periphery, Afghan women stand centre stage in the full glare of world opinion. Since the takeover of Kabul by the Taliban Islamic Movement, the women's issue has been raised to a pinnacle with equal fervour by both the Taliban and the international community. Each stands steadfast on foundations of fundamental principles guaranteeing women a dignified place in society. Yet they stand poles apart. The avowed purpose of the Taliban Islamic Movement is to complete the unfinished agenda of the jihad: to install a pure Islamic state, cleansed of evils perpetrated by their predecessors. Great stress is placed on the creation of secure environments where the chasteness and dignity of women may once again be sacrosanct. When they first appeared, the Taliban acted against a Mujahideen commander in Kandahar who had reportedly abducted, raped and killed three women in mid-1994.

**The Decrees**

The first decrees announced after each major takeover require women to curtail their movements in public, and then only when decently covered and in the company of close family relations (mahrammat). As an extension of these restrictions, female work outside the home is proscribed and girls' schools are closed. Not so well publicised, but upsetting to women, was the closing of women's bath houses (hammam) in Herat and in Kabul where, on 19 October 1996, the municipality closed 32 public baths reserved for women. Initially, these instructions on work and education were enforced in a haphazard manner, varying from region to region. Through patiently dialogue, aid providers operating in provincial Taliban-held Pushtun communities, where secluded female behaviour was already the norm, were frequently able to continue their programmes after an initial hiatus.

In many provincial areas, central administrative control was and is still indifferently imposed; policies are unclear; and individual lattitudes among local authorities reflect a wide spectrum of personal opinion, from ultraconservative to moderate.

The aid providers within the international community have doggedly sought clarifications since 1994, particularly regarding education and employment for women. With equal consistency, the Taliban, on all levels, have insisted that the movement considers it an Islamic duty to provide education for all, including women, as long as Islamic rules and regulations are properly followed.

When after a year no policy changes were forthcoming, the international community took action. On 10 November 1995 UNICEF issued an official communique announcing that it was suspending assistance to education programmes in those parts of Afghanistan where girls were excluded from education. In taking this position UNICEF cited its commitment to the principles of the UN Convention on the Rights of the Child, to which Afghanistan is a party.

This argument made no impression, for the Taliban recognise only the validity of the Sharia; they do not feel bound by UN human rights instruments, which they regard in good part as vehicles of Western cultural imperialism. Not surprisingly, the written response to UNICEF called the UNICEF action 'unfortunate and unjustifiable', adding, rather unkindly, that as their assistance was 'a lot of paperwork and a few vehicles', UNICEF should reconsider its position, do something practical and stop indulging in politics.

By the beginning of 1996 with the 'temporary' bans yet to be lifted and as restrictions on the employment of women as well as their access to basic services worsened, the Save the Children Alliance in Afghanistan announced the suspension of its operations in Herat on 4 March 1996. On 8 March, Save the Children called for all humanitarian aid organisations to follow UNICEF and consider the suspension of every non-emergency programme in sectors where women's employment was prohibited?

Female education was encouraged and thousands of women worked in government offices, but occasional constraints were imposed for reasons of female propriety. In July 1995, the Women's High Association in Kabul hosted 300 women at a 3-day workshop to prepare guidelines for the Afghan delegation to the Fourth World Conference on Women in Beijing on 4 September. As they were about to depart on 31 August, the Deputy Foreign Minister, Abdul Rahim Ghafoorzai, announced that the government had cancelled the delegation because 'there are a lot of issues to be discussed that the High Council considers are against the basic Islamic principles governing life in the Islamic society in Afghanistan. We are concerned, about a number of issues that we consider un-Islamic. They include the question of parental control over their children, the right of a husband to control the women of the family, matters of family planning, including abortion, and the concept of premarital relations for boys 'and girls.'

As Taliban challenges increased, harsher restraints were implemented. In November 1995 the Eastern Shura in Jalalabad banned women from working. The NGOs negotiated and continued -for their programmes; the UN suspended all Afghan female employees, earning a flurry of well-publicised reproof from female activists in the . United States to On the whole, however, the Western media reported on women only peripherally from the end of 1994 until the Taliban swept into Kabul on 27 September 1996. Then, suddenly, Afghanistan, Kabul and women were at the top of every agenda and the real clamour began.

Predictably, within hours after they took Kabul, orders from the High Council were announced over Radio Kabul instructing women to cease attending workplaces, to move outside the home only when necessary, and then only with faces covered and accompanied by a male family member (mahram). Schools were closed.

**Role of UNESCO**

World leaders launched a barrage of statements throughout October. The Director-General of UNESCO, Federico Mayor, called for a spirit of tolerance. The European

Commissioner for Humanitarian Aid, Emma Bonino, feared that Afghanistan's new rulers were set to take the country 'back to the Dark Ages'. The Secretary-General of the United Nations, Dr Boutros Boutros-Ghali, pointed out that the United Nations system is obliged to be guided by the norms stated in its Charter and that the restrictions imposed by the Taliban could have serious repercussions on the ability of the United Nations to deliver programmes.

The UN High Commissioner for Human Rights, Jose Ayala. Lasso, only mildly noted that Afghanistan was party to various conventions protecting women's rights. Dr Norbert Holl, the UN special peace mediator, warned that it was not up to Taliban leaders to rule on human rights, since 'Whoever is controlling Afghanistan is bound by the Charter of the UN.

While the US Permanent Representative to the UN (now Secretary of State), Madeleine Albright, dubbed the Taliban decrees 'medieval and impossible to justify or defend' a State Department spokesman warned that the Taliban should not expect recognition unless they showed respect for women's rights, observing that Taliban 'directives threaten to generate international isolation, which would deny Afghanistan international assistance'.

Even Maulana Fazlur Rahman, Chief of Jamiat-a Ulema-i Islam, the alleged patron of the Taliban, criticised the regime 'for their unrealistic attitude towards women.' Taliban officials were stung by the outcry. Their only purpose, they said, was 'to protect their sisters from corrupt people'. Some bristled at the arrogance of outsiders in assuming that Western standards must be imposed. It soon became clear that threatening, international disapprobation and cuts in assistance would not move they authorities toward moderation.

In Kabul, at a meeting on 8 October 1996 with the Acting Foreign Minister, Mullah Mohammad Ghaus, the aid community observed that humanitarian projects dependent on' female staff would be suspended unless UN and NGO female employees were allowed to work, and that this would badly affect some 30,000 widows who were the sole earners in their families. The Minister expressed his 'astonishment' at the level of internation concern for 'such a small percentage of the working population' an stressed the fact that the movement was still coming to grips with establishing a government.

Privately, not a few in positions of authority sincerely fear individuals within the young Taliban militia who have never be exposed to urban living may easily be led astray. They point to equally inexperienced young Mujahideen who came to Kabul in 1992 with similar ideas about upright female behaviour: 'good' women stay home, 'bad' women expose their faces and mingle with men in public places. Young immature Mujahideen who had grown up on battlefield under the influence of conservative leaders marvelled at unveiled Afghan female newsreaders on TV, concluded they must promiscuous, and-Kalashnikovs at the ready-waylaid the ladies at the studio gate saying, 'Tonight you are mine'. Several former celebrities have told me how relieved they were when the Rabbani government finally put a ban on female TV appearances, an denounced by Westerners as being discriminatory to women.

**New Laws**

Initially women in Kabul were terrified of these zealous Mujahideen but; time, because the former regime was lax in its vigilance, women shed their fear and began to act more assertively, moving about the ci they had in the past. The change was rapid and extraordinary.

At first so terrified they dared not leave their homes, a scant four months later women walked the streets with confidence, returning measure for measure when young men deigned to question the appropriateness of their apparel. At the same time, the Mujahideen lost their fervour, became weak, gave in to the lures of women and succumbed to corrupt city ways. The authorities are dependent on their young militia as a base of power, but they are less than sanguine about their real ability to control them. Nor do they dare risk losing the loyalty of these fighting forces by modifying their stand on women, an important symbol of the movement's Islamic legitimacy.

Then, of course, there are those who simply have no doubt that women appearing in public in any capacity are instruments of moral corruption and agents of sexual anarchy. Whatever the reasoning, many in the leadership worry that women could be sexually dishonoured.

The movement would then be sullied. To avoid this, women must be kept covered, out of sight and off the streets. By imposing strict restraints directly on women, the society's sensitive component symbolising male honour, the regime sends a message of its intent to subordinate the personal autonomy of every individual, thereby strengthening the impression that it is capable of exercising control over all aspects of social behaviour, male and female.

In short, although official pronouncements regarding women may be couched in Islamic rhetoric, the web of hidden attitudes governing official actions and colouring public statements is woven of many complexities.

The Taliban vigorously enforce the requirement that women wear the chadari, a voluminous head-to-toe pleated covering, also referred to by the Arabic term burqa. This garment totally encompasses the body, leaving only a mesh square over the eyes to permit minimal vision. The *hejab*, adopted by many refugee women on orders from the Mujahideen is not acceptable 'because it is not from our culture and because it does not conform to Islamic Sharia since it is very smart and draws attention', according to Haji Mawlawi Qamaluddin, Deputy Director, Amr bil-Maroof wa Nahi An il-Munkir, the department responsible for the Promotion of Virtue and Suppression of Vice, a religious police force which is one of the most powerful arms of Taliban Movement. Kejab is a general Arabic term for body covering. Various forms are worn in the Middle East.

The style of hejab that evolved in Pakistan among Afghan refugees consisted of ankle-length, long-sleeved coat worn with a waist-length head, which is drawn across the face just below the eyes when moving in the streets or in mixed gatherings. These hejab were typically black or navy blue. Even little girls in primary schools run by the politic parties wore uniforms in this hejab style. Many women, a majority, who objected to the hejab because it was a foreign import, wore instead the traditional Afghan chader, a large shawl-like headscarf draped over the hair and falling to cover about three-quarters of body. The chader leaves the face open, although it also can be drawn across the face when needed.

In July 1996, after Gulbuddin Hekmatyar became Prime Minister in June, he warned women they would be required to wear black hejab if they wished to continue working. Many women in Kabul at that time were already wearing the long coat over Western-style suits and dresses, under which they had added the *shalwar* (full trousers). Headcoverings were sometimes so small, however, they covered the hair inadequately. The new Taliban dress codes and restrictions on movement were alien to women in Kabul; many were slow to comply. Daily confrontations between women and young Taliban militia resulted in insults and beatings. These incidents, captured on TV and graphically described by Western journalists, hardened Western attitudes toward Taliban. Women adapted quickly out of fear of the consequences, but the beatings continue, often for such inconsequential reasons as length of the chadari or the colour of the shoes. Seldom do women suffer extensive physical injuries from these beatings. The intent is humiliate. This, of course, causes considerable psychological damage. Thus cosmopolitan Kabul has reverted to the days before 195 when the government of Prime Minister Daoud Khan announced the voluntary end of seclusion and removal of the veil. The key word then was voluntary; whether to shed the veil and move in public was strictly up to individual families to decide. Those who did come out, however, were immediately and fully prepared to make significant contributions since governments from 1929 onward had strongly supported women's education and employment in separate institutions, even while keeping women in *purdah*

Literally meaning curtain, refers to the practice of secluding women inside their homes, and includes veiling in public places. King Amanullah urged women to come out from purdah, and many elites did so. The conservative tribesmen who overthrew Amanullah in 1929 put women back into purdah and the chadari.

Nadir Shah and his successors until 1959, reap sing that their base of power was too weak to confront conservatives on this sensitive issue, kept women behind the veil, in seclusion away from the public domain. After 1959, women in ever-increasing numbers took education and professional careers for granted, a trend that escalated after 1978.

Of the many rules and regulations governing women, the international community has reacted with the greatest concern to restrictions on education and employment. The dilemma is to find ways in which congenial environments can be created where assistance may be delivered according to internationally recognised human rights standards without compromising national cultural perspectives. To these ends, the issue of female education is hit hard by both sides.

According to a UN survey conducted in May 1996, Kabul had 158 public schools accommodating 148, 223 boys and 103,256 girls, taught by 11, 208 teachers of whom 7, 793 were women. Because of the high percentage of female teachers, the restrictions effectively deprived boys as well. Efforts to reactivate the shattered education sector remain deadlocked. The voices of moderates are muted; the hard liners dominate. Contradictions and inconsistencies abound; hopes rise only to evaporate.

In December 1996, there was a flurry of optimism that the ban on girls' schools would be lifted after the winter recess. In meetings with the Ministry of Education, UN agencies declared themselves ready to commit an estimated $300,000 toward the rehabilitation of schools, provided half of the facilities would be utilised for girls.

The final government document, beginning with an introduction flaying former regimes for damaging the entire education system by utilising a foreign curriculum, simply requested repairs for buildings, furniture and funds to print textbooks. The expected commitment for girls was nowhere mentioned. On 9 March 1997 when the schools opened, headmasters were directed not to register girls; Kabul University opened with no female teachers or students.

**Role of Kandahar Governor**

The most recent round on education took place in Kandahar on 1213 May 1997 at which the Governor of Kandahar, Mullah Mohammad Hassan, candidly observed that in the overall scheme of things, the conclusion of the war and the establishment of law and order are uppermost priorities, against which the question of girls' education is a 'minor matter.' Because so little action has been taken, the early optimism generated by conciliatory remarks apparently designed to mollify Western critics and the aid community is rapidly turning into cynicism.

Slightly better progress can be noted regarding women's

employment, although initially many distressing incidents occurred. Various reports estimated that anywhei : from 40,000-150,000 women, including teachers plus doctors, nurses, administrators and other civil servants, were affected by the prohibition on women's employment. Three days after taking Kabul, Mawlawi Wakil Ahmad, member of the Central Shura and Senior Adviser to the founder of the movement, Mullah Mohammad Omar, announced that the government would continue to pay female government employees, but that 'we stand by our decision that women cannot work in government offices in the future.

Kabul is overcrowded with Internally Displaced Persons and homeless returning refugees reeling under the affects of escalating inflation in an environment with limited earning opportunities. Government services have mostly collapsed, and the safety net of traditional closely-knit extended family support networks has been severely damaged. For the first time in its history, beggars roam the streets of Kabul or huddle outside relief agencies. A high proportion are children and women, many of whom are widows or those responsible for disabled men unable to work. A January 1997 survey by ICRC recorded the presence of 50,000 widows, each with an average of 7-9 children.

Restrictions on female employees drastically interfered with the, ability of many organisations to continue delivering emergency assistance to this vulnerable population, as well as services for others in need of assistance in the deteriorating economic environment': Without female staff it was impossible to access families or monitor' programmes. Programmes were scaled down; some suspend operations altogether. Conditions in hospitals where women were forbidden to be seen by male doctors became desperate without female medical professionals.

Continually pressured on these matters, a set of eleven rules for female medical personnel, signed by Amir al-Momineen Mullah Mohammad Omar as well as the Minister of Public Health, was issued in November 1996; a comprehensive set of regulations for both men and women was announced on 17 December by the Amr bil-Maroof wa Nahi An il-Munkir. These cleared the way for women to work in the medical sector, as long as they dressed appropriately, 'in simple clothes ... with no cosmetics and make-up', worked in segregated spaces and travelled with escorts.

Of the general regulations, only three pertained to women. Number: 1 stated that in order to prevent 'sedition and uncovered females', no drivers were allowed to pick up females wearing the Iranian burqa, which did not cover the face, or seductive clothing, or those' unaccompanied by a mahram. In case of violation the driver would be imprisoned and the husbands would be punished. Number 12 required? that it should be announced in all mosques that women found washing clothes in the river would be picked up in a 'respectful Islamic ,manner' and taken to their homes where their husbands would be severely punished. Number 15 announced that tailors found taking ,a female body measurements and displaying fashion magazines would be imprisoned.

The emphasis on punishing males for infractions committed by females reflects the universal acceptance of male responsibility for females, which is a natural consequence of the belief that males have a duty to exert control over female members of their families. Even under normal circumstances evidence of a loss of male control affects family as well as individual standing within the community. Female behaviour therefore becomes the ultimate determining factor of family status.

Summarily dismissing the letters of authorisation, the guards publicly insulted the women over a loudspeaker, calling them prostitutes because they worked for foreigners, and proceeded to strike them several times with a metre and-a-half-long whip made of metal and leather. The ladies escaped unhurt but badly humiliated, the driver was arrested, and apologies were eventually extended by the Deputy Director of the religious police, with the explanation that the action had not been authorised. Work resumed. The ladies now carry yet another letter of authorisation, from the Amr bil-Maroof wa Nahi An il-Munkir.

This incident vividly illustrates several important realities. First, unacceptable acts are being carried out by individuals without the sanction of the authorities, either because of a misguided sense of righteousness or, very often, simply because of personal whims and grudges. It is against official policy to punish women in the streets, but incidents continue to be reported. Rank-and-file members of the religious police are especially notorious for being undisciplined often act counter to official policies as they cruise about in jeeps patrolling the streets.

**New Regulations**

Regulations are often misunderstood misinterpreted by this poorly-educated mass of militia. But the Taliban are not a homogeneous monolith. There are moderate Taliban in the government who seek equitable alternatives, as well as men who are not taliban, numbers of whom are distinguish professionals, who do not approve of the excesses. But with ultraconservatives entrenched at the higher echelons of power, that efforts must for a time be kept at a low level if they are eventually, to persuade.

Second, women work at risk. They have no security for they may be beaten without provocation even when wearing the chadari and carrying credentials. Thus there is danger that women may be sacrificed to worthy principles during this period of violent transition. It is important for all aid providers to be aware of, and remain sensitive to, all the nuances of the volatile environment in which women they wish to help must move.

Third, the incident is a sterling example of increasing antipathy toward foreigners, especially regarding their influence on women Distrust of foreign cultural encroachments thought to be inimical Islam has festered ever since Afghanistan's ruling elites turned toward the West at the beginning of the century and largely isolated themselves from values cherished outside Kabul. Westernised parliaments, constitutions, architecture, city plans, dress, education, literature, food, music, entertainment were all part of the government's modernising zeal, with highly visible women at the centre of the whirl. For women of this era, Western dress, with skin to the knee and heads uncovered, was a symbol of emancipation, as potent as Islamic dress is for the Taliban.

Current pressures by Westerners are also viewed as aggressions against Islam, deepening Taliban convictions that the society is in danger from outsiders. Referring to their Western critics, Mullah Mohammad Hassan Akhund, number three in the ruling hierarchy, told a group of Pakistani academics in Kabul: 'They won't be satisfied unless we obey them and turn our face from Allah, but we do not care about anybody, as long as the religion of Allah is maintained.' The Acting Deputy Foreign Minister, Sher Mohammad Stanekzai, put it more bluntly: 'This is our country and we know better what to do with our women, do not interfere in our internal affairs.'

Rural and nomadic women do not typically wear the chadari, unless they have travelled to the city or their husbands have acquired education or secured government employment, in which case they wear it proudly as a symbol of status and sophistication.

Instead, women in each tribal or rural ethnic group wear distinctively designed veils. All are draped over the head and can be demurely pulled over the face for modesty as occasion demands; many are of bright colours, some are heavily embroidered with silk and set with small mirrors. The cut, the colour, and the decoration are expressions of group identity and individual creativity. The purpose is modesty, not effacement. But in Kabul the Taliban have attempted to impose a measure of standardisation by insisting on the chadari. They equate it, perhaps, with greater anonymity and thus more effective protection and 'dignity.' But women are already making their own fashion statements, despite the fact that the prices of chadari can amount to more than an average month's salary which is next to intolerable for many families. Burnt orange and forest green are fashionable in Jalalabad; various clear shades of blue accented by an occasional canary yellow flit about Kabul; black was never usual, except among some groups in Herat. Made mostly of soft artificial silk, the veils shimmer and billow with a certain mysterious seductiveness. This, of course, is far from the intent of the authorities.

Restrictions on movement ; inhibit women fiom seeking necessary medical treatment, for themselves and for their children; attendance at prenatal and postnatal, facilities is down; family nutrition worsens because inflation keeps prices high and women are restricted in shopping for their families.

While improvements in physical security are appreciated, the absence of economic security is universally deplored. To watch their children suffer because of deteriorating family income is heartbreaking. Women are angry beneath their veils. Tensions are being held under great pressure which could erupt at any time, but so far few have been emboldened to stage overt group expressions of discontent inside Afghanistan. Those that have erupted 'have been quickly quelled, because there is no effective leadership to sustain them. As usual in Afghanistan there is always an exception. Early in 1996, 150 women demonstrated in front of the Governor's office in Kandahar. These were poor beggar women objecting to shopkeepers who refused to accept bank notes of small denominations. That night the Governor announced over the radio that shopkeepers would accept the notes, or be closed down.

**The Demonstration**

The Taliban staged a women's demonstration on their own behalf, in Kabul, on 17 October 1996, to protest against foreign interference. It was a half-hearted affair with both men and women, and lots of energetic little boys, attending. Following this; on 23 October, women rallied for five hours in Mazar-a Sharif raising slogans such as 'Taliban law is not Islamic law' under the inspiration of a lady judge ' in General Dostum's administration. In Herat a demonstration on 21 December 1996 by 50 women protesting the closing of-women's bath houses turned ugly. Twenty were arrested and several others were hospitalised after being beaten.

In Pakistan, the politicised Revolutionary Association of the Women of Afghani (RAWA) continues to hold demonstrations in Islamabad, Pesha war and Quetta, from which they inevitably emerge bloodied by Pakistani police lathi charges. They have now transferred their vitriolic the from their erstwhile enemy, Gulbuddin Hekmatyar, to the Taliban. Other Afghan women's groups engage mainly in forming networks which periodically hold seminars and issue statements

Afghan women are fortunate in enjoying the staunch support one male-directed agency, the Cooperation Centre for Afghanistan based in Peshawar, which publishes and holds seminars on lit, rights in addition to implementing women's projects inside Afghanistan. Aside from CCA and a handful of others quietly working on in-country programmes benefiting women, most Afghan males are conspicuously silent. Some frankly observe that since enjoy so few rights, they see no reason why such a fuss should made over women. Truly, it must not be forgotten that Afghan m are being disadvantaged as well. Nevertheless, most Afghans,' believe, agree that women are being disadvantaged to a greater extent. The community seems to be rather evenly split between those who believe the Taliban should be given the benefit of the doubt and tire in which to resolve their problems by themselves, and those who view all Taliban promises with cynical scepticism. 'Give them time' We have. All we get with time is worse than before. When changes are always negative, hope must die.'

Even men who may be sympathetic hesitate to speak publicly' partly because they fear to do so may jeopardise their projects Taliban-held areas. Looking deeper, one sees more significant reasons for their reticence. Many sophisticated professionals, technicians, administrators and managers, within the UN and NGO systems, prefer to keep their wives and daughters safely secluded within prescribed social networks which do not include mixed study or working environments, particularly where there are foreigners. This mirrors prewar attitudes. Even during the freedom of the 1960s, working women were expected to socialise within the family, rather than with their colleagues. Women then, as now, chafed under traditional attitudes which bound them too tightly to family choices, a state they described as 'family sickness'.

Nomadic and rural women have been little affected by the controversies. Rural women mostly live in secure kin-related settings where they move about with considerable freedom. When they venture beyond these protected areas, they travel swathed in chaders escorted by male relatives. Handicrafts are made at home; when they work outside, women work in family groups. Above all, their primary ambition in life is to become a mother, preferably of many sons. Through motherhood, the creativity of handiwork and efficient household management, rural women achieve status and a sense of personal fulfilment. For all Afghans, rural and urban, the family functions as the paramount social institution to which individuals look for rights and owe recognised obligations. For women, a primary obligation is to uphold family honour by conforming to accepted behavioural norms. Although rules governing female behaviour vary from group to group, Afghan society is consistent in its innate belief in male superiority, giving to men the prerogative to determine the dos and don'ts for women.

The Taliban resent these disparaging characterisations and expound repeatedly, on their commitment to female education and promises to provide some female employment-whenever the situation is secure. They ask for time. Some would give them that time. Others at sceptical, convinced that Taliban procrastination and inconsistency belie their sincerity. At least some tendencies toward positive action are needed before the negative images can be redrawn; visible action not rhetoric is required. The Taliban must come to realise that one can be a good Muslim without a beard or a chadari.

The Taliban also seem not to appreciate that war and exile have fostered expanded expectations. Before the war neither the education nor the health system stretched very far into the rural areas. Only about three per cent of school age females went to school; preponderantly in urban areas, mostly in Kabul; in some provinces virtually no girls were enrolled. Infant and maternal mortality rates were, and still are, the second highest in the world; the highest next Africa. But now women have learned that health services can ease their suffering, that they need not grieve over so many infants. They have seen the benefits of education. They have experienced the satisfaction of raising livestock and poultry, of growing kitchen gardens and learning skills for better child care and extra income.

While the public skirmishes take place at the upper levels, the a programmes that quietly function in districts held by the Taliban build on these heightened expectations. Steady progress at community levels occurs when aid providers are willing to be flexible in seeking imaginative alternatives and, equally important, when communities learn to persuade authorities to modify the harshness of the restraints. While some programmes function semi-clandestinely ultimate success is possible only when communities commit themselves to action by presenting their desires to local authorities. Evidence suggests that numbers of communities are doing so.

Many donors such as the Nordic countries have clearly stated that they will not support programmes if women's rights are not respected. Yet they recognise that under current circumstances flexibility is required and thus agree to endorse programmes as long as it can be demonstrated that they form part of 'broader strategies benefiting females'. Such ambiguity clouds assistance delivery. Lack of consensus is a continuing problem, lofty statements calling for 'one voice' notwithstanding. Both sides have dug in their heels. In the standoff, one can imagine each side asking of the other, 'Will they never learn?

Since access to women under the Taliban is so perplexing, it is useful perhaps to view the totality of Afghan women as a pyramid. The sound base is broad and consists of a majority who live in rural areas cherishing aspirations that are almost exclusively oriented toward children and family. Their needs lie in all aspects of basic and nonformal education, in health and in skills training for better family welfare.

At the tip are the small number of Western-oriented, assertive working women who have taken a leading part in the emancipation process begun in 1959. They have become accustomed to formal employment in mixed environments, often in association with foreigners who are now joined in battle on their behalf. These women call for the right to participate fully at all levels of decision-making. They bear the full brunt of Taliban ire.

In the centre is the solid core of professional teachers, medical practitioners, engineers, judges, administrators, businesswomen, social workers and civil servants of every sort which has grown in magnitude and strength since the beginning of the century. Largely from middle class, conservative but progressive families, these women neither wish to deny their society's values nor compromise Islam. Over the years, they have shown by their comportment that Afghan women can function in the public sphere with no loss of dignity to themselves, their families or the nation.

Tragically, many have been lost to Afghanistan through resettlement. Many thousands remain, nevertheless, and thousands of others are being trained even though opportunities for utilising their training looks bleak. It is this strong central core that most urgently needs to be uncaged if Afghanistan is to recover and move forward.

**Human Rights for Women**

During the Taliban era, the human rights situation for women was extremely poor with widespread and widely accepted societal discrimination throughout the country. Violence against women remained a serious problem. Women and girls were subjected to rape, kidnaping, and forced marriage. The Taliban increased enforcement of strict dress codes and maintained the prohibition against women working outside the home except in strictly limited circumstances in the health care field and in some humanitarian assistance projects. The Taliban appeared to reverse a 2-year trend of relaxing enforcement of restrictions on women and girls and increasingly restricted female education and participation in the labor force. Although girls were prohibited formally from attending school, some organisations clandestinely operated elementary schools and home schools with girls in attendance.

The Taliban detained persons because of their ethnic origins. Worker rights were not defined. Reports from refugees and others indicate there was widespread disregard for and abuse of internationally recognized worker rights. Child labor persisted. The human rights situation in areas outside of Taliban control also were extremely poor, and Northern Alliance members reportedly committed numerous, serious abuses. Opposition forces continued sporadic rocket attacks against Kabul and bombarded civilians indiscriminately.

Various factions infringed on citizens' privacy rights. Armed units of the Northern Alliance, local commanders, and rogue individuals were responsible for political killing, abduction, kidnaping for ransom, torture, rape, arbitrary detention, and looting.

**Political Killings**

Taliban forces committed a large number of political and other extrajudicial killings, both within the country and in the refugee community in Pakistan during the year. In September 2001, agents believed to be associated with Usama bin Laden's al-Qaeda organization and working with the Taliban killed Northern Alliance Defense Minister and key military leader Ahmed Shah Masood. The agents disguised themselves as journalists to gain access to Masood and concealed explosives in their camera equipment, which they detonated in Masood's presence. The perpetrators also were killed in the explosion.

Much of the political and extrajudicial killing in Afghanistan during the Taliban era occurred in connection with the renewed conflict between the Taliban and the Northern Alliance. The conflict was characterized by sporadic, indiscriminate shelling and bombing, as well as mass killings. According to Human Rights Watch, the killings apparently were intended as collective punishment for local residents, whom the Taliban suspected of cooperating with the Northern Alliance, and to deter such cooperation in the future. The Taliban denied responsibility but barred journalists from the area.

From August 9, 2000, through September 5, 2000, when the Taliban captured it, there was intense fighting around and in the town of Taloqan. During the offensive to capture Taloqan, Taliban aircraft bombed the city many times. No statistics are available regarding civilian casualties in Taloqan, but 60,000 to 75,000 persons left their homes in Taloqan and other areas in the northern part of the country to flee the fighting. Amnesty International reported that during the fighting in Taloqan, the Taliban bombarded a village, burned all of the houses there, and killed some of the villagers.

When they recaptured Bamiyan in 1999, the Taliban forces carried out summary executions upon entering the city. Amnesty International reported that hundreds of men, and in a few instances women and children, were separated from their families, taken away, and killed. There was no investigation by the Taliban of these widely publicised allegations. The Taliban also took no action and conducted no investigation into allegations by Amnesty International that dozens of noncombatants were killed systematically by Taliban forces when they captured most of the Shomali valley in late July 1999.

**Summary Trials**

The Taliban employed swift summary trials and

implemented strict punishments in accordance with Islamic law. Executions, whippings, and amputations at times took place before crowds of up to 30,000 persons. Amnesty International has reported that From 1998 to 2000, dozens of Afghan leaders and intellectuals living in Pakistan had received death threats, and several had been killed. Many believe that these political killings occurred at the direction of the Taliban. A number of moderate activists left Pakistan for other countries, partly in reaction to these killings.

Opposition forces also reportedly committed extrajudicial killings during the year, according to press reports. In November 2001, Northern Alliance forces killed approximately 100 to 300 Taliban fighters in the city of Mazar-e-Sharif, when it shelled a former girls' school that was being used as a military barracks by the Taliban. On November 25, Northern Alliance forces reportedly killed at least 120 Taliban prisoners in Mazar-e-Sharif, allegedly during the suppression of a riot. Opposition forces fired rockets into Kabul on a number of occasions. In many of these attacks, civilians were killed or injured. Taliban soldiers reportedly were killed and injured by landmines laid by the Northern Alliance as they advanced in the Shomali plains.

On December 4, 2000, United Front Commander Abdullah Jan Wahidi reportedly was killed in an ambush. Northern Alliance military leader Ahmed Masood's forces executed the individuals allegedly responsible for the ambush on December 6, 40 hours after their arrest, and denied charges by Amnesty International and the individuals' relatives that the accused had been tortured. The Northern Alliance also claimed that a civilian rather than a military court tried the accused.

**Mass Executions**

In 1998 the UN found several mass graves connected with the massacre of Taliban soldiers near Mazar-i-Sharif in 1997, which contained evidence consistent with mass executions. Independent investigations of these and other killings, including killings by the Taliban, were hindered by the continuing warfare and the unwillingness of local commanders to allow investigators to visit the areas in question. The Taliban leadership had indicated in several of these cases that investigations were underway or that investigations would be permitted. However, according to neutral observers, no real progress was made by the Taliban in facilitating investigations, and mass and other killings from 1997 and 1998 have not been investigated fully.

The strict security enforced by the Taliban in areas under its control had resulted in a decrease in abductions, kidnapings, and hostages taken for ransom. However, there are credible allegations that Taliban forces were responsible for disappearances, abductions, kidnapings, and hostage-takings, and that the Taliban maintained private prisons to settle personal vendettas in areas it controlled.

Amnesty International reported that hundreds of persons were separated from their families in the Taloqan area during the Taliban's 2000 summer offensive, and that these persons were taken away and are believed to have been killed. There were unconfirmed reports that some Taliban soldiers abducted girls and women from villages in the Taloqan area during fighting from June through October 2000.

There also were reports of the abduction of women by the Taliban in August 1999 when the Taliban retook the Shomali plains; women reportedly were taken in trucks from the area of fighting and were trafficked to Pakistan and to the Arab Gulf states. In 1998 there were credible reports that the Taliban detained hundreds of persons, mostly ethnic Hazaras, after the takeover of Mazar-i-Sharif; the whereabouts of many such persons remained unknown at year's end. There were unconfirmed reports that some Taliban soldiers abducted girls and women from Hazara neighborhoods in Mazar-i-Sharif in 1998.

There were credible reports of some instances in which Taliban soldiers arrested individuals, often from minority ethnic groups, to extract ransoms. Abductions, kidnapings, and hostage-taking for ransom or for political reasons also occurred in non-Taliban areas, but specific information regarding such acts was unavailable.

**Women in Northern Areas**

According to the UN, in northern areas women were at risk of being raped and kidnapped. There have been unconfirmed reports that forces on both sides kidnaped young women. Some of the women reportedly then were forced to marry their kidnapers; others remained missing. To avoid this danger, some families reportedly sent their daughters to Pakistan or to Iran.

Groups in Russia listed nearly 300 Soviet soldiers formerly serving in Afghanistan as missing in action or prisoners of war (POW's). Most were thought to be dead or to have assimilated voluntarily into Afghan society, although some are alleged to be held against their will. A number of persons from the former Soviet Union missing since the period of the Soviet occupation are presumed dead.

The Taliban reportedly tortured opponents and beat some persons detained for political reasons. In July 2000, the UN Special Rapporteur on Human Rights in Afghanistan met in Iran with a former governor of Herat, General Ismail Khan, and two of his colleagues. The three stated that they were detained in a Kandahar prison on political grounds for 3 years prior to their escape in March 2000. They were kept in windowless cells and shackled the entire time.

The Taliban detained and tortured persons who they believed were being helpful to Western journalists. In July 2000, a Western journalist observed his Afghan associate being beaten severely. The associate subsequently was detained and beaten routinely until he was able to escape from prison. All Afghan factions were believed to have used torture against opponents and POW's, although specific information generally was lacking. Torture did not appear to be a routine practice in all cases.

Some of military leader Ahmed Masood's commanders in the north reportedly used torture routinely to extract information from and break the will of prisoners and political opponents. In December 2000, following the ambush of United Front commander Abdullah Jan Wahidi, Masood's forces arrested six persons.

The Taliban ruled strictly in areas that it controlled, establishing ad hoc and rudimentary judicial systems, based on its understanding of Islamic justice. Taliban courts imposed their extreme interpretation of Islamic law and punishments followed swift summary trials. Murderers were subjected to public executions, a punishment that at times was inflicted by the victims' families. Thieves were subjected to public amputations of one hand, one foot, or both. Adulterers were stoned to death or publicly given 100 lashes.

Taliban forces, particularly religious police, threatened and beat women for what they considered immodest dress, including failure to wear a full body covering. Religious police also assaulted men for immodest dress, incorrect beard length, and long hair. In one incident in 2000, a visiting Pakistani soccer team playing in Kandahar had their heads forcibly shaved in the middle of a match by Taliban authorities.

Prison conditions were poor. Prisoners held by some factions were not provided food; this generally was the responsibility of prisoners' relatives, who were allowed to visit to provide them with food once or twice a week. Prisoners with no relatives had to petition the local council or rely on other inmates.

Prisoners lived in overcrowded, unsanitary conditions in collective cells. There have been credible reports that torture occurred in prisons under the control of both the Taliban and the Northern Alliance. Local authorities maintained prisons in territories under their control and reportedly established torture cells in some of them. The Taliban operated prisons in Kandahar, Herat, Kabul, Jalalabad, Mazar-i-Sharif, Pul-i-Khumri, Shibarghan, Qala-e-Zaini, and Maimana.

The Northern Alliance maintained prisons in Panjshir and Faizabad. According to one credible report, prison authorities in Badakhshan Province routinely used rubber and plastic bound cables in beatings. According to Amnesty International, there were reports that the Taliban forced prisoners to build a new story for the Kandahar prison building, and that some Taliban prisoners held by Masood's forces were forced to work in life-threatening conditions, such as digging trenches in mined areas.

The International Committee of the Red Cross (ICRC) continued to visit detainees throughout the year; however, intensified fighting and poor security for foreign personnel limited the ability of the ICRC to monitor prison conditions.

In the absence of formal legal and law enforcement institutions, justice was not administered according to formal legal codes, and persons were subject to arbitrary detention.

There are credible reports that both Taliban and Northern Alliance militia extorted bribes from civilians in return for their release from prison or to avoid arrest. Judicial and police procedures varied from locality to locality. Little is known about the procedures for taking persons into custody and bringing them to justice.

The Taliban reportedly detained approximately 60 civilians when it reoccupied Bamiyan's Yakawlang district in June; their whereabouts remained unknown at year's end. In August the Taliban jailed eight foreign workers associated with Shelter Now International, a German NGO, on charges of proselytizing. They also arrested 48 Afghan employees of the organization on unspecified charges, reportedly including apostasy, which is a capital crime. The foreign volunteers initially were denied consular access and not permitted to see their relatives or consult with an attorney. In addition, they were not informed of the specific charges against them or of the legal procedures under which they would be tried.

**Arrests and Detentions**

Taliban arrests and detentions of journalists increased during the intensified military conflict late in the year. The Taliban also harassed and detained NGO workers throughout their rule. On July 9, 2000, the Taliban's PVSV jailed for several days a foreign aid worker who had lived and worked in Afghanistan for several years, as well as a number of her Afghan associates. The aid worker and her associates promoted home-based work for women and home schools for girls. She was expelled from the country shortly after her release on July 12, 2000. She returned to Kabul in late September 2000, but again was ordered to leave the country; she departed on October 6, 2000.

Amnesty International reported that the Taliban had taken children hostage in an effort to compel their fathers to surrender; the fathers of such children generally were reported to be political opponents of the Taliban. The families of these children have been told that the children would be released when their fathers surrendered to the Taliban. The UN Special Rapporteur on Human Rights in Afghanistan met in July 2000 in Iran with a former governor of Herat, General Ismail Khan, and two of his colleagues. The three claimed that they were detained in a Kandahar prison on political grounds for three years prior to their escape on March 26, 2000. They were kept in windowless cells and shackled for the entire time.

The General's colleagues reported their own torture by the prison authorities, and all three reported the torture of other prisoners, including being hung upside down by the legs while being beaten with cables. A number of persons arrested by the Taliban in 1998 for political reasons were believed still to be in detention until the fall of the Taliban late in 2001.

Both the Taliban and the Northern Alliance held thousands of combatants. The Northern Alliance reportedly held a number of Pakistanis and other third country nationals, along with several hundred Taliban soldiers, as POW's. In June 2000, the Taliban and the Northern Alliance sent delegations to inspect each other's prisoners in advance of an exchange of prisoners; however, the prisoner exchange initiative ended when fighting resumed in the summer of 2000.

With no functioning nationwide judicial system, many municipal and provincial authorities relied on some interpretation of Islamic law and traditional tribal codes of justice. The Bonn Agreement called for the establishment of a Judicial Commission to rebuild the domestic justice system in accordance with Islamic principles, international standards, the rule of law, and Afghan legal traditions.

The Taliban used Islamic courts in areas under their control to judge criminal cases and resolve disputes. According to the UN, the Taliban asserted that there was a lower court and a higher court in every province, and a Supreme Court in Kabul. According to press reports, in 1999 Mullah Omar promulgated a decree ordering the Supreme Court and military courts not to interfere with one another. The courts reportedly dealt with all complaints, relying on the Taliban's extreme interpretation of Islamic law and punishments, as well as on traditional tribal customs.

Punishments handed down by the courts included execution and amputation. In cases involving murder and rape, convicted prisoners generally were ordered executed, although relatives of the victim could instead choose to accept other restitution or could enforce the verdict themselves. Decisions of the courts were reportedly final. The courts reportedly heard cases in sessions that lasted only a few minutes.

**Amnesty International**

According to Amnesty International, some judges in these courts were untrained in law and at times based their judgments on a combination of their personal understanding of Islamic law and a tribal code of honor prevalent in Pashtun areas.

In August 2001, eight foreign aid workers were arrested on charges of promoting Christianity. Their trial began, but immediately was adjourned. The UN warned the Taliban that it was violating international norms by refusing to let the detained foreign aid workers consult with representatives of their governments or lawyers. The aid workers eventually were freed by opposition forces on November 15.

Little is known about the administration of justice in the areas that were controlled by the Northern Alliance. The administration and implementation of justice varied from area to area and depended on the inclinations of local commanders or other authorities, who summarily executed, tortured, and meted out punishments, including executions, without reference to any other authority. Following the ambush of a Northern Alliance commander in December 2000, six prisoners were arrested and executed within 40 hours of their arrest.

Continued fighting often resulted in the homes and businesses of civilians being invaded and looted by forces on all sides. Some armed gunmen reportedly acted with impunity, due to the absence of a responsive police force or legal protection for victims. It was unclear what authority controlled the actions of the Taliban militiamen who patrolled the streets of cities and towns.

A number of incidents were reported in which Taliban soldiers, persons masquerading as Taliban, or foreign volunteers fighting alongside the Taliban, entered private homes without prior notification or informed consent. In Kabul soldiers allegedly searched homes for evidence of cooperation with the former authorities or for violations of Taliban decrees, including the ban on the possession of depictions of living things, including photographs, stuffed animals, and dolls. At various times, the Taliban also banned certain traditional recreational activities, such as flying kites and playing chess.

**Religious Police**

The Taliban's religious police arrested or assaulted individuals on the streets for infractions of Taliban rules concerning dress, hair length, and facial hair, as well as for the violation of the prohibition on women being in the company of men who were unrelated to them. The Taliban required women to wear a burqa, a tent-like outer garment that covers a woman from head to toe, when in public. Men were required to wear their beards a certain length or longer, not to trim their beards, and to wear head coverings. Men whose beards did not conform to the guidelines on beard length set out by the Taliban were subject to imprisonment for 10 days and mandatory Islamic instruction. The Taliban reportedly also required parents to give their children "Islamic" names.

There were also reports that the Taliban forcibly conscripted or attempted forcibly to conscript persons, and that in several instances such attempts were resisted. Resistance to forced conscription resulted in an increased Taliban dependence on foreign volunteers. There were reports that some prisoners of the Taliban, including the sons of families that had opposed Taliban social restrictions, were drafted forcibly and sent to the front. The Taliban reportedly followed a longstanding practice of forcibly expelling ethnic Hazara and Tajiks from areas controlled by the Taliban, and otherwise harassing these minorities. The Taliban posed serious obstacles to the efforts of international aid organizations to deliver food aid and other humanitarian assistance. UN-led negotiations to obtain Taliban permission for delivery of food and nonfood aid across the front lines into the Panjshir Valley and the Dara-i-Suf area remained at an impasse during the period that the Taliban controlled these areas.

The Taliban imposed severe restrictions on international assistance activities, severely hampering personnel and limiting their effectiveness. It also restricted the ability of women to take advantage of the limited aid available by restricting their movement, and at times banned or limited deliveries into areas inhabited by non-Pashtun groups.

In October, 2001, Taliban soldiers seized food warehouses of the UN World Food Program (WFP) in Kabul and

Kandahar, seizing approximately 7,000 tons of food. According to a WFP spokesperson, the WFP regained control of the warehouse shortly following the takeover. On October 16, Taliban members reportedly intermittently looted the offices of the Swedish Committee for Afghanistan over a period of 2 days in five separate Afghan cities—Mazar-i-Sharif, Pul-e-Khumri, Kunduz, Taloqan, and Ghazni. According to the organization's director, Afghan staff of the committee were beaten and forced to flee, fuel reserves were set on fire, and nearly half of the committee's 80 vehicles, as well as computers, printers, photocopying machines, telephones, and furniture, were removed.

Various other forces also reportedly harassed or otherwise interfered with the operation of humanitarian relief organizations. On October 13, a group of approximately 20 armed men entered the Kandahar offices of the Islamic Relief Organization, demanding vehicles at gunpoint. Taliban security forces intervened, and a clash ensued. One vehicle was taken from the compound by the unidentified armed men. On November 9, Northern Alliance forces reportedly seized a 10-truck, 200-metric-ton UNICEF supply convoy, which was carrying 300 water pumps and 150 family tents with heaters. There were reports in 1999 that some individual Northern Alliance commanders in the northeast were "taxing" humanitarian assistance entering Afghanistan from Tajikistan, harassing NGO workers, obstructing aid convoys, and otherwise hindering the movement of humanitarian aid.

During most of their rule, Taliban continued internal conflict resulted in many instances of the use of excessive force. They frequently bombed cities held by the Northern Alliance resulting in the deaths of civilians, property damage, and the displacement of residents. They reoccupied Bamiyan's Yakawlang district in June and destroyed public, residential, and commercial buildings and detained approximately 60 civilians, whose whereabouts remained unknown at year's end. As many as 50,000 residents were displaced. The Taliban units involved in the action reportedly included a large number of foreign volunteers, who were responsible for a disproportionate percentage of abuses committed by Taliban forces.

According to the UN mine-clearing experts' reports

Afghanistan is the most heavily mined country in the world. The UN estimates that there are 5 to 7 million landmines and over 750,000 pieces of unexploded ordnance throughout the country, planted mainly during the Soviet occupation. However, some NGO's estimate that there may be fewer than 1 million mines. There have been claims that 162 of 356 districts are mine-affected. The most heavily mined areas are the provinces bordering Iran and Pakistan. The landmines and unexploded ordnance caused deaths and injuries, restricted areas available for cultivation, and slowed the return of refugees.

In 1999 the NGO Halo Trust estimated that mines covered more than 420 square miles, including over 285 square miles of grazing land, over 100 square miles of agricultural land, almost 25 square miles of roads, approximately 7.5 square miles of residential area, and over 2 square miles of irrigation systems and canals. From 1995 to 1997, new mines were believed to have been laid over 90 square miles of land, reportedly mostly by the Northern Alliance in the western provinces of Badghis and Faryab. Additional newly mined areas were reported but not confirmed in 2000 and during the year in the conflict areas north of Kabul.

One positive action by the Taliban in the areas they occupied was the banning of drug trafficking. Drug addicts were to be arrested and a proper investigation made to reach the supplier, who was to be severely punished. This fact was reiterated by Mullah Mohammad Rabbani, Chairman of the Caretaker Council of Afghanistan, while giving his government's policy at the Extraordinary Session of the OIC held at Islamabad on 23 March 1997. However, directives on banning poppy cultivation were not implemented as that was the only source of revenue for many in Afghanistan.

**Role of Mullah Omar**

The Taliban leader Mullah Omar reportedly banned the use, production, trade, and stockpiling of mines in 1998. Despite the general prohibition on the depiction of living things, the Taliban reportedly once allowed the visual depiction of persons in demining educational materials. An estimated 400,000 Afghans have been killed or wounded by landmines. Casualties caused by landmines and unexploded ordnance are estimated at 10 to 12 per day.

In some parts of the country, including Herat and Kandahar, the presence of landmines causing bodily harm and restricting travel affected almost 90 percent of households. An estimated 96 per cent of civilian mine and unexploded ordnance casualties are male. Approximately 53 per cent of mine and unexploded ordnance casualties occur in the 18 to 40 age group, while 34 per cent of the casualties involve children, according to the UN Mine Action Center. With funding from international donors, the UN has organized and trained mine detection and clearance teams, which operate throughout the country. Nearly all areas that have been cleared are in productive use, and approximately 1.5 million refugees and internally displaced persons (IDPs) have returned to areas cleared of mines and unexploded ordnance. Nonetheless, the mines are expected to pose a threat for many years.

Under the Taliban Rule, there were no laws that effectively provide for freedom of speech and of the press, and senior officials of various warring factions attempted to intimidate journalists and influence their reporting. There were fewer than 10 regular publications in the country. All other newspapers were published only sporadically, and for the most part were affiliated with different factions. Various factions maintained their own communications facilities.

The Taliban selectively banned the entry of foreign newspapers into their territory. Many foreign books were prohibited. The Taliban radio station, the *Voice of Shariat*, broadcast religious programming and Taliban pronouncements. Radio Kabul changed its name to *Voice of Radio Shariat*. No music and songs are broadcast from the new radio station. This, according to the Taliban elders, is in keeping with the Quranic verse *Amr Bil Maruf Wa Nahi anl Munkir*. The sixteen-point set of rules incorporating most of the points mentioned above, was handed over to the UN agencies, foreign funded NGOs, and all the concerned government departments. Cinemas have been closed and their buildings turned into mosques. Taking photographs and displaying portraits, posters, and pictures is banned to prevent idolatry. Video shops were destroyed not only in Taliban- controlled areas but also in Zhob, where they were raided by the Taliban and forced to shut down. No cassette was to find its way into shops, hotels, vehicles, or anywhere else.

All factions attempted to pressure foreign journalists who reported on the conflict. The Taliban initially cooperated with members of the international press who arrived in Kabul, but later imposed restrictions on them. The Taliban banned all foreign journalists from filming or photographing persons or animals and required them to be accompanied at all times by a Taliban escort to ensure that such restrictions were enforced. Foreign male journalists were not permitted to interview women.

In August 2000, the Taliban introduced additional strict regulations governing the work of foreign journalists in the country. A list of 21 points "to be respected" was provided to foreign journalists upon arrival. The list included an item requiring journalists "not to offend the people's feelings." Journalists were required to inform the Taliban authorities when they traveled outside of Kabul and to stay out of prohibited areas. Journalists could work only with approved interpreters and local assistants, were required to renew their work permits every year, and were required to register all of their professional equipment. The Taliban also required most journalists to stay at the Intercontinental Hotel in Kabul, allegedly for security and economic reasons.

**Action Against Journalists**

The Taliban had arrested an estimated 34 journalists since it took control of Kabul in September 1996. In March the Taliban authorities expelled a BBC journalist for what it considered biased reporting on the destruction of the statues of the Buddha in Bamiyan.

Taliban arrests of and restrictions against journalists increased during the intensified military conflict late in the year. Beginning in September, 2001, the Taliban banned foreign media from areas under their control, and stated that they would not issue visas. In September the Taliban arrested British journalist Yvonne Ridley, along with two Pakistani guides, Gul Muhmand and Jan Ali. Ridley was held for 10 days on charges of spying. She was released on October 8. Muhmand and Ali were released on November 13. On October

9, the Taliban arrested French journalist Michel Peyrard, who illegally had entered the country disguised in a burqa, and a Pakistani reporter, Mukkaram Khan, and a Pakistani guide, Mohammad Irfan. The three were charged with spying. Peyrard was released on November 3, Irfan was released on November 10 and escorted to the Pakistani border, and Khan was released on November 12 and returned to Pakistan. On October 22, the Taliban arrested a Japanese journalist, Daigen Yanagida, in Asadabad. Yanagida was imprisoned until November 16, then released.

In July 2000, a Western journalist, while being detained, observed his Afghan associate being beaten severely. The journalist subsequently was expelled from the country, and his associate was detained and beaten routinely until he escaped from prison. In August 2000, the PVSV arrested three foreign journalists, allegedly for photographing a soccer match in Kabul. The journalists were interrogated for 2 hours, after which their film was confiscated. PVSV officials stated that taking pictures of living things was forbidden. A number of journalists were killed during the intensified fighting late in 2001. On November 11, Taliban forces fired on a Northern Alliance military convoy, killing three journalists—Pierre Billaud, Volker Hankloik, and Johannes Sutton—who were riding with the Northern Alliance soldiers in an armored personnel carrier. The convoy was advancing toward Taliban positions near the city of Taloqan. On November 19 in Mnangarhar Province, armed men forced four journalists, Harry Burton, Maria Grazia Cutuli, Julio Fuentes, and Azizullah Haidari, out of their convoy of vehicles and executed them. On November 26, in an apparent attempted robbery, armed gunmen broke into a home in Taloqan in northeast Afghanistan in which Swedish journalists were sleeping. The gunmen killed journalist Ulf Stromberg. The intruders demanded money and stole equipment, including cameras, computers, and a satellite phone.

In 1998 the Taliban had banned televisions, satellite dishes, videocassette recorders, and video and audio cassettes. On July 12, 2001, the Taliban banned use of the Internet. On July 19, the Taliban banned the import of 30 items it claimed were "un-Islamic," including musical instruments, cassettes, and computer discs. There have been numerous threats to Afghan journalists working in exile in Pakistan; the United Nations High Commission for Refugees (UNHCR) has assisted approximately 10 Afghan journalists in relocating to Western countries from Pakistan. Many believe that Taliban authorities made these threats in response to critical reporting. For example, in July 2000, Inayat-ul-Haq Yasinin, a journalist in Peshawar, received death threats for publishing the results of an opinion poll on Afghan refugees living in Peshawar.

War, tenuous security, and likely opposition from local authorities seriously inhibited freedom of assembly and association in areas that were under Taliban control. The Taliban has used excessive force against demonstrators. All factions harassed and interfered with the operations of domestic and international NGO's, including aid organizations.

The Taliban interfered consistently with the operations of the UN and NGO's. The Taliban reportedly required NGO's to undergo burdensome registration procedures to obtain permission to operate and attempted to exert control over NGO staffing and office locations, especially in Kabul. Other Taliban restrictions on freedom of association included threatening to impound vehicles of NGO's that did not work on projects approved by the Taliban and forcing organizations to employ Taliban supervisors or workers.

In September, 2001, the Taliban occupied the offices of many NGO's throughout the country, including the WFP, restricting communications to foreign headquarters but generally allowing local staff to operate the organizations. Almost all foreign personnel of NGO's in the country had left areas under Taliban control when the US-led coalition military operations began in October, either on their own or after being expelled by the Taliban. Foreign personnel had begun returning to Kabul and other major cities where security conditions permitted their return by year's end.

In May religious police raided an Italian-funded hospital in Kabul, assaulted staff members, and forced the hospital to suspend operations because male and female staff allegedly mixed in the dining rooms and operating wards. The Taliban detained the director of one NGO and impounded all of the NGO's equipment in an effort to increase Taliban control of the organization. In August the Taliban arrested 8 foreign aid workers and an estimated 48 Afghan employees of the NGO on charges of proselytizing; they were freed by opposing forces on November 15.

The Taliban announced in March 1998 that foreign Muslim women, including UN workers, would be allowed to perform their jobs only if accompanied by a male relative, a decision that continued to hamper NGO and relief operations during the year. The UN withdrew its personnel from southern Afghanistan in late March 1998 to protest the assault on a U.N. worker by the Taliban governor of Kandahar Province and the interference with its work by the Taliban. After reaching agreements with local officials, the UN returned to Kandahar in May 1999.

On June 15, 1999, members of the Taliban detained and beat staff members of an international NGO in Bamiyan Province. After the incident, Mullah Omar issued an edict stating that any person causing annoyance to a foreign worker could face punishment of up to 5 years in prison. However, in November 1999, UN properties were targeted in organized demonstrations in several cities when UN sanctions related to terrorism were imposed on the country. Certain key issues, including the mobility of international female Muslim staff and access by Afghan women and girls to programs, remained unresolved at year's end. There were reports in 1999 that military leader Ahmed Masood's commanders in the northeast were taxing humanitarian assistance entering Afghanistan from Tajikistan, harassing NGO workers, obstructing aid convoys, and otherwise hindering the movement of humanitarian aid.

**Freedom of Religion**

Freedom of religion was restricted severely. Due to the absence of a constitution and the ongoing civil war, religious freedom is determined primarily by the unofficial, unwritten, and evolving policies of the warring factions. For most of the year in most parts of the country, the Taliban vigorously enforced its extreme interpretation of Islamic law. Sunni Islam of the Hanafi school of jurisprudence traditionally has been the dominant religion, and the Taliban also nominally adhered to the Hanafi school. The Taliban claimed in mid-1999 that it was drafting a new constitution based on the sources of Islamic religious (*Shari'a*) law (the *Quran*, the Sunna, and Hanafi jurisprudence.)

Custom and law required affiliation with some religion, and atheism was considered apostasy and was punishable by death. Licensing and registration of religious groups do not appear to be required by the authorities in any part of the country. The small number of non-Muslim residents remaining in the country may practice their faith but may not proselytize.

The country's official name, according to the Taliban, was the Islamic Emirate of Afghanistan; according to the Northern Alliance, it was the Islamic State of Afghanistan. These names reflected the desire of both factions to promote Islam as the state religion. Taliban leader Mullah Omar carried the title of Commander of the Faithful. The Taliban ruled strictly in areas that it controlled, establishing ad hoc and rudimentary judicial systems. The Taliban established Islamic courts to judge criminal cases and resolve disputes. Taliban courts imposed their extreme interpretation of Islamic law and punishments following swift summary trials.

The Taliban sought to institute its extreme interpretation of Islamic observance in areas under its control and declared that all Muslims in areas under Taliban control must abide by the Taliban's interpretation of Islamic law. The Taliban announced its proclamations and edicts through broadcasts on the Taliban's Radio Shariat and relied on a religious police force under the control of the PVSV to enforce rules regarding appearance, dress, employment, access to medical care, religious practice, expression, and other behavior.

Members of the PVSV, which was raised to the status of a Ministry in May 1998, regularly monitored persons on the street to ensure that individuals were conforming to Taliban edicts. Persons found to be in violation of the edicts were subject to punishment meted out on the spot, including beatings and detention. In practice the rigid policies adopted both by the Taliban and by certain opposition groups had a chilling effect on adherents of other forms of Islam and on other faiths. Enforcement of Taliban social strictures was erratic; Taliban edicts generally were enforced in the cities, especially in Kabul, but enforced less consistently in rural areas, in which more discretion was permitted based on local custom.

**Sunni in Majority**

About 85 per cent of the population are Sunni Muslim and most of the remaining 15 per cent are Shi'a. Shi'a, including the predominately Shi'a Hazara ethnic group. are among the most economically disadvantaged persons in the country. There also are small numbers of Ismailis living in the central and northern parts of the country. Ismailis are Shi'a, but consider the Aga Khan their spiritual leader.

In the past, small communities of Hindus, Sikhs, Jews, and Christians lived in the country, but most members of these communities have left during the Tabliban rule. Almost all members of the country's small Hindu and Sikh populations, which once numbered about 50,000 persons, have emigrated or taken refuge abroad.

In March, 2001, the Taliban, acting on what it claimed to be religious grounds, completely destroyed two giant statues of the Buddha dating from pre-Islamic times, which were carved into the cliffs near Bamiyan. The statues had been damaged in the past, but the Taliban claimed that the damage was unauthorized vandalism committed by a soldier, and that they would protect the statutes from further damage. The destruction of the statues received worldwide criticism, including from numerous Islamic authorities.

On February 26, 2001 Mullah Omar had ordered the destruction of all statues in the country. The Taliban also claimed to have destroyed statues and images in the collections of the Kabul Museum and elsewhere dating from the pre-Islamic period. There reportedly are no practicing Buddhists in the country; however, the Bamiyan statues and the collection of pre-Islamic images, most dating from the classic Gandhara period, are widely considered to be important cultural artifacts and religious symbols. On May 23, the Taliban decreed that Hindus and Sikhs would be required to wear a piece of yellow cloth attached to their clothing to identify their religious affiliation. The Taliban purportedly imposed this system of identification to spare non-Muslims from the enforcement of rules mandatory for Muslims and from harassment by agents of the PVSV. The requirement later was suspended, and an identity card was to be issued instead. On July 3, the Taliban announced that Hindus would be consulted before ordering them to wear any distinctive mark to differentiate themselves from Muslims.

In September 1999, the Taliban issued decrees barring non-Muslims from building places of worship but allowing them to worship at existing holy sites; forbidding non-Muslims from criticizing Muslims; ordering non-Muslims to identify their houses by placing a yellow cloth on their rooftops; banning non-Muslims from living in the same residence as Muslims; and requiring that non-Muslim women wear a yellow dress with a special mark so that Muslims could keep their distance.

In Taliban-controlled areas, the Taliban had decreed that all Muslims were required to take part in five daily prayers. Those who were observed not praying at appointed times or who were late attending prayer were subject to punishment, including severe beatings. Friday noon prayers at mosques reportedly were compulsory for all Muslim men; women and girls reportedly were forbidden to enter mosques and thus were forced to pray at home.

On January 7, 2001, the Taliban issued a decree calling for capital punishment for any Afghan who converted from Islam. Decree 14, which was issued in June and related to foreigners in Afghanistan, stated that those preaching other religions to Afghan Muslims would be deported after being imprisoned for 3 to 10 days. Taliban officials subsequently stated that the initial decree was only a guideline. A small number of foreign Christian groups were allowed in the country to provide humanitarian assistance; however, they were forbidden to proselytize. Conversion from Islam was considered apostasy and was punishable by death.

The Taliban reportedly had a long history committing numerous human rights violations against the mostly Shi'a Hazaras, including summary executions, massacres, and mass arrests. There were reliable reports that the Taliban summarily executed approximately 300 Hazara men and boys after recapturing Yakawlang in early January. There were reports of mass arrests by the Taliban in Hazara neighborhoods of Kabul in January 1998. There also were credible reports of the massacre of thousands of civilians and prisoners by the Taliban during and after the capture of Mazar-i-Sharif in August 1998; this massacre reportedly was aimed at ethnic Hazaras.

In September 1998, approximately 500 persons were killed when the Taliban took control of the city of Bamiyan. The Hazaras regained control of Bamiyan in April 1999 following prolonged guerrilla-style warfare; however, the Taliban recaptured Bamiyan in May 1999 and reportedly killed a number of Shi'a residents.

There were reports during 1999 and 2000 that there were forced expulsions of ethnic Hazaras and Tajiks from areas controlled or conquered by the Taliban, as well as harassment of these minorities throughout Taliban controlled areas.

The Ismaili community fought for the Northern Alliance against the Taliban and suffered when the Taliban occupied territories once held by Ismaili forces. There were reports of mistreatment of Ismailis at the hands of the Taliban and destruction of some of their cultural monuments. The Taliban, following its extreme interpretation of Shari'a, required women when in public to wear a head-to-toe garment known as the burqa, which has only a mesh screen for vision. The requirement to wear the burqa represented a significant change in practice. According to a decree announced by the religious police in 1997, women found outside the home who were not covered properly would be punished severely, along with their family elders. In Kabul and elsewhere, women found in public not wearing the burqa, or whose burqas did not cover their ankles, were beaten by Taliban militiamen.

According to Taliban regulations, men's beards were required to extend farther than a fist clamped at the base of the chin. Men also were required to wear head coverings and to wear their hair short. A man who had shaved or cut his beard was subject to imprisonment for 10 days and required to undergo Islamic instruction. All students at Kabul University reportedly were required to have beards in order to study there. There also were credible reports that Taliban members gave forced haircuts to males in Kabul.

In March, 2001 religious police reportedly ordered all students across the country to wear turbans in class. Students from grades one to six reportedly were required to wear black turbans and students in higher grades to wear white turbans.

Students who did not follow the instructions were turned away from their classrooms. At various times, the Taliban banned certain traditional recreational activities, such as flying kites and playing chess. Dolls, stuffed animals, and photographs were prohibited under the Taliban's interpretation of religious injunctions against representations of living beings; in search of these objects, Taliban soldiers or persons masquerading as Taliban members reportedly entered private homes without prior notification or informed consent.

Although in principle male citizens have the right to travel freely both inside and outside the country, their ability to travel within the country was hampered by warfare, brigandage, landmines, a road network in a state of disrepair, and limited domestic air service, complicated by factional threats to air traffic. Some Afghans reported difficulty in receiving necessary permits to leave the country for tourism or business purposes, while others reported no such difficulty.

The Taliban's restrictions on women further curtailed freedom of movement. Despite these obstacles, many persons continued to travel relatively freely, with buses using routes in most parts of the country. However, due to intensified fighting, international aid agencies often found that their ability to travel, work, and distribute assistance was hampered severely.

International travel continued to be difficult as both the Taliban and the Northern Alliance threatened to shoot down any planes that flew without their permission over areas of the country that they controlled. UN Security Council sanctions imposed because of the Taliban's links to international terrorism eliminated landing rights for the Afghan airline Ariana at non-Afghan airports and urged member states to restrict the entry into their territories of senior Taliban officials.

Afghans continued to form one of the world's largest refugee populations, and the number of refugees increased as a result of the intensified military actions in 2001. According to the UNHCR, at year's end more than 3.5 million Afghans remained outside the country as registered refugees: Over 2 million in Pakistan; more than 1.5 million in Iran; and some in Russia, India, and Central Asia. Women and children constituted 75 per cent of the refugee population. In addition there were a reported 1.1 million IDP's following years of fighting and drought, even before the events of the latter part of the year. A total of 4,069,000 Afghan refugees have been repatriated since 1988, with over 1.5 million returning to the country in the peak year of 1992.

All the neighboring countries of Afghanistan officially closed their borders to refugees, citing both security reasons and an inability to absorb more refugees. According to the UNHCR, during the first 6 months of the year, the Government of Iran deported an estimated 82,000 Afghans, and on July 15, announced that it would deport any Afghan who lacked documentation or who had failed to register. In addition, on September 25, Iranian newspapers reported that 248 Afghans who had fled from Afghanistan because of fears of a US-led military action on the country were arrested and returned to Afghanistan. In 2000 133,600 refugees were repatriated voluntarily from Iran under a UNHCR-Iran program, and another 50,000 are estimated to have returned outside the programme. In October, 2001, the Government of Iran set up two camps for Afghan IDP's who were attempting to flee to Iran from territory that was then controlled by the Taliban.

During the Taliban era, there was no functioning constitution or legal provisions prohibiting or protecting against discrimination based on race, sex, religion, disability, language, or social status. However, the December 5 Bonn Agreement stated that the 1964 Constitution of Afghanistan would apply on an interim basis until the adoption of a new constitution. Those provisions of the 1964 Constitution relating to the monarchy and to the executive and legislative bodies would not apply; however, provisions prohibiting discrimination based on race, sex, and religion would be in effect. Despite the legal primacy of the 1964 Constitution at year's end, local custom and practices generally prevailed. Discrimination against women remained prevalent throughout the country. Its severity varied from area to area, depending on the local leadership's attitude toward education for girls and employment for women and on local attitudes.

Historically the minority Shi'a faced discrimination from the majority Sunni population. There was greater acceptance of persons with disabilities as the number of persons maimed by landmines and warfare increased, and as the presence of persons with disabilities became more widespread. In 1998 and 1999, the Taliban on several occasions sought to execute homosexuals by toppling walls on them.

As lawlessness and interfactional fighting continued in some areas, violence against women occurred frequently, including beatings, rapes, forced marriages, disappearances, kidnapings, and killings. Such incidents generally went unreported, and most information was anecdotal. It was difficult to document rapes, in particular, in view of the social stigma that surrounds rape.

The enforced seclusion of women within the home greatly limited the information available on domestic violence and marital rape. In a climate of secrecy and impunity, it was likely that domestic violence against women remained a serious problem.

Women accused of adultery also were subjected to violence. Adultery was punishable by death through stoning. In 2000 at least one accused adulteress was sentenced to 100 lashes; a female accomplice was sentenced to 30 lashes. Overall, the situation of women and girls remained mostly unchanged under Taliban rule, as the Taliban generally continued to apply its ultra-conservative interpretation of Islamic law.

Following the Taliban's fall from power and the signing of the Bonn Agreement and easing of restrictions on women, some Afghan women made tentative steps towards resumption of public life. However, lack of education and unavailability of jobs remained significant problems for many women seeking greater opportunity despite the removal of the Taliban.

Discrimination against women in areas under Taliban control was particularly harsh. The Taliban initially excluded women from all employment outside the home, apart from the traditional work of women in agriculture; women were forbidden to leave the home except in the company of a male relative. In urban areas, and particularly after the Taliban took Kabul in 1996, the Taliban forced almost all female professionals and clerical workers, including teachers, doctors, nurses, bank tellers, and aid workers, to quit their jobs. In a few cases, the Taliban permitted women to work in health care occupations under restricted circumstances.

In July 2000, the Taliban issued a decree banning women's employment by UN agencies and NGO's. Implementation remained erratic, but the UN and NGO's nonetheless required their female staff to remain at home to avoid open confrontation with the Taliban. The prohibition on women working outside of the home was especially difficult for the large numbers of widows left by 20 years of civil war; there were an estimated 30,000 widows in Kabul alone.

Many women reportedly were reduced to selling all of their possessions and to begging to feed their families. On August 6, 2000, the Taliban issued an order closing down the 25 widows' bakeries operated by the WFP, which provided food to the neediest citizens, including many war widows and other female-headed households. The Taliban reversed its decision the next day, apparently accepting the WFP's explanation that female staff of the bakeries were not direct hire WFP employees and therefore not subject to the July 6 order.

Girls formally were prohibited from attending school, apart from instruction provided in mosques, which was mainly religious in content. Some girls were educated in formal, community-based or home schools operated in country by international NGO's; however, their activities were restricted severely during the year. Some home schools also existed, but were forced to operate clandestinely. Students, teachers, and their families were subject to punishment if discovered. By year's end, some girls were returning to schools; however, the lack of teachers and materials remained deterrents to girls' education.

Most citizens lack any access to adequate medical facilities, and the provision of health care under Taliban rule remained poor. Such conditions particularly affected women. Life expectancy was estimated at 45.1 years for women and 46.6 years for men. In most regions, there was less than 1 physician per 10,000 persons. Health services reached only 29 percent of the population and only 17 percent of the rural population. Clean water reached only about 12 percent of the population.

Taliban actions significantly reduced women's access to

health care. In practice women were excluded from treatment by male physicians in most hospitals. These rules made obtaining treatment extremely difficult for most women, and especially for widows in Kabul, many of whom have lost all male family members, who would be needed to escort them to any visit to a male doctor. In addition, even when a woman was permitted to be treated by a male doctor, the doctor was prohibited from examining her except if she were fully clothed in Taliban-approved garb, as well as from touching her, thus limiting the possibility of meaningful diagnosis and treatment.

Participants in a 1998 survey of 160 Afghan women reported little or no access to healthcare in Kabul. Most of the participants also reported a decline in their mental health. There were credible reports that the restrictions on women's health care were not applied in practice and that there were some improvements in access to health care for women in 1999 and 2000.

By the end of 1999, all Kabul hospitals apart from the military hospital reportedly treated women. Rabia Balkhi Women's Hospital in Kabul provided a full range of health services to women, although there was only one maternity hospital in the country.

The Taliban decreed what women could wear in public. Women in public spaces were required to wear a burqa, a loose, head-to-toe garment that has a small cloth screen for vision. While in many, particularly rural, areas of the country, the burqa was the customary women's outer garment, the requirement for all women to wear the burqa represented a significant change in practice for many women, particularly in urban areas. According to a decree of the religious police in 1997, women found outside the home who were not covered properly would be punished severely, along with their family elders.

In Kabul and elsewhere women found in public who were not wearing the *burqa*, or whose burqas did not cover their ankles, were beaten by Taliban militiamen. Some women could not afford the cost of a burqa, and thus had to remain at home or risk beatings if they left their houses uncovered. During 1999 there were reports of differences in the enforcement of the requirement for women to wear the burqa.

Enforcement reportedly was relatively lax in rural and non-Pashtun areas, and there were reports that some women in Herat and in rural areas cover their heads with large scarves that leave the face uncovered without reprisal. However, there were credible reports that the Taliban increased enforcement of the dress code during the year. The Taliban's dress code for women apparently was not enforced strictly upon the nomad population of several hundred thousand or upon the few female foreigners, who nonetheless had to cover their hair, arms, and legs. Women in their homes could not be visible from the street; the Taliban required that homes with female occupants have their windows painted over.

Women were expected to leave their homes only while escorted by a male relative, further curtailing the appearance and movement of women in public even when wearing approved clothing. Women appearing in public without a male relative risked beatings by members of the Taliban. Some observers reported observing fewer and fewer women on the streets in Taliban-controlled areas. Under the Taliban, women were not permitted to drive, and taxi drivers reportedly were beaten for taking unescorted women as passengers.

On June 21, religious police arrested four female Afghan WFP employees in a taxi outside the WFP office because they were not accompanied by a male relative. The women were detained for 2 days. In October 2000, taxi drivers were warned by the PVSV not to pick up unaccompanied female passengers at risk of having their driving privileges revoked. Women could ride only on buses designated as women's buses; reportedly there were not enough such buses to meet the demand, and the wait for women's buses could be long. In December 1998, the Taliban ordered that bus drivers who took female passengers must encase the bus in curtains and put up a curtain so that the female passengers cannot see or be seen by the driver. Bus drivers also were required to employ boys under the age of 15 to collect fares from female passengers; neither the drivers nor the fare collectors were to mingle with the passengers.

Amnesty International reported that the Taliban ordered the closure of women's public baths. Women were also forbidden from entering mosques or other places of worship unless the mosque had separate sections for men and women. Most women prayed at home alone or with other family members. Women also reportedly were prohibited from appearing on the streets for certain periods during the month of Ramadan.

**Restrictions**

The Taliban's restrictions regarding the social behavior of men and women were communicated by edicts and enforced mainly by the PVSV. The UN and numerous other sources noted that the edicts were enforced with varying degrees of rigor throughout the country. The restrictions were enforced most strictly in urban areas, where women had enjoyed wider access to educational and employment opportunities before the Taliban gained control. Even with the fall of the Taliban by year's end, Afghanistan's poverty and lack of employment opportunities remained deterrents for women seeking to return to work.

After her 1999 visit, the UN Special Rapporteur on Violence Against Women noted some improvements in the status of women, including the existence of home schools as well as limited primary educational institutions for girls run by the Religious Ministry in Kabul, increased access of women to health care, and the permission for widows to work. The Special Rapporteur also noted continuing violations of the physical security of women and the practice of lashings and public beatings, violations of the rights to education, health, employment, freedom of movement, and freedom of association, and of family rights, including the existence of polygyny and forced marriage. She also noted that minority women sometimes were subject to forced displacement and that there were some cases of trafficking in women and children.

Local administrative bodies and international assistance organizations undertook to ensure children's welfare to the extent possible; however, the situation of children was very poor. Approximately 45 per cent of the population were made up of children age 14 or under. The infant mortality rate was 250 out of 1,000 births; Medecins Sans Frontieres reported in 2000 that 250,000 children per year die of malnutrition. One-quarter of children die before the age of 5. These figures most likely have increased due to another year of drought, intensified fighting, and massive displacement.

The Taliban's restrictions on male-female medical treatment, and on the movement of women and girls in areas under its control, hampered the ability of UN agencies and NGO's to implement effective health and education programs and had a detrimental effect on children. Physicians for Human Rights reported that children at times were denied medical care when the authorities did not let male doctors visit children's wards, which in some instances are located within the women's ward of a hospital, or did not allow male doctors to treat children accompanied only by their mothers.

An UNICEF study reported that the majority of children is highly traumatized and expect to die before reaching adulthood. According to the study, some 90 per cent have nightmares and suffer from acute anxiety, while 70 per cent have seen acts of violence, including the killing of parents or relatives.

According to a report of the Gender Advisor to the UN system in Afghanistan, the educational sector suffered from: Limited human and financial resources; the absence of a national educational policy and curriculum; the inability of authorities to rehabilitate destroyed facilities; and discriminatory policies banning the access of females to all levels of education. Female literacy is approximately 4 per cent, compared with 30 per cent for males. There were reports that the ban on women working outside the home hampered the education of boys, since a large percentage of the country's teachers were women prior the advent of Taliban rule.

The Taliban's implementation of educational policy was inconsistent and varied from region to region, as well as over time. The Taliban had eliminated most of the formal opportunities for girls' education that existed in areas it had taken over; however, some girls' schools still operated in rural areas and some towns. Some girls received an education in informal home schools, which were tolerated to varying degrees by the Taliban around the country. During 2000 there were reports that the number of children reached by these home schools was increasing as was the attendance of girls in various educational settings, including formal schools;

however, during the year the authorities increasingly restricted the activities of home schools.

In September 1999, the UN Special Rapporteur on Violence Against Women noted the existence of home schools and also of limited primary educational institutions for girls run by the Religious Ministry in Kabul. The Taliban told the Special Rapporteur in 1999 that primary education was available to girls between the ages of 6 and 10 and that such education was provided in mosque schools under the Ministry of Religious Affairs.

Approximately three-fourths of the curricula in the Ministry of Religious Affairs schools reportedly dealt with religious and moral subjects. Taliban-sponsored public schools, at both the elementary and secondary levels, provided education only to boys and also emphasized religious studies. However, schools run by NGO's and international donors mostly were open to both boys and girls.

UNESCO reported in 2000 that as few as 3 percent of Afghan girls were receiving primary education as opposed to up to 39 percent of boys. However, the Taliban's increasingly anti-education policies further reduced educational opportunities, even for males. Credible sources reported that during the year Taliban elements pressured a Turkish NGO, which had long been present in the country, to close its six secondary schools for boys, most of which operated in Turkic speaking areas.

The Taliban reportedly also barred Afghan students from traveling abroad, even to Islamic countries, to complete their education, although this restriction reportedly was not always enforced in practice, and a number of children, including many females related to the Taliban leadership, were able to obtain a foreign education.

Prior to the Taliban takeover in 1996, more than 100,000 girls reportedly attended public school in Kabul in grades kindergarten through 12, according to a UN survey. During 1999 approximately 300,000 to 350,000 school-age children attended schools run or funded by various assistance agencies and NGO's. In 1999 the Swedish Committee for Afghanistan reported that it served 170,000 students in 567 schools; most of these were formal schools, although 39 were home schools.

In a few areas, over 50 per cent of students reportedly were girls. The SCA reported that 20 per cent of the students in its formal schools, which mostly were located in rural areas, were girls. In March the SCA signed a protocol with the Taliban that was to benefit the SCA's primary schools. Many boys also were being educated in home schools because of administrative problems in the Taliban-run schools, including problems in the payment of teachers' salaries.

In 1999 in areas that had been newly captured by the Taliban, some communities successfully petitioned Taliban representatives to reopen the schools. In Herat, which was captured by the Taliban in 1995, girls' schools remained closed, except in the refugee camps maintained by international NGO's. Nonetheless, approximately 5 percent of girls were enrolled in school in Kandahar and approximately 20 percent of girls were enrolled in Herat.

The Taliban had banned certain recreational activities, such as flying kites and playing chess. In October 2000, the Taliban banned youths from playing soccer in Kabul on Fridays. Dolls and stuffed animals were prohibited by the Taliban as a result of its interpretation of religious injunctions against representations of living beings. Many Afghan women are still subject to the same abuse as under the ousted Taliban and in some regions, such as the west of the country, face increasing harassment. The New York-based human rights group concedes that conditions for women have improved and they are allowed to go to school and to work. But in many areas they suffer serious restrictions by government troops and local officials, who invoke vague "Taliban-era" edicts on dress and behavior.

Ismail Khan's government has opened few jobs to women and has pressured them not to work with foreign aid groups or the United Nations. The United States and other countries involved in Afghanistan to stop military assistance to local commanders, such as Khan, and to coordinate any future aid through the Kabul government. While maternal death rates vary considerably from region to region and are significantly higher in rural areas than in cities and towns, they are overall among the highest in the world, the researchers found. In rural Badakshan province in northern Afghanistan, mothers are dying while giving birth at the highest rate ever documented - 6,500 maternal deaths for every 100,000 live births, according to their survey.

Widespread women's rights violations are partly to blame for high maternal mortality rates in Afghan women, according to a study appearing in the September 11 issue of the Journal of the American Medical Association. Researchers from Boston's Brigham and Women's Hospital and Physicians for Human Rights interviewed 4,886 women from the northwestern Afghan province of Herat. They estimated that 593 out of 100,000 Herati women die during pregnancy or childbirth. Countrywide, Afghan maternal mortality rates are the second highest in the world (Sierra Leone is highest) with 1,700 deaths out of 100,000 Afghan pregnancies compared to 12 out of 100,000 in the US.

A study explained that trained professionals and medical facilities and supplies are scarce, plus many roads are inaccessible in the war-ravaged nation. In Herat, 35 physicians serve a population of 793,214. No hospitals exist in 20 of Afghanistan's 31 provinces. Amowitz also cited the lack of women's rights in hindering women's access to medical care and family planning. In some cases, husbands force their wives to deliver in their own homes, because the culture considers treatment by strangers in public places "shameful."

In addition, the study also noted that 80 percent of the women interviewed considered sex with their husbands obligatory. Nearly half said that a husband had the right to physically abuse his wife for disobedience. The United Nations is guiding the rebuilding of Afghanistan, with significant financial help from Washington, after decades of internal warfare, years of drought and a U.S.-led bombing campaign that drove the Taliban from power after the Sept. 11, 2001, hijack attacks on the United States

The Afghan Supreme Court has dismissed a female judge for not wearing an Islamic headscarf during a meeting with President Bush and his wife last month, government sources said on Saturday. Marzeya Basil was among a group of 14 female government officials who attended computer and management courses in Washington at the invitation of the U.S. government and who met Bush and his wife, Laura.

Pictures of Basil and several other course participants standing with Bush without a headscarf were carried by world media. The 44-year-old Basil, a mother of several children, was sacked days after her return to Kabul before the end of last month for not wearing her scarf during the meeting, said the sources, who did not want to be identified.

The lives of women remain vulnerable and there are reports of killings of women by their family members in the name of morality. Despite interventions by local NGOs the authorities have looked away, and have taken no action to investigate such murders. Such gender-based impunity by any State is a clear discrimination of the right to life of women

Some Afghan Muslim women have stopped wearing the coverall burqa required by the fundamentalist Taliban who were overthrown with the help of U.S. air power late last year. The U.S.-backed government of Hamid Karzai has relaxed many of the Talibans more strict decrees, but some in the administration have opposed liberalization. Karzais government includes mujahideen (holy warriors) who enforced strict dress codes for women themselves when in power before the Taliban takeover Afghan Women Remain Victims of Hope Unfulfilled

Under the religio-psychotic Taliban, Afghan women inhabited a unique and living hell. Now the Taliban are forgotten, though not entirely gone. And yet, girls and young women in Herat, on Afghanistan's southwestern border with Iran, are drenching themselves in gasoline and setting lit matches to their clothes. George Bush vowed a year ago to wreak vengeance on Osama bin Laden, destroy the al-Quaeda network, rebuild Afghanistan so that it would never again serve as a hatchery for insane mass murderers ---and, by George, to liberate the women.

The media feasted on pictures of Afghan women in Kabul throwing off their burqas, and on the photogenic little girls grinning rapturously on their first day back at school. We all had a pleasant snapshot of triumphant liberation . before our attention drifted elsewhere. Meanwhile, the life expectancy for Afghan women is 40 to 45 years; maternal mortality is probably the highest in the world. The U.N. says 70 per cent of Afghans suffer from malnutrition. Although almost half the girls in Kabul are attending school, outside the capital the numbers fall to a puny 9 per cent. In a town west of Kabul, the local Taliban has just blown up a girls' school and vowed to kill any woman who goes to school or work.

It will take rivers of money and years of education to scrub away the toxic legacy of male domination in the Afghan culture. "Even now, you can hear five year old boys talking so horribly to their mothers, ordering them to be silent, to hide themselves, fetch this, do that," Armstrong said. The women barely have time or energy to resent such injustices when merely keeping themselves and their children alive is an exhausting struggle.

Many women in Afghan, continue to wear the *burqa* (in self-protection from armed and fanatical men), it has been easy for outside observers to conclude that the Afghan women consented to their own subjugation. But the opposite is true. In self-preservation, they are grimly biding their time.

**Threat to Security**

In 2001, November U.S.-led alliance toppled the Taliban in November 2001, women and girls in Afghanistan have gained greater freedom to participate in public life and access to education, health care, and employment. This is the case particularly in the capital, Kabul, where the deployment of foreign military forces under the International Security Assistance Force (ISAF) has helped bring much-needed security.

Even in Kabul, however, many Afghan women still face constant threats to their personal security from other civilians or armed men belonging to various political factions. Outside Kabul, the situation is one of acute general lawlessness and insecurity, as there is no ISAF presence and rival warlords control security conditions. In these areas, more than in Kabul, Afghan women continue to face serious threats to their physical safety, which denies them the opportunity to exercise their basic human rights and to participate fully in the rebuilding of their country. The danger of physical assault is evident throughout northern Afghanistan, where ethnic Pashtuns have been specifically targeted for violence and harassment, including sexual violence.

During February and March 2002, Human Rights Watch

documented cases of sexual violence against Pashtun women perpetrated by the three main ethnically based parties and their militias in the north. Many women described how they had to fight off attackers or hide young female relatives out of fear of rape.

These attacks took place immediately following the fall of the predominantly Pashtun Taliban on November 9, 2001, in Mazar-i Sharif (hereafter, Mazar), the largest city in northern Afghanistan, leaving it and the surrounding areas in the control of the three main rival factions competing for territory. These factions include the predominantly ethnic Uzbek Junbish-i Milly-yi Islami of General Abdul Rashid Dostum the predominantly ethnic Tajik Jamiat-e Islami led in Mazar-i Sharif by Ustad Atta Mohammad, and the ethnic Hazara Hizb-i Wahdat, led in the north by Haji Mohammad Mohaqiq. These three factions signed a U.N.-backed agreement on February 3, 2002, establishing a 600-person multi-ethnic security force for the city, headed by Junbish commander Majid Rouzi. However, general lawlessness and insecurity prevail.

Although lawlessness is a critical issue for all Afghans, the lack of physical security has affected women in gender-specific ways, making them especially vulnerable to rape and other sexual abuse. Although Pashtun women in the north have been specifically targeted for sexual violence, during February and March 2002, Human Rights Watch researchers also gathered credible evidence of continuing politically or ethnically motivated sexual violence against women and girls of other ethnicities in Mazar.

Women in Mazar reported that they live under constant fears of physical assault and feel compelled to limit their movement, expression, and dress to avoid becoming targets of such violence by armed civilians or armed men aligned with the three main ethnically based parties. Gender-specific violence has also taken on a potentially deadly dimension elsewhere. Women continue to be assaulted or abused for not adhering to former Taliban edicts that strictly controlled women's behavior, dress, expression, and movement. In the second week of April, for example, an acid attack on a female teacher in Kandahar, after handwritten pamphlets were found circulating in the city warning men against sending their daughters to school or their wives to work.

**Afghan Laws Still Repress Women**

Refusing suitor, leaving husband bring jail time

KABUL, Afghanistan—Shazia is only 13. Her voice is barely audible. Around adults, she bites her nails and tugs at her black chiffon scarf, covering her face and hazel eyes.

She is one of the hardened criminals inside the dank and forbidding walls of Kabul's Provincial Jail for women. Her crime: running away from the 45 year-old husband she was forced to marry.

In fact, the jail is filled with teenage girls accused of crimes ranging from falling in love to having illicit affairs, from leaving unbending parents to running away from abusive husbands.

Taliban-style executions may be gone, but Islamic law and rigid cultural traditions persist in Afghanistan. The country still relies on Islamic law dating to the 7th Century.

The U.S.-supported government of interim Prime Minister Hamid Karzai says it still will uphold these laws, although perhaps not as strictly as the Taliban. Islamic laws allow women the right to turn down their parents' choice of husbands, but enforce harsh punishment for sex outside marriage.

Tribal laws, on the other hand, allow relatives to imprison and even kill young women who lose their virginity, bring shame to their family by falling in love with unacceptable suitors or even seek a divorce.

"I want a divorce," said Shazia, who like many Afghans does not have a last name. "My husband beats me. I'm not happy with him."

**Taliban Punishments Halted**

In its zeal to enforce Islamic law, the Taliban chopped off the hands of thieves in public stadiums and had family members shoot down murderers. If a woman were to run away from her husband, she, too, would have been executed, said the deputy of security in Kabul, Lt. Gen. Mohammed Khalil Aminzada. A married woman who committed adultery would be stoned to death.

"Right now, we don't do that," Aminzada said. "We put them in prison for three to four months. This is an Islamic society. If we let people do whatever they want, half of society will soon suffer from AIDS."

There is little information about AIDS here, but the World Health Organization reports 10 known cases in Afghanistan.

Aminzada said Kabul's police don't go out of their way to arrest runaways or adulterers unless they feel it will create a threat to security or if family members turn them in.

"Unless people complain, we do nothing," he said.

Among its many tasks, Afghanistan's interim government was supposed to create a commission to plan the rebuilding of the criminal justice system and to restore human rights as part of the Bonn agreement last fall. The commission has yet to be established.

In the absence of new laws, the country's high court has gone back to using the old Shariah laws of Islam, those in place before the Taliban. But they say they will apply them more compassionately.

Since the Taliban's departure, there have been no stonings or whippings. Those punishments could occur again some day, legal officials said, for repeat offenders or if the evidence is strong in a case.

For example, under the strict standard set by Shariah law, a married man or woman will be stoned to death for committing adultery if the accusation can be substantiated by four male eyewitnesses.

Under the Taliban, says the head of Afghanistan's high court, Fazal Hadi Shinwari, they didn't wait for four witnesses.

"It's very difficult to find four witnesses who can confirm the act," said Shinwari, who has a long white beard, a copy of the Koran sitting on his desk and a leather whip hanging on his wall.

"Of course the Taliban executed them without evidence, without any confirmation. They did not use the real Shariah. They just wanted to scare people. We're softer than them," he said.

Being softer in this case means imprisoning women for months or years rather than killing them.

**Teen jailed by Family**

So in the empty, dreary cells of the Kabul Provincial Jail sit young women like Farayba, 19.

She and her lover went to the Taliban, hoping the former

rulers would marry them against their families' wishes. Instead, Taliban officials gave them 5 year jail sentences.

When the Taliban abandoned Kabul five months ago, Farayba escaped with 71 other women in the jail.

Her family was relatively wealthy; her father had been a commander in the Ministry of Defense before the Taliban. When she chose to marry a poor man's son, Farayba brought shame to her family, who wanted her to marry a cousin. When she refused, her father, cousins and brothers beat her boyfriend's father.

Fearing for their lives, the young lovers turned again to authorities, this time from the interim government. "The police officials told me to marry my cousin," she said. "I refused and so they said I should serve the rest of my 5 year sentence. I don't think there's any difference between this regime and the Taliban regime."

**Families Face Penalties**

Adiba, 14, was forced at gunpoint to marry a 30-year-old Talib who broke into her father's house one night. She says family members in her husband's house tried to force her into prostitution.

When the Taliban left Kabul, she escaped from her husband's home. He, in turn, had her uncle and a cousin arrested, which is why she turned herself in to police.

In this tribal society, badal, or revenge, is a common theme. Often, families can have relatives of the guilty party arrested until the accused turns himself or herself in or pays compensation to the victim's family.

Nasreen, 30, has been in jail for months because her brother-in-law ran off with a girl. The girl's father had Nasreen, a widow with five children, arrested in his place.

In all, there are 14 women in the jail, sharing two tiny cells.

The jail provides only bread and water for most meals. The women buy their own tea and sugar. On good days, a family member may bring meat and rice, which prisoners often share.

The women do little except sit and talk, or perhaps walk in the courtyard. They stare out a window with iron bars and a ripped screen.

Bugs crawl in the reeking cells, where the women sleep with thin mats on the hard ground. Their blankets and pillows have not been washed in months.

Despite everything, some say they would rather be here than out on the streets of Kabul.

"Outside of the jail, they'll be killed by their families," said a jail guard, Khatool. "They feel it's safer to be in jail."

*"Give me security, then I will remove my burqa"*

*The News International,* January 31, 2002

Mazar-i-Sharif, Afghanistan : The fall of the Taliban has brought an unexpected windfall to stall-holders in the northern Afghan city of Mazar-i-Sharif, sales of burqas are sky-rocketing.

The burqa, an allencompassing garment women were forced to wear by the Taliban, was seen as a symbol of the oppression exerted by the fundamentalist regime. But now the Taliban have been driven from power, sales could not be better, said a delighted Udut Qarizada at his stall in the Mandavi market in central Mazar-i-Sharif, the main city on the northern plains.

"Under the Taliban, I sold approximately 50 per day, now it's up to 120-140," he said, as the generator providing electricity to the market stopped and started in a sign that not everything was perfect. Mondays and Thursdays are best for sales when villagers descend from the surrounding mountains to do their shopping in this city of about 200,000 people.

"I sell much more burqas than before because the women are now free to go out alone and choose their clothing for themselves," another stall-holder Karim Wahid, 28, said. He carries a stock of 1,000 burqas, in blue and in white, and said he was selling " 100- 120 a week compared to 10 in the time of the Taliban," who were driven out of the city by Northern Alliance ground forces on November 7.

With the lifting of the strictly enforced Taliban laws, which banned women from working and from going outside unless accompanied by a male relative, Wahid finds he has "more sales and thus more money."

In his office several blocks away, city mayor and former fighter Ishaq Raeguzar said one of the first directives after the Taliban fled was "to give women permission to work everywhere, including in official organisations."

This order, plus the arrival of international aid, the presence of many humanitarian organisations and the return of refugees from Iran and Pakistan gave a small boost to the economy. Schools for girls, music and kites, all prohibited under the Taliban's puritanical interpretation of Islam, have reappeared in the rejuvenated city but the burqa remains essential for most women at present.

"Give me security, then I will remove my burqa," said 40-year-old Nasrim. Hidden beneath her white garment, with a small mesh area in front of the eyes to look through, she told of crimes by the soldiers now in control of the city after the Taliban left and before the arrival of foreign troops.

**Inside Afghanistan: Behind the Veil**

An undercover documentary film about the Taliban movement in Afghanistan has shown shocking footage of mass executions, and an insight into the oppression suffered by Afghan women. Dressed in an Afghan veil, reporter Saira Shah used a hidden camera to film life for ordinary Afghans under the Taliban. "I had to wear the burqa which looks like a great big tablecloth. It covers absolutely everything" Saira Shah told the BBC.

The Channel Four crew went undercover because of restrictions on their visa, saying they were only allowed to film inanimate objects.

They were helped by an underground women's group, the Revolutionary Association of Women of Afghanistan (RAWA), which runs secret clinics and schools for girls.

From the moment that I was across the border I felt the restrictions on women," said Ms Shah, a British journalist who is half Afghan.

She described how the veil was so thick that it was difficult to breath, and the little crocheted grill for her eyes made it difficult to cross roads.

If she tripped and showed her face or ankles, she risked arrest.

The woman next to her in the car was violently car sick, but was still not allowed to take her head out of her veil.

"I suddenly wasn't an objective reporter anymore; I was someone actually participating in this, I was actually being subjected to the same restrictions," she said.

**Female Resistance**

In disguise, Ms Shah was able to gain unique access to women's lives, and record the horrendous conditions in which they live.

"The first thing you notice when you come into Kabul is the ghost-like figures in their blue shroud-like burqas, begging in the streets," she told the BBC.

In Kabul alone, she said, there are over 40,000 widows as a result of the war.

Because the Taliban forbid women from working, they are forced into begging - and sometimes prostitution - in order to support themselves and their families.

But the film, Behind the veil, also documents the resistance of some women.

Memebers of the opposition group, RAWA, risk their lives to run secret schools for girls, giving them educational opportunities they would otherwise be denied.

Some women also set up underground beauty parlours in their apartments. Even wearing nail varnish is a crime in Afghanistan.

"You can make a woman wear a veil, but this is our way of showing they haven't crushed our spirit," said a woman in the beauty parlour.

**Executions**

The crew also acquired secretly-filmed footage of a public execution in a football stadium financed by the West.

The footage shows a veiled woman dragged to the centre of the pitch, and forced to kneel facing the goal posts.

She is shot dead to the cheers of the watching crowds.

The team then ventured to the north-west corner of the country, which is still in the hands of the opposition.

Earlier in the year, the Taliban briefly took control of four villages.

The survivors told stories of how dozens of civilians were rounded up and executed.

Footage obtained from a local wedding photographer showed the villagers burying their dead.

Three girls sitting hunddled in brightly coloured veils outside one house described how they saw their mother being shot dead.

Their father said they have not stopped crying for weeks.

**Shining Brighter Than the News They Cover**

*Los Angeles Times, August 24, 2001*

Nor will you see Saira Shah. Along with producer Cassian Harrison and cameraman James Millet', she exposed herself to substantial risks while gathering evidence of terror, squalor and despair inside Taliban-ruled Afghanistan for a chilling news report that aired two months ago on Britain's Channel Four.

The same hour, titled "Beneath the Veil," is scheduled to air Sunday on CNN.

Reporter Shah is a Britisher whose father is from Afghanistan, where women are oppressed and rendered all but invisible by the rigid Islamic regime. She and her crew were not the first Westem journalists allowed inside Afghanistan by the Taliban, but some of the secret footage she brought back may break ground. Supplied by the underground Revolutionary Association of the Women of Afghanistan (RAWA), it shows executions being carried out before cheering throngs in a Kabul football stadium against veiled women and others for crimes unknown.

Shah notes how distant this is from her "liberal Islam" upbringing. As is a secret schoolroom for girls that she visits, its teacher saying that merely organizing the class is a hanging offense. Then comes "the most subversive place of all," an underground beauty parlour where women paint the faces they are forbidden to display in public.

Later, Shah and her crew arrive at a village where they are told of recent alleged massacres by Taliban as part of ethnic cleansing. Supporting the charges is footage of strewn bodies almost too grisly to witness, including a youth's skull said to have been skinned by his murderers.

Now cut to three young sisters. Tears rolling down her cheeks, one tells Shah their parents were murdered before their eyes.

The experienced Shah has put in years reporting from hot spots for British TV. Yet even if she were an American, she wouldn't have the star wattage to crash tonight's lineup.

**Review**

*The Times (U. K.), June 27, 2001*

Saira Shah, in Beneath the Veil (Channel 4), is the latest reporter with hidden cameras to enter Afghanistan to expose the repressiveness of its Islamic government. Shah, being half-Afghan and often dressing in robes that left only a letterbox slit for her eyes, had an advantage in being able to visit areas that would be impossible for a Westerner such as Langan.

But at the same time, being a woman - and not an identifiably Western woman once she had left her film crew behind - she was at the mercy of any officials who unmasked her.

Many of the most horrific clips that Shah showed us were filmed by members of the Revolutionary Association of the Women of Afghanistan, who risked execution to collect their secret footage. They have filmed scenes at football stadiums of women being led out into the penalty area and shot like stray dogs; of men hanging from nooses strung over the goal's crossbar. Shah talked to women who had become beggars because the Taliban government forbids them to work: their children starve or, if they are lucky, subsist on mouldy breadcrumbs. Children spoke of their civilian parents being slaughtered by the Taliban, and their villages razed.

Peculiarly shocking was Shah's visit to a secret classroom, where women who lost their teaching jobs when the Taliban took power, educate teenage girls. Girls over 12 are barred from school. If these teachers and pupils were caught, says Shah, they would be hanged.

**Misery brings down Bride Price in North Afghanistan, UN**

*Deutsche Presse Agentur, June 22, 2001*

Islamabad (dpa) - Misery caused by drought and conflict has brought the bride price down in northern Afghanistan, a United Nations office in Islamabad said Friday. Families in Balkh and Baghlan provinces are having a hard time finding enough to eat and are "giving away their daughters at greatly reduced bride prices and at a young age", the office of the U.N. Coordinator for Afghanistan said in a statement.

"Some of these families have coped as long as they can. Now, they are simply at the end of their rope," the deputy coordinator, Antonio Donini, said.

"People are suffering because of war, drought, and widespread poverty that is, itself, an outcome of the deepening crisis," said the regional coordinator based in Mazar-e-Sharif, capital of Balkh province. He called for "immediate action" by the aid community.

**Taliban Orders Women Aid Workers to Stop Driving**

*Reuter, May 31, 2001*

The ruling Taliban's religious police have ordered foreign women providing humanitarian aid in Afghanistan to stop driving on grounds they are damaging the society, aid workers have said.

They said the foreign ministry had proclaimed the ban on women driving after it received the orders from the Taliban's Ministry for the Promotion of Virtue and Prevention of Vice.

"It has been seen that some foreign women drive cars in the cities, which is against Afghan tradition and has a negative impact on the society," said the letter issued on May 24.

"Therefore, you (foreign ministry) are requested to inform the relevant foreign aid agencies that in future foreign women must not drive cars and must observe the tradition of our country and abide by the regulations of the Islamic Emirate," it added.

The ban on all women driving, similar to laws in Saudi Arabia which often reflect a similar interpretation of Islam, contrasts with the common pre-Taliban practice of women driving in Afghanistan.

Reports of the order came a day after the United Nations said aid workers no longer could walk on streets in Afghanistan because of increasing threats from foreign "guests" of the Taliban from Arab and other countries.

Taliban foreign minister Wakil Ahmad Muttawakil, to whom the United Nations complained, said on Wednesday both foreign aid workers and the foreign Muslims associated with the Taliban were guests.

"They suspect each other. They fear each other. Muslims say the westerners are spying on them and the latter in return say they are terrorists. We do not allow anybody to harass each other," Muttawakil told reporters.

**Women at Risk in Afghanistan**

As Afghansstruggle to shape their country's future, US

foot-dragging on peacekeeping there threatens to preclude democracy and close off opportunities for women. Unless the United States shifts its security policy in Afghanistan, American commitments to the human rights of Afghan women will amount to little more than rhetoric.

Since Sept. 11, 2002 the US administration has repeatedly pledged its commitment to Afghan women. President Bush made the case strongly in his June commencement speech at West Point: "A thriving nation will respect the rights of women, because no society can prosper while denying opportunity to half its citizens."

However, America's Afghan policy is, in effect, selling women out. The United States has fostered the increasing power of the Afghan warlords and provided only minimal support to the fledgling Afghan government.

Moreover, it has opposed the expansion of the International Security Force, which could neutralize the power of those with guns and allow other voices to be heard.

A US- and UN-guided process helped ensure women a place at the table as ministers in the temporary Afghan administration and participants in the emergency grand council, or loya jirga, which met in Kabul in June. During that assembly, women demonstrated why Afghanistan needs them to create democracy. Though a scant 10 per cent of those assembled, with no troops or guns at their disposal, female delegates challenged with unparalleled candor the misogynist warrior ethos of both the Taliban and the warlords now in power and said they were looking for a leader who would make human rights a priority.

The female presidential candidate, Massouda Jalal, injected a modicum of democracy into the process, lining up the necessary signatures to run as male candidates fell by the wayside.

The women's urgent need for accountable government drew them together in a unity that bridged tribal and ethnic differences.

However, at the end of the day the men with guns had, with apparent US acquiescence, greatly increased their power within the Afghan administration and were escalating the intimidation of "dissenters." During the loya jirga, the Afghan defense minister, Field Marshal Mohammed Fahim, assailed the husband of Massouda Jalal for his wife's temerity in running for president. Accusations of blasphemy pursued Former Vice President Sima Samar, who was driven from her post as women's affairs minister. Interim government ministers with civilian rather than military credentials were dismissed, Chief Justice Shinwari, who publicly upbraided Samar and has called for full support of Sharia, or Islamic law, was reappointed; and the majority of the Judicial Commission, responsible for reconciling Islamic principles with other legal traditions, are graduates of religious schools, called madrassas, with no further education.

Returning home from the loya jirga, many women faced the threat of violent backlash. Their joy at the promise of freedom and pride in finding a public voice conflicts with the fear of pervasive lawlessness. Taliban-style sexual policing still thrives in a number of places under the aegis of the US Northern Alliance partners as well as in former Taliban strongholds. Taliban pamphlets warn of reprisals for "spreading indecency and vulgarity" by "sending women to offices and daughters to schools." In much of the country outside of Kabul, the crossfire of rival factions has left women immensely vulnerable and victimized anew by a wave of rapes and other forms of sexual violence.

The US failure to support the Afghan administration materially or militarily has blighted early opportunities for women and the rule of law. While spending more than $2 billion a month on its pursuit of Al Qaeda and the Taliban and channeling money and technical assistance to local military leaders, the United States pledged only $2 million this year to help the Afghan administration build a national army. Most important, while anarchy grows, the United States has opposed the expansion of the international security force, essential for establishing national order outside of Kabul.

Rooting out Al Qaeda is an unquestioned American priority, but it falls far short of what we need to achieve in Afghanistan. To lay the groundwork for peace and reconstruction in the aftermath of the loya jirga, the United States must signal its commitment to the rule of law by pushing for the immediate deployment of international security force throughout Afghanistan. We will not measurably increase our security from terrorism unless we keep our promises to help win the peace - and to the participation of women of rebuilding their country.

**Afghan Women Still Languish**

Rights: Despite Western pressure for greater attention, many laws have not changed since the Taliban left, and jails are refilling,

**RAWA Interview with some Prostitutes**

Among the outcomes of more than two decades of war and destruction in Afghanistan, especially in the last decade when the reign of terror of Jehadi fundamentalists and their brother-in-creed Taliban were prevailing over the sky of our country, prostitution among our widows is a tragedy that can never be forgotten. Unfortunately, as prostitution is illicit and secretive, there are no exact facts and figures to show the actual number of prostitutes. However, in keeping with the reports of RAWA members who are in touch with some of them, the number definitely exceeds thousands.

One of the projects of RAWA inside Afghanistan is to help the hundreds of thousands of miserable widows, some of whom have turned to prostitution and to rescue them from his filthy occupation. Fortunately, our members have succeeded in getting in touch with many of them and enrolling them in literacy and tailoring courses. Those women who are taking RAWA's tailoring courses are given one sewing machine free, so that by using it they can stand on their own feet and come back from prostitution to the normal and honourable life which is the desire of every woman. It is worth mentioning that in the past few months RAWA has distributed food to a number of these women.

In June 2002, two members of RAWA in Kabul interviewed around 60 women and recorded their conversation on video. Below we share a few translated parts of the videos. The pain and misery of most to these women are alike; the majority of them have lost their husbands at the hands of fundamentalists in the war and had no other way of life except to turn to prostitution. Their only desire is to find some sort of help and to return to a life worthy of human beings.

Your aid and support will give us the capability of

rescuing even more of these helpless and oppressed women and saving the future of them and their children.

Due to request of those women who have been interviewed, we have censored their pictures and have used abbreviations instead of their full names.

**MH**: She is a widow around 33 years old. She lost her husband four years ago in the war and has six children who are between 4 to 14 years of age. She was crying as she said: "Because of my children I could not even commit suicide. For the last couple of months I have not paid rent on the house and every day the owner is threatening that he will evict us by force. I have not paid off the electricity bill yet, and make excuses every time the clerk comes for money.

During the regime of the Taliban, as there was no other way to make a living, I turned to prostitution. I was in contact with a Talib whose name was Sakhi Dad; he gave me ten lack (one lack= 100,000) Afghanis (US$1=42,000 Afghanis) per week. However, six months ago, Sakhi Dad left Kabul and I am in great trouble. My only hope is to find a job. I regret being a prostitute but it was the hunger of my children that pushed me to this. My older daughter is in the fourth class and I have tried hard to keep her ignorant of these facts".

**FA**: She is a 35-year old widow with five children. She lost her husband in the war between the Taliban and the Wahdat Party in Dara Soaf. Her eyes were full of pain and sorrow and with her eleven year old daughter by her side she said: while she was working in the field the Taliban attacked, killed people and destroyed the farms. They killed my husband in his field, and destroyed our houses. They killed my brother-in-law in the same spot.

We came to Kabul. There was no other way to feed my five children except prostitution. My eleven-year old daughter knows about my contacts. I have arranged an engagement for her with a boy about whom I don't know much, so that she would not face what I am going through now. My husband's family is poor and can't help. I am shattered and very worried about the fate of my children.

**NH**: She looks about 35 years old. She is from Paghman Province. She is the mother of six children; her older daughter is eleven years old. She is saying: "I studied in school till the eighth class, but when I got married my husband did allow me to study further. Two years after we got married my husband became addicted to drugs. He beat me daily and made life bitter for me. He wanted me to work and earn money to feed the children. When I was seven months pregnant he divorced me. I begged and washed clothes but that was not enough to fulfill our necessities. Nine months ago I turned to prostitution. I know that my life and my children's lives will be affected; if any one wants to help, I will leave this disgraced occupation without any hesitation.

**FH**: She says: "I am from Shamali. When the Taliban attacked our village, they destroyed everything. Everyone escaped to somewhere. The Taliban killed my father while he was working in the field. I moved to Kabul with my three children from three to seven years old. From that day my brother and husband are missing; perhaps they might be among the dead. In Kabul I was working as a servant in one of the houses from where I started prostituting. Nowadays I am in touch with a jeweller who gives me money when I visit him. I am suffering from stomach pain and do not like to have sexual relations with too many people.

**RA**: She is the mother of three children, the oldest one five years old. When I asked her age, she smiled and said: I have forgotten my name and you are asking about my age; perhaps 21". She is also from Shamali.

"I lost touch with my husband in Shamali. We escaped to Kabul, but on the way there, the Taliban separated men from women. My husband belonged to Panjsher and my guess is he might have been killed there. I was two months pregnant when we left our ruined village. I have been a prostitute for the last five months; there is a woman who guides me in this field. I have contact with a number of men who give me five to six lack Afghanis each week. My mother is a widow, too, but she doesn't know about what I am doing. I regret what I am doing but there is no other way out.

**SH**: I am from Panjsher valley but lived most of the time in Kabul. I had three children; two girls and one boy. I had a good life with my husband. But after seven years of togetherness my life took a new turn. Recently my two children died due to chickenpox. My husband blamed me for their deaths and used this as a pretext to leave me. He didn't take his son from me. I started this dirty business in the last few months.

I was living with my mother for some months but at last started begging. One day a shopkeeper made an offer and I accepted. Each week he gives me one and a half lack Afghanis. I don't know where he is from and whether he has a wife and children. I don't take any kind of pleasure in sexual relations with him, but it is forced on me. I used condoms to prevent getting pregnant, but in spite of that, I am four months pregnant now. My mother doesn't know anything about my relationship with that man.

**WH**: I have been doing this for the last two years; I am widowed and must feed my children. I started with cooking and washing clothes but our condition was very bad. At last I got in touch with a woman who was a prostitute for a long time discouraged me to leave that hard job and do this business, which is full of money. My first reaction was to refuse, but later on, when our condition worsened, I accepted. When I did it for the first time, I felt very bad and cried for many days. I am in contact with a number of men who give me money. I have been forced to do this and feel no joy while doing it. I am taking pills to keep myself from becoming pregnant. I always fear letting anyone, including my children and neighbours, know about my relations. If the neighbours find out they will throw me out of this area.

I am very afraid of getting AIDS or any other sexual disease; that is why I do this only in time of need. I am in touch with many women who are doing this dirty business and all of them are widows. I know Jamila who was killed by one of the Taliban's commanders. She had a relationship with the commander but when he found out that she had relations with other men, he killed her.

**AH**: My husband divorced me five years ago. I gave birth to two daughters but he wanted a son. With two daughters I faced a lot of problems. I started with washing clothes but at the end fell into this net. I have been doing this for more than two years and I am in contact with a man who has a showroom and he gives me money in return for sexual relations. He has a family, wife and children. I am using pills to avoid conception and I am a heart patient as well.

My older daughter is 14. In order to keep her safe from these things, I arranged her marriage. But because of bad luck, her life is more bitter than mine. Her husband is young and inexperienced and he and his mother do very cruel things to her. My daughter usually comes to share her pain with me. She is now a teacher in a RAWA literacy course.

**FA**: I have two daughters and two sons. I am illiterate. My father died some years back, my mother is alive. I was very young when I got married. We lived in happiness for some years but then my husband went to Pakistan and did not return. My life took a shocking turn after the loss of my husband. I have a brother-in-law who is jobless, poor and a weak man. I started doing it [prostitution] three years back when I found no other way out. I had nothing, no food, and no clothes for four small children.

I first started this with the shopkeepers. They gave me food for free.

Sometimes they gave me three or four lack Afghanis as well. They took me into many places, in a hotel for some hours or a vacant home. I am using the coil to prevent conception. My brother-in-law is unaware of all this. But, if he comes to know about it, he will not care because he cannot help. My brother usually comes home only at night for sleeping. He does not know anything about it either, because I am home at night. One of my children is weak and suffering from malnutrition. I took him to the hospital but it did not help.

**AA**: I am from Panjshir and living in the Saraji section of Kabul in a rented house. I am the mother of five children. I married one of my cousins who has been missing for the last two years. He was in Panjshir and worked with Taliban who captured him and did not kill him but rather forced him to work for them. I had another husband before this who was a Mullah and died due to illness. I have three children from him and one from my younger husband. I lived with my young children in one home but they forced me to leave as they could not bear my expenses. When I left that house, they fought among themselves. Finding no one to help me, I decided to go with this dirty business. Washing clothes and doing household chores for people was not enough. Whenever I go with someone, he gives me three or four lack Afghanis. I am still doing this twice or thrice a week.

**SA**: I am from Shakar Dara but have lived mostly in Kabul. My husband, who was from Saraei Khoja, lost his life three years ago when a rocket hit him and two of my children together. During the war we all had escaped the city to our village. We had a house there but Taliban burned that too.

After all these events (three years ago) I was left alone in this world with my two sons and one daughter, and I was forced to do this. My expenses were more than what I earned from clothes washing. I started begging at first. One day I went to a jeweller's shop to beg for money. The jeweller said : "what a pity! Begging is not worth your doing." He asked me why I am begging, and I told him that you don't know the pain which is crossing my heart. He said he wanted to take me to his house for washing clothes. The next day when I reached his home, when I entered his house nobody else was there and he locked the room and raped me forcibly. I could do nothing and he threatened me not to tell anybody and also gave me some money in return. I lost my honour, the only thing which I had left in my life.

Now, I am having contact with this man only. No one knows about this. His wife is a rich lady and often takes me to do household chores for her. I earn 8 to 10 lack Afghanis each month. God should not make any woman a widow. Nobody helps, neither kith nor kin.

I am using injection for contraception. I know the injection has its own side effects and that is why I am usually suffering from headaches. But, what should I do? Sometimes when I go to shops for begging, in order to pass the time shopkeepers will keep talking to me and give me a little more money. I am working for relatives as well, to feed my three orphan children.

**GM**: My husband is a driver and has been addicted to drugs for the last twenty years. I married 15 years ago. Actually one of my other cousins was supposed to marry my husband but she refused and my parents forced me to marry him. My husband, from the very first days of our marriage, mostly is out of the home. When he is home I usually find him nervous and in bad health. I have often asked my brother-in-law about my husband's addiction. I had three children, one died due to chicken pox and the other two due to pneumonia. Now I have only one daughter who is 9 years old.

I started doing this in 1989. My husband was asking me for money every time he needed it for drugs. One day he sold off my daughter to a stranger. Fortunately I saw the man taking my daughter and running away, and I chased him. Another man who was passing by witnessed the scene and caught the man. I got my daughter back. After that day, my daughter is very scared of her own father; she does not even want to see him. My husband says it does not matter to him how I earn money. In search of money sometimes even I go from Kabul to Panjshir. But I do take care to go to people who do not know me and are not relatives. My husband cannot live for a day without drugs and medicine. He is on his bed all the time like a small baby.

We are living with my sister-in-laws in the same house. Certainly, I do not want them to know about my relations and make different excuses when I leave the house. The men take me to strange places where I have never been before. I usually do this three or four times a week otherwise my husband will kick me out of his home.

**HA**: I am an orphan. My mother brought me up in a very good manner. I was able to go to school until class six in Kabul. My mother loved me very much. I had a happy and excellent life after my marriage. I am mother of two sons and a daughter. Then two years ago my husband got sick and died.

For one year I was able to earn my living in a very honourable way. But the situation becomes much tougher with the passage of time. Everyone forgot me. I was no longer able to feed my children. At last I began begging. A tailor by the name of Noor Ali (probably from Shamali, valley) called me many times and promised to give me a good amount of money. At first I turned down his offers, but then later I accepted to go to him for money. He promised to give me money weekly or monthly. I am still having contact with this man but my children are unaware of it. I have my father and mother-in-law alive but they do not help me. I would like to become literate, learn something, and earn money through honourable ways.

***Sun Journal, July 27, 2002***

KABUL, Afghanistan- Wrapped in blankets and bright scarves, the six inmates are scattered like wallflowers on the side of a cell inside Kabul's women's prison.

Twenty-eight-year-old Marzia's husband won't give her a divorce. She says the 55-year old chained her feet and locked her in a small damp room in his house for a month.

Nilofar, 16, and Fariba, 19, fell in love with boys next door and tried to elope. When Fariba refused to marry a cousin, she says, her father threatened to chop her up "and give me to my cousin in pieces." The cousin sent her a message in jail that he would kill her as soon as she was freed.

On Nov. 13, when the Taliban left Kabul, the women's jail emptied. But in the past six months, women and teen-age girls have started trickling back in, arrested for many of the same crimes that got them jailed during the Taliban era.

Of 29 prisoners, the majority were jailed for eloping or leaving their homes, half a dozen were accused of adultery, one was charged with murder and one was charged with theft.

Despite Western pressure for greater attention to the rights of women in Afghanistan, many laws pertaining to women have not changed, and there is confusion as to what the law is.

Afghanistan runs under a dual legal system, with sharia, or Islamic law, and some parts of the civil code that existed before the Taliban took control in 1996 and burned all the contemporary laws, legal records and books.

Under sharia, a man's word is worth twice that of a woman's. Convincing a court that a woman has been beaten by her husband or raped or needs a divorce is difficult.

A woman or girl who reports a rape but fails to prove she did not consent may risk a charge of fornication. Rana, 40, Kabul's senior female police investigator, who also held the position under the Taliban, argues that rape is physically impossible and that the crime cannot exist. Rana is responsible for investigating all crimes involving women. Peering through thick, black-rimmed glasses, she compares rape with a needle and thread.

"Can you force the thread through the needle if the needle is jerking around?" she asks, suggesting that no man could force sex upon any woman who really struggled.

Sherin Aqa Manawee, deputy of Afghanistan's Supreme Court, says that under sharia, a man or woman is entitled to choose a spouse, provided it neither is engaged - and the woman's father has no legal right to interfere.

But it rarely works out that way. The law clashes with the long-held Afghan tradition that families select the spouse. Women and girls who run away from the homes of their fathers, husbands or other male relatives are arrested and taken to jail, where they stay unless claimed by a male relative.

Martin Lau, an Islamic law specialist at the University of London's School of Oriental and African Studies, says some offenses - such as "honor crimes," in which male relatives dishonouring the family - are more a matter of tradition than law.

"It's custom here. It's not Islamic law," he says. "There is nothing in Islam that says a betrayed husband has the right to take the law into his own hands. "

The detention of women for running away from home is part of a culture that treats them as though they were minors, their lives ruled by their male relatives. Under the law applied by the Taliban and still widely in force, a woman has to be represented by her male guardian or husband in all legal proceedings. In a country where clan connections are all-important, a woman must rely on her male relatives to push her cause with police and court officials. For Afghan women, the legal system is opaque and terrifying.

Marzia spent eight months in prison because she wants a divorce. A month ago she was released pending the divorce trial, but she may be sent back to her husband if the court refuses a divorce.

She is living with her one male relative, a 95-year-old uncle. She has been twice married. Her first husband married a younger woman, divorced Marzia, and he and his new wife took her 2-month-old girl. She never saw the child again.

When she was 18, a shopkeeper 27 years her senior took her as his second wife, but she says he never consummated the marriage. "He said he'd not married me to have children. He'd married me to work for his first wife," she says.

Several years later, when the government of Burhanuddin Rabbani ruled Kabul, bringing in fundamentalist Islam, she tried to get a divorce. Her husband refused and had her jailed for 18 months. Eight months ago, Marzia says, she again sought a divorce after her husband, who she says was often angry and violent, chained her in a dark, wet room.

"I was hungry and thirsty. The other wife brought me something secretly," Marzia says. "I respect her very much, Like a mother."

When her husband refused again to divorce, she ran away. He went to authorities and had her jailed a second time. Rana, the investigator, corroborated Marzia's version, saying her husband, the shopkeeper, is a powerful figure with good connections.

After returning to her husband's house the first time, Marzia says, he beat her frequently, "almost every day."

"If I'd have argued with him, that would be one thing," she says. "But I never spoke out against him. I never screamed because I was frightened. I felt guilty. I felt ashamed. I was very afraid that he would kill me."

Three years ago, she says, he broke her ribs with a full Coca-Cola bottle because she put fresh yogurt into a bowl instead of leaving it in a bag in a cool place. Another time he hit her with the handle of a shovel.

Manawee, 35, appointed to the Supreme Court after the fall of the Taliban, says getting a divorce should be difficult.

"Have you noticed the problem in the West, that there's more divorce cases in foreign countries than in Afghanistan? We don't want these unfavourable changes or the experiences that Westerners face," he says.

The girls and young women jailed in Kabul for eloping have all the defiant love and bravery of heroines in romance novels but come across as shy. Nilofar, from provincial Ghorband, hangs her head and retreats under a long pale blue shawl as she tells the story of her love for Anjamuddin, 20, a driver who lived next door. She says she was determined not to marry the cousin her father chose: "When my mother married a relative, she did not have a good life. My sister also married my father's relative, and she is not happy either. "

The couple saw one another over an adjoining wall and whispered for two hours each night. Finally, they ran away but spent only nine hours together before they were arrested at a relative's home.

"I know it's a scandal for the family, but I do not regret it for any reason. I still want to marry him," Nilofar said in her cell in April. But Rana said the family would never agree to the marriage and added there is a risk the male relatives would kill the girl.

Asked whether she wanted to be a good wife and mother, or whether she wanted other things as well, Nilofar did not have a chance to answer.

"What can she be?" said Rana, amazed at the question. "She's not educated. What can she be except a housewife?"

In the end, the older woman was proved right. Nilofar's will broke while she was in prison, and she bent to her father's demand to give up the boy she loved and marry the cousin she does not. As soon as she agreed, one month ago, she was freed.

*Robyn Dixon is a reporter with the Los Angles Times, a Tribune Publishing newspaper.*

# 5

# Women's Participation in Government

Violence against women and girls occurs in almost all countries, in all regions, and in every segment of society, though the forms and incidence of such violence are variable. Often, violence is not random - women and girls are victims simply because they are female. Thus, gender-based violence is an expression of gender inequality but it also may serve to bolster wider patterns of gender discrimination and injustice. Too often, violence is visited upon women as though it were a right of men to inflict it and the obligation of women to suffer it. Such thinking must be rejected categorically. In recent years, the existence of gender-based violence has gained greater public acknowledgement in many countries but denial of its scope and seriousness remains widespread. Its victims, moreover, may prefer silence, especially when prevailing social customs, powerful institutions and the legal system do little or nothing to afford protection.

Gender-based violence has immediate and far-reaching consequences affecting women's and children's development, health, mental and physical well-being, and life prospects. By 'children', of course, we mean both boys and girls, whether they are the direct victims of violence or are exposed to it. Despite its pervasive presence in human history, we are only just beginning to reach a fuller understanding of the causes and effects of violence. Much more research and investigation are needed if we are to understand how violence affects the behaviour, emotions, attitudes and personal development of its direct victims and its witnesses.

However, crucial though they are, increased knowledge and understanding are not enough, nor should they be the first response. The key immediate action in all cases is to stop the violence before it does any further damage. Violence feeds upon itself and therefore has the potential to escalate. Stopping the violence, therefore, is urgent and vital. But it too is not enough. For the cycle of violence to be decisively broken, its recurrence must be prevented. This applies as much to political violence as it does, say, to domestic violence. Effective prevention must take specific and appropriate forms but a factor common to many different approaches is the strengthening of the resilience and coping capacity of the victims of violence.

UNESCO believes that supportive learning environments are very important in this regard, as are particular strategies for promoting peace, conflict resolution, human rights, tolerance and democracy through education.

Without in any way diminishing the importance of other situations around the world, allow us to take the example of Afghanistan, where until recently women and girls were victims of systematic marginalization and discrimination at the hands of the Taliban regime. Afghanistan under the Taliban became justifiably notorious for its denial of women's fundamental human rights, particularly the right to education, health and work.

**Policy of Taliban**

The Taliban officials beat up five Afghan women workers employed by a foreign aid agency in Kabul. The women who worked for the CARF International Agency were traveling in the agency's car on Saturday when they were stopped by the officials of the Taliban's department for preventing vice and fostering virtue.

Besides imposing other restrictions on individual freedom, the Taliban in Afghanistan, have banned the keeping of pigeons and playing with the birds, describing it as un-Islamic. The violators of the ban, according to a report from Kabul will be imprisoned and the birds shall be killed. The kite flying has also been stopped. Another interesting rule on the subject related to what it described the promotion of Islamic hairstyle. They have advised the Afghans not to go for the

American and British hair styles which could land them in jail. The concerned department has also authorized to shave the hair of such people and charge expenses. The male tailors have been banned from sewing ladies dresses and taking their body measurements, adding that if any woman or magazines were found at the tailors shop, the owner will be arrested.

Afghan ambassador to Islamabad Maulvi Shahabuddin Dilawar has ruled out holding of elections in Afghanistan saying that the people of the war-ravaged country have already given a verdict in favour of Taliban.

**Forced Abortion**

On May 29, [1997] Layla living in Khairkhana, Kabul, who was five months pregnant left her house for a routine pregnancy check-up at the nearby Parwan Maternity Clinic. She was dressed head-to-foot in the prescribed chadari [also called burqa] which only allowed a grill through which she could look out but even her eyes could not be seen. She had to wrap her self carefully in the chadari, as allowing her dress to be seen was against the imposed dress code. Halfway to the clinic she felt suffocated and felt an urgent need for fresh air. Turning into a deserted lane she raised her veil and drew deep breaths, relishing the feeling of relief. Suddenly a scourge-wielding Taliban militiaman screaming abuse materialised out of nowhere. "Why have you bared your face! Why have you bared your face!" he kept screaming while he poured out the vilest invectives. His whip hand was raised and before Layla could say anything the blow landed on her distended abdomen. Layla could only scream "Bradar jan, [brother, dear], don't hit me, I am with child, I am going to the clinic" but the frenzied Taliban kept raining down blows on the miserable woman. The pain and the terror made Layla sit down on the dirt and the Taliban went away after a few more vicious blows of the lash. None of the few passers-by could dare to intercede. By now Layla was bleeding but both she and one or two passers-by knew that she could not hope for a helping hand as there were no women around and it is against Taliban 'ethics' and edicts for a male to touch any female other than close family members. Any man extending a helping hand to a woman in need was sure to receive the same treatment that had been meted out to Layla a moment ago. Layla could only drag herself to the clinic where she passed out. When she came to she was drenched in blood and the nurses told her that she had had a miscarriage. They sounded very worried about her own condition and it was not long before she lost consciousness again. The following day she developed a soaring temperature and doctors diagnosed peritonitis. They recommended abdominal surgery but before they could obtain the necessary go-ahead from the Taliban authorities Layla breathed her last.

On the July 20 [1997] Taliban forces attacked Takana and Jalrez [some 150 kilometres to the west of Kabul, inhabited mostly by ethnic Hazaras]. The Wahdat forces [a politico-military group composed of Hazaras] retreated into the valleys in their rear but in a surprise counter-attack caught the Taliban off-guard and seized some 70 Taliban fighters alive. They rounded up their hostages, then doused them with petrol and set them on fire alive.

When the Taliban got to know of the fate of their comrades they swept down on Hazara villages in the vicinity and carried off some 30-40 Hazara women. These women were repeatedly and systematically raped by Taliban force. A week later Wahdat fighters led by Commander Qambar, known as Qambar the Lame, swept down on villages in the proximity which were inhabited by Pashtoons [the Taliban are predominantly ethnic Pashtoons] and carried away some 40-50 Pashtoon women in revenge. The Pashtoon women were subjected to the same treatment the Hazara women were receiving at the hands of the Taliban. To the filing of this report none of the women have been freed from either side.

On Nov. 13, when the Taliban left Kabul, the women's jail emptied. But in the past six months, women and teen-age girls have started trickling back in, arrested for many of the same crimes that got them jailed during the Taliban era. Of 29 prisoners, the majority were jailed for eloping or leaving their homes, half a dozen were accused of adultery, one was charged with murder and one was charged with theft.

Despite Western pressure for greater attention to the rights of women in Afghanistan, many laws pertaining to women have not changed, and there is confusion as to what the law is. Afghanistan runs under a dual legal system, with sharia, or Islamic law, and some parts of the civil code that existed before the Taliban took control in 1996 and burned all the contemporary laws, legal records and books.

Under *sharia,* a man's word is worth twice that of a woman's. Convincing a court that a woman has been beaten by her husband or raped or needs a divorce is difficult. A woman or girl who reports a rape but fails to prove she did not consent may risk a charge of fornication. Rana, 40, Kabul's senior female police investigator, who also held the position under the Taliban, argues that rape is physically impossible and that the crime cannot exist. Rana is responsible for investigating all crimes involving women. Peering through thick, black-rimmed glasses, she compares rape with a needle and thread. Under *sharia,* a man or woman is entitled to choose a spouse, provided neither is engaged - and the woman's father has no legal right to interfere. But it rarely works out that way. The law clashes with the long-held Afghan tradition that families select the spouse. Women and girls who run away from the homes of their fathers, husbands or other male relatives are arrested and taken to jail, where they stay unless claimed by a male relative.

The lives of women remain vulnerable and there are reports of killings of women by their family members in the name of morality. Despite interventions by local NGOs the authorities have looked away, and have taken no action to investigate such murders. Such gender-based impunity by any State is a clear discrimination of the right to life of women

The detention of women for running away from home is part of a culture that treats them as though they were minors, their lives ruled by their male relatives. Under the law applied by the Taliban and still widely in force, a woman has to be represented by her male guardian or husband in all legal proceedings. In a country where clan connections are all-important, a woman must rely on her male relatives to push her cause with police and court officials. For Afghan women, the legal system is opaque and terrifying.

**Condition of Women**

Women in war-shattered Afghanistan are dying during childbirth at a staggeringly high rate, U.N. and U.S. researchers reported on Wednesday, recommending broad improvements in maternal health care. While maternal death rates vary considerably from region to region and are significantly higher in rural areas than in cities and towns, they are overall among the highest in the world, the researchers found. In rural Badakshan province in northern Afghanistan, mothers are dying while giving birth at the highest rate ever documented -- 6,500 maternal deaths for every 100,000 live births, according to their survey.

Widespread women's rights violations are partly to blame for high maternal mortality rates in Afghan women, according to a study appearing in the September 11 issue of the Journal of the American Medical Association. Researchers from Boston's Brigham and Women's Hospital and Physicians for Human Rights interviewed 4,886 women from the northwestern Afghan province of Herat. They estimated that 593 out of 100,000 Herati women die during pregnancy or childbirth. Countrywide, Afghan maternal mortality rates are the second highest in the world with 1,700 deaths out of 100,000 Afghan pregnancies compared to 12 out of 100,000 in the US.

In some cases, husbands force their wives to deliver in their own homes, because the culture considers treatment by strangers in public places "shameful." In addition, the study also noted that 80 percent of the women interviewed considered sex with their husbands obligatory. Nearly half said that a husband had the right to physically abuse his wife for disobedience

**Role of U.N.O.**

The United Nations is guiding the rebuilding of Afghanistan, with significant financial help from Washington, after decades of internal warfare, years of drought and a U.S.-led bombing campaign that drove the Taliban from power after the Sept. 11, 2001, hijack attacks on the United States. Access to any type of health care at all was a key gauge of maternal survival. While in Kabul, there was at least one functioning maternity hospital, health care access in Badakshan was "profoundly limited," the study found.

A newborn baby had only one chance in four of surviving until its first birthday if its mother died in childbirth, the study found. "Most of these infants died in the first month of life from acute malnutrition due to lack of breast milk." Only 5 percent of the women studied could read or write and only 36 percent of the families interviewed owned a radio, the researchers found.

In addition to generally improving health services and increasing access to skilled caregivers, they recommended that women be taught ahead of time about healthy pregnancies and delivery and be screened for preventable causes of maternal complications such as pre-eclampsia, malaria and anemia.

The five men who raped 14-year-old Fatima, her mother and two younger sisters last month have no fear of the law. For eight hours, they took turns assaulting her, her mother, Nazu, and sisters Bibi Amina, 10, and Bibi Aisha, 12, all the while training a Kalashnikov assault rifle on the girls' disabled father, Jamaluddin. Before they left, the men took the family's life savings -- about $142 -- and a carpet from the living room.

They returned the next day to warn them not to go to the authorities. "They said that they would kill us if we told anyone," Jamaluddin said. The family says the rapists were soldiers of Gen. Abdul Rashid Dostum's army, the Junbish-e-Millie (National Movement), which has been terrorizing thousands of civilians in the northern province of Balkh since the fall of the Taliban in November.

Although the war is over, some of Dostum's soldiers, who are mostly ethnic Uzbeks but include ethnic Tajik fighters, go out almost nightly to rob and rape Pashtuns, the ethnic group that composed most of the Taliban militia but is a minority in the north. Such abuses are a clear illustration that the interim government of Prime Minister Hamid Karzai has been unable to stem lawlessness throughout much of Afghanistan.

Fear over the widespread persecution has overcome even international aid workers, who are virtually tight-lipped when asked about it.

The ruling Taliban's religious police have ordered foreign women providing humanitarian aid in Afghanistan to stop driving on grounds they are damaging the society, aid workers have said. They said the foreign ministry had proclaimed the ban on women driving after it received the orders from the Taliban's Ministry for the Promotion of Virtue and Prevention of Vice.

**Taliban Rules Weigh on Afghan Women**

The Taliban, who control 90 percent of the country, say

the streets were not safe from marauding bands of men who would steal and rape. But for women, it seems the movement's puritanical edicts are taking a toll on their mental health.

At Kabul's only mental health hospital, Dr. Shaheen Shah Wasah, says since the Taliban takeover the number of women patients is on the increase. Theirs is a small, shabby ward. Even behind closed doors several women bury themselves in their burqa, lying listlessly on the bed. Some moan and rock back and forth. Others squat in a corner.

On 20th July 1998 Taliban conducted a house to house search for televisions, VCRs, dish antennas, tape recorders and cassettes. Taliban's women folk were also participating in the search. While searching a house in block 14 of third Macroryns, these female Taliban stole 40,000 Rupees (Pakistani) from a family. A woman of the family complained that the female Taliban had stolen her money. However the Taliban started beating her up and were saying to her "you have no shame, accusing angels".

According to eye witnesses these "angels" are involved in robberies all over the city of Kabul. The thefts and robberies are so common that the Taliban have been forced to make radio announcements and blame the crimes on people impersonating Taliban.

On 23 August members of Fostering Virtue and Suppressing Vice were searching the shops, and implemented Sharia in the Mariam high school market. A woman, with her burqa (veil) pulled up, was talking to a shopkeeper. Taliban started beating the women and were calling her names for not being accompanied by her Mahram (close male family member) and not covering her face.

While shaking from pain and anger and not being able to stand properly, the women took her burqa off and throw it away. Being enraged and disgusted she shouted and abused the Taliban and Mullah Omar, calling them gutless and lackeys to Pakistanis. She was cursing their law and Sharia, and swore by Quran not to wear the burqa again. The woman was so enraged that she cursed Kabul's women for putting up with their miseries. The Taliban surprised by the sudden rage of the woman hastily retreated and left the shop and the woman in her pain and suffering. For several days a group of Fostering

Virtue and Suppressing Vice was patrolling the high school market from 11 am to 6 pm, and were beating any woman that they saw there. They even tried to make the market for men only. When Taliban took the .power in Kabul, a number of Pakistani spies (similar to Russian advisers during Purchami and Khalqi regimes) entered the city under the guise of religious preachers. They positioned themselves in busy mosques around the city, and generally, they are carrying out the following three activities 1- preaching and recruiting for Wahabite sect, 2- Degrading the religious people of Kabul, 3- investigating families especially about their adult male members.

Also, they are duty bound to send people into mosque for morning and evening prayers. These so called preachers go to people's houses before morning and evening prayers in groups of five or six accompanied by a Taliban youth as guide. In each house, they ask for a male member of the house. After a short and brief speech on Islamic values they turn to Pakistan's and Iran's politics toward Afghanistan, and, make Pakistan appear as innocent and clean. After they "convert" that man, in their terms, to a Muslim, they ask for another man in the house. At the same time, they stop any educated or elderly person passing by and preach them too.

On 11th August 1998 in Ali Chopaan locality in Mazar-e-Sharif Province, three Taliban entered a house to conduct search. The house belongs to a mother from Hazara ethnicity who lives there with her two young daughters.

The mother beseeched the Taliban for mercy and told them that her husband and son are innocent and wrongly imprisoned and begged for their freedom. However, the Taliban raped the two daughters in front of their mother, and told her if she dared to mention a word of this incident to any one, they would kill her husband and son in the prison. Finally before leaving the area, to deceive the women, they give her a piece of paper and told her to take the paper to the prison and they would free her husband and son.

**Atrocities**

On 27th August 1998 a mother and her two daughters were walking back home from the city in Ali Chopan village, on the way they came across a filthy Chali (another term used for young Taliban). He forced the three into a house and locked the mother in one room and the two daughters in another and right away left the house to inform his accomplices of his 'hunt'. However the two girls managed to break the door and escape, and from terror of the situation they even forgot about their mother. However no one knows of the where about the 65-year-old mother.

The greatest tragedy is that there seems no end to the sufferings of Afghan women. As a result, the majority of the Afghan women are suffering from mental disorder and have become a burden for their own parents. An Afghan refugees says that all the time he is worried about his three daughters. There is no law to check crimes against women in Afghanistan. In many cases women in the recent past were raped and tortured by unknown criminals in various parts of Afghanistan.

The recovery of mass graves of women near Kabul about four months ago is a glaring proof of the sort of agony Afghan women were passing through. "To protect the honour of my daughters, I want my daughters to be married as early as possible. No matter whether she is nine years old or 12 years old," says a man.

A RAWA report claims that on September 15,1993 several women with worn-out dresses were seen in Bagh-e-Bala. The women, according to the report, told that they had escaped from a jail, controlled by a group which was later ousted from Kabul. The report says that there has been an incident in which a father killed his daughter to escape cruel treatment at the hands of criminals. The report alleges that in the absence of any law, criminals break into houses of people for looting and dishonouring the women.

War has so badly devastated the Afghan nation where suffering has reached unprecedented heights. The Afghan feel so helpless - in Peshawar an Afghan refugee, Habibullah, was seen selling his two-year-old grandson. The man said that all his family members had been killed in the war. "I am an old man and there is no one to look after the child", he says that he does not want money, but is looking for someone who could guarantee this grandson's well-being. There are numerous similar painful stories of Afghan women and children.

There is no right of safe return to Afghanistan for women living in Pakistan, especially widows. Widows have no protection, no right to employment or benefits and no guarantees of security. Women could be targeted for revenge killing by a particular party or tribe or just because they are educated.

Widows living in Pakistan whose husbands were members of the former communist-backed regime consider themselves to be in great danger of execution if they try to return to Afghanistan. Widows in Afghanistan are often forced to marry their brother-in-law or other relative in their husband's family. In a village near Mazar-i-Sharif, village women claimed that a year ago a widow was hung for refusing to marry her deceased husband's cousin.

The Taliban have been responsible for the killing of hundreds of innocent people in indiscriminate rocket attacks against residential areas in and around Kabul. Their leaders have frequently ordered the execution of suspected opponents - in July this year, 30 young men were executed in Herat in one night. Retreating soldiers, and those who surrendered to the Taliban in Herat last year where also summarily executed.

Civilians in areas already taken over by the Taliban have been denied basic and fundamental human rights. Arbitrary punishment such as stoning and amputations have been introduced, and severe restrictions placed on women.

Today, women are reclaiming their rights to education and employment, schools for girls are reopening and women are returning to their former jobs.

In whatever way it can, UNESCO is supporting these efforts, recognizing that Afghan women themselves must take the lead in identifying their own needs and priorities. The end of all forms of gender-based violence is likely to figure prominently among those priorities. The collapse of the Taliban regime has removed a major impediment to Afghan women's recovery of their rights but other obstacles stubbornly remain.

However, women face considerable challenges in this process, which include entrenched traditional attitudes in Afghanistan constraining women from participating in political processes, as well as security concerns inhibiting women from traveling to regional centers to cast ballots. Such representation is crucial to ensure that women's rights are at the core of all governance arrangements, including post-conflict reconstruction, justice, and accountability.

Both Interim Administration officials and senior United Nations (U.N.) representatives emphasized this point at a meeting on March 8 in Kabul to commemorate International Women's Day, when they stressed that a peaceful and secure environment is necessary to implement reconstruction and rehabilitation programs designed for women.

In Mazar, women expressed fears of leaving the security of their homes. However, the security situation was so acute that women who had been raped or otherwise sexually abused had typically been attacked in their own homes. Some had been gang-raped. The identities of the perpetrators were difficult or impossible to discern, even to the victims.

Women described attackers as men wearing traditional clothes (loose trousers and a long shirt), or a military-style camouflage jacket, sometimes carrying arms, and often with a turban pulled across their faces. Sometimes, women could identify their attackers' ethnicity by their facial features or speech, and so the armed political group to which they probably belonged. In December 2001, fourteen armed Hazara men from the Wahdat party raped three sisters, ages twelve-, fourteen-, and twenty-years-old from Char Rahi Haji Ayub, a neighborhood in Mazar.

Security forces under the command of Majid Rouzi1arrested four men who were released a few days later. One day after this incident, General Dostum called on all his forces to "respect the honor of all women." The manager of the hospital records where this case was registered and where the girls sought medical treatment, explained that when she followed up with the family about their case, they told her that the authorities said they could not do anything because the responsible soldiers belonged to another faction.

In the atmosphere of generalized insecurity in Mazar, fears for personal security severely restrict Afghan women's ability to function and participate in public life. Women feel compelled to abide by the Taliban edicts severely restricting the role of women in public life or risk abuse and even assault. A.P., a forty-five-year-old school administrator, stressed that women are, therefore, still reluctant to abandon their chadari or to travel unaccompanied and independently in the city. She explained:

"We have experienced many problems [in the past] and are happy that some changes have come and the life of girls has gotten better, but still nothing has been done about our security problems. Both before and during the time of the Taliban, political rivalries led to local conflicts and the winner did not consider the rights of the loser. After the Taliban, there is still abuse of the rights of all people and of women. I am free inside the house but not outside in the city."

A woman working as a teacher and community worker in Dasht-i Shour, located in the southwestern outskirts of Mazar, expressed similar concerns when she spoke of the insecurity in her area and the consequences this has for women's mobility:

"The Taliban government was strict and bad things happened then, but now the security is a problem, especially at night. For women the situation in the case of education and employment was worse under the Taliban. I am a widow, and so it was difficult for me to work. Now it is better, and I am working as a teacher. Women can go out now and have the opportunity to get an education, but still while wearing a chadari. Older women are free to go without a chadari. This is because of the security situation [in Mazar]."

The reasons for women's fears in Kabul stem mainly from their personal experiences of violence and discrimination during 1992 to 1996, and since that time under the Taliban regime. Women feared being attacked or harassed by men who supported the former Taliban edicts that had restricted women's behavior, dress, expression, and movement; and of being physically assaulted by armed groups from the different factions that were responsible for the reported abductions and rapes of women and girls in Kabul between 1992 to 1996. Most women in Kabul, as in Mazar, continue to wear the chadari.

For example, on January 10, 2002, in Kabul, a woman nongovernmental (NGO) worker accompanied by another woman and a male colleague were forced to stop their vehicle by three men in another vehicle; the men then questioned the man about the women appearing in public with their faces uncovered. The woman told that the men were clearly from among the armed forces from the north that had captured Kabul; they wore camouflage jackets and trousers, pakuls.

**Overthrow of Talibans**

The overthrow of the Taliban in November 2001 raised hopes that women in Afghanistan would rapidly regain their human rights. But the continuing threat to their security that women face in the north and elsewhere has in large measure rendered women's participation in public life almost impossible.

The Interim Administration has only limited effective authority outside Kabul, and the government that replaces it will have to address these issues. Extensive and sustained support from the international community is required.

The international community should take urgent action to improve security conditions throughout Afghanistan, and help end ethnic and gender-specific violence if women are to play a full and constructive role in the rebuilding of Afghan society.

Afghan women will not be able to participate in a meaningful and sustained way in the rebuilding of Afghanistan. Yet, the goal of long-term peace and security can only be realized if fundamental human rights are fully respected and past human rights abuses are addressed, including accountability for abuses against women.

**Women's Security**

Afghan women of all ethnicities have been compelled to restrict their participation in public life to avoid being targets of violence by armed factions and by those seeking to enforce repressive Taliban-era edicts.

Trafficking in women and girls has increased. Girls are purchased in Afghanistan, trafficked through Pakistan and sold into prostitution or marriage in the Persian Gulf countries.

Very few of the men in the interim administration believe there should be a Women's Ministry. These are not for the most part liberal, progressive men; many of them have similar attitudes to the Taliban. Process up to the end of the Loya Jirga has been guided by the international community and has been positive for women, including:

2 women were ministers in Afghan Interim Authority out of 30 members.

- A woman stood for presidency at the Loya Jirga in June 2002. Finished second, but ahead of two men
- 3 members of the Special Independent Commission for the Convening of the Emergency Loya Jirga were women.
- 11% of Loya Jirga seats were guaranteed to women.
- 200 women were elected to the Loya Jirga (14%).
- All Loya Jirga delegates had a 3-hour training session on gender sensitivity.
- Female delegates at the Loya Jirga have spoken out about other delegates who had been heavily involved in the conflict and destruction of the country.

For the first time in history, Afghanistan has a Women's Ministry, which will be key to promoting and achieving Afghan women's rights. The Women's Ministry has a payroll of 200 civil servants and a building to work in. A woman heads up the new Human Rights Commission. As of June 2002, 2 women are cabinet ministers (Public Health and Women's Affairs). There are also women in positions of Deputy Minister for Education and junior minister for Women's Affairs. Positive involvement of women's groups and activists internationally in getting issues such as women's political participation onto the political agenda.

There are UN plans to set up a network of women in the regions to act as "local leaders". The UN Secretary General has recommended that the Afghan Transitional Government ensures the full participation of women in the assessment of short, medium and longterm priorities in all sectors.

Process up to the end of the Loya Jirga has been guided by the international community and has been negative for women, including:

- Only 2 of 26 cabinet ministers are women.
- There is no democratic process for the women elected to the Loya Jirga to move into the Transitional Government (TG) - all members of the TG are hand-picked by the President.
- There is no minimum quota to ensure that women will be represented in the TG, or on any bodies which are set up by the TG, such as the Constitutional Commission.
- Negatives for women associated with the political process so far have been:

- In many rural areas, local authorities and commanders tried to intimidate potential female candidates and many women were openly threatened during the process. UN envoy to Afghanistan Lakhdar Brahimi ssaid: "Voting for the Loya Jirga has been plagued by violence and vote-buying... There were attempts at manipulation, violence, unfortunately. Money was used, threats were used."
- The Ministry of Women's Affairs had called for 25% women's representation on the Loya Jirga. 11% was disappointing as a target, and the 4% who came through other channels showed that a more ambitious target could and should have been set.
- Known human rights violators were involved in the Loya Jirga process.
- Most women delegates felt they had been sidelined in the Loya Jirga process and were expected to rubber stamp decisions made behind closed doors.
- Fundamentalist leaders branded critics of the warlords who participated in the Loya Jirga as traitors to Islam and a petition was circulated at the Loya Jirga.

# 6

# National Policy

Several measures have been undertaken as national policy for the Welfare of Women.

- Commitment within Afghan Transitional government and international community to an inclusive Constitution entrenching women's rights.
- Afghanistan has ratified virtually every human rights treaty, including the International Covenant on Civil and Political Rights (ICCPR) which prohibits discrimination against women and establishes the equal right of women to participation in public life.
- Afghan Women Lawyers and Professionals Association emerged in January after four years underground. Planned activities include:
  - Setting up a training centre in Kabul and information offices around Afghanistan.
  - Working on securing women's rights in the new Constitution.
  - Training 40 women in basic human rights practices.
  - Establishing a resource centre for comparative Islamic, national and international law.
- Afghanistan's Constitution of 1964 exists as a positive model which can be developed.
- A Human Rights Commission has been established, headed by a woman, which will look at transitional justice and begin working this month on a 2-year programme. The HRC will have a formal secretariat, including 34 staff in Kabul plus regional satellite offices, entirely financed by external donor support.

**UN Mandate**

- The UN Secretary General has recommended that women are well represented as members of the Judicial Commission, the Civil Service Commission and the Human Rights Commission; that a gender perspective is taken into consideration when developing the mandates of these commissions and that that urgent measures be taken to repeal all edicts and orders that discriminate against women.
- Taliban decrees and laws discriminating against women remain in force.
- Existing legal structures are poor and women's rights are rarely recognised or upheld. In some parts of the country there is no functioning legal system.
- The Minister of Justice is reported to be a hardliner on justice issues and to have a negative attitude towards equality before the law for women.
- Women continue to serve and receive extreme sentences for "crimes" such as seeking to marry a man of their choice, attempting to leave partners, and criticizing their husbands.
- There is a possibility that, unless international pressure remains strong, conservatives will win the argument on continued implementation of strict Sharia law. A strict following would include death by stoning for a married woman guilty of committing adultery and 100 lashes for a single woman. The new Chief Justice of the Supreme Court was quoted in press interviews in January as saying that Sharia punishments including stoning and amputation would be retained, albeit with stricter due process guarantees than under the Taliban.
- There is no national consultation process on the Constitution committed to taking on board the views of women, and no obligation for women to be represented on the Constitutional Commission.
- There are concerns that the Human Rights Commission may not be independent and free to advocate for justice, particularly for women, as well as reconciliation.
- Although the Human Rights Commission is not looking at granting immunity for war crimes, there is widespread

fear that warlords will not be brought to justice, and that violence will carry on as ever.

- It is procedurally unclear where the Human Rights Commission fits into Afghanistan's present or future legal structure.
- Action on "human rights" may be seen as taking care of women's rights.
- The HRC does not have great capacity and it will bear the brunt of much hostility, yet the international community is not taking responsibility for monitoring violations of human rights or women's rights until it is functional - and it is clear that there are many violations taking place.
- Although Afghanistan has ratified most human rights conventions, it has yet to commit to the Convention on the Elimination of all forms of Discrimination Against Women (CEDAW). This is an important symbol of commitment to lasting and positive change for women.

**Results of Efforts**

- Only 1-2% of women in Afghanistan have identity cards and 98% have no formal papers, citizenship or identity.
- No obligation to include women in representative numbers in the Constitution-making process.
- No plan for a national consultation process on the Constitution which will consult with women or guarantee that the constitution will be informed by best practice from Islamic countries.
- CEDAW still not ratified; CEDAW defines what constitutes discrimination against women and sets up an agenda for national action to end such discrimination.
- Absence of guarantee for appointment of female judges.
- No guarantee of adequate resourcing and established political status of Human Rights Commission, nor of security for its members.

***Women's Freedom of Expression and Participation in Civil Society***

- Intensive civil society activity has begun, with Afghan women coming together in their thousands and producing coherent and consolidated policy demands. These are being are taken seriously by the international political community and used by international civil society to advocate for Afghan women. Eg. Afghan Women's Summit for Democracy, Brussels, 4-5 Dec, 2001 and 1000 Women conference in Kabul, 7-9 Jun 2002.

- Women teachers and lawyers who have worked undercover for years are now openly practising their profession.
- In January 2002, Hamid Karzai signed "The Declaration of the Essential Rights of Afghan Women"
- In March 2002 celebrations were held in Kabul for International Women's Day. Women issued a plan of action and demands to the Interim Authority and international community to include women in reconstruction.

**Negative**

- 80% of a survey of more than 1,000 Afghan men and women living in Afghanistan living under the Taliban agreed that women should be able to move about freely and that the teachings of Islam do not restrict women's human rights.
- In most parts of the country, women are still unable to move around freely and express themselves freely. Those who do draw attention to themselves (eg Sima Samar, former Minister for Women now head of the Human Rights Commission) and become targets for abuse and threatened or actual violence.
- Fragmentation and factionalisation of Afghan society also applies to Afghan women, where there is an urgent need for resources to build bridges in order to, for example, resolve tension between returnees and women who have remained in Afghanistan over the years.
- Although women's rights workers are returning to Afghanistan from exile, they mostly continue to keep a very low profile - there is no confidence that things have changed for good.
- Women and girls are being denied the right to move around freely and to seek out education and work.
- Attitudes and behaviour of men towards women developed over years of conflict and condoned and strictly enforced by the Taliban remain ingrained.

- Inadequate freedom for women to speak out and no action taken when their freedom of expression is denied.
- Absence of training and support to women's organisations to assist development of local and regional networks.
- Absence of leadership training for women.

***Education***

- Huge enthusiasm for education, repeatedly highlighted in reports and media and sense that women want to be trained in professional skills and English.
- For the first time in five years, in Feb 2002 Afghan women took university entrance examinations. 1,000 women took part.
- In March 2002 girls began to re-enrol in primary schools. In the Kabul area around 50% of those newly enrolled were girls.
- 1.6 million more children are being educated since the fall of the Taliban out of a possible 4.4 million.
- Women can now teach in public schools again.
- The opportunity for primary education is currently about 39% for boys and 3% for girls.
- Only about 16% of women over 15 years old are literate.
- Education remains extremely under funded. Estimated shortage of teachers is 100,000 and conditions for teaching are exceptionally poor.
- The rural-urban divide in terms of education is huge.
- Outside cities, there are reports that a majority of men are still very reluctant to allow education of women and are forbidding girls to go to school.
- International community has not delivered on aid pledges.

*Negative*

- Inadequate provision of training and education programmes for women.
- Women and girls are often not genuinely free to attend courses and schools.

**Employment**

- Women are now officially permitted to work outside the home.
- Organisations and facilities for women are beginning to operate openly, including newspapers and magazines (e.g.

"Roz") radio stations, (e.g. Radio Voice of Peace), beauty salons etc.

- Some humanitarian and reconstruction projects are targeting women, e.g. Women's Bakery Project in Kabul run by the World Food Programme, currently 318 staff, plans to expand to employ 500 more women.
- Employment opportunities overall are limited, and lack of security and attitudes of male family members mean that many women are still confined to their homes.
- Three years of drought have led to widespread food shortages.
- Women have suffered huge financial losses as a result of the Taliban-imposed ban on work.
- Absence of official data relating to women's employment.
- Challenges for women's employment include cultural social acceptance.

**Forced Marriage and Early Marriage**

- Afghan women are campaigning on this issue. E.g. The 7-9 June 1000 women conference in Kabul, issued a statement including an appeal that forced marriage of women should be condemned as a criminal offence and that women subjected to forced marriages should be granted the status of victims.
- The conflict in Afghanistan during the Taliban rule and the militarization of society led to an increased number of abductions of young girls and women by Taliban fighters. The exact numbers are unknown, as families have been reluctant to come forward and report cases of abductions for fear of reprisals and due to the social stigma attached to a daughter or sister kidnapped or sold for sex.
- Girls continue to be forced/sold into marriage - at least in part to provide sustenance for their families. In February it was reported that girls as young as 10 have been sold as "brides" for a 100kg sack of flour.
- More than 50% of girls in Afghanistan are married by the age of 15.

**Health**

- Health projects are central to the reconstruction efforts and are a priority for donors and non-governmental humanitarian organisations.

- The UNFPA are carrying out a survey of Afghanistan's health facilities and resources, particularly related to maternal mortality and morbidity.
- There is a critical lack of data on health issues for women that do not relate to reproduction. Psychological trauma, for example, is widespread and related to many other health problems.
- There will be $600,000 less in Afghanistan's health budget if the US withdraws funding from UNFPA
- There are 17 maternal deaths per 1,000 live births in Afghanistan (one every 30 minutes), the second highest rate in the world. 12% of women have access to healthcare while internally displaced women have almost no access to health care.
- There is a danger of women coming "last in the line for foreign assistance, as needs like children need seem to be drawing the bulk of public health aid."
- International community not delivering on aid pledges.

**Widowed Women**

- Theoretically, widows are now able to work.
- The NGO community is beginning to recognise the needs of widows and acknowledge the crucial role they could play in reconstruction efforts. Advocacy on this is now underway at the national and international level.
- Data on widows is extremely limited, despite the huge proportion of adult women who fall into this category: of Afghanistan's population of around 24 million, it is estimated 36% are widows.
- In Kabul there are around 40,000 widows.
- Lack of a male intermediary in the current climate in Afghanistan affects widows' access to services, shelter, food, health care, counselling, training, extension services, income-generating projects and legal representation.
- Girl children of widows are, because of family poverty, less likely to be sent to school and more likely to be found working in high-risk informal sector undertakings. They are more vulnerable to prostitution, trafficking and forced marriage.
- No developed aid/development action plan for the involvement and incorporation of widows in reconstruction.

**Women, Aid and Transparency**

- In January 2002, $4.5 billion in aid was pledged over 5 years by the international community, including $1 million through the United Nations Development Fund for Women (UNIFEM). $2.1 billion of this is from the EU and member states, and includes a commitment to paying "special attention to the inclusion of women in Afghan society at all levels".
- There is some tying of aid to women's inclusion.
- The European Parliament has called for Afghan women to be the direct beneficiaries of between 25% and 30% of the economic aid provided for reconstruction.
- Processes are underway to try and create a more consolidated approach to Aid. As of June, UNDP is supporting the Afghan Assistance Coordination Authority (AACA) to take the lead in the tracking and analysis of aid flows.
- Of the $1.8 billion due in 2002, the UN has received only $870 million.
- By June, the Afghan Interim Administration had received only $45 million out of the $460 million pledged to arrive by this time. There is a serious knock-on effect on humanitarian programmes and reconstruction stability.

**Negative**

- There is little donor accountability on whether money is being spent on women: the UN channels most money and the vast majority of reporting is not transparent in this respect.
- Lack of code of conduct is leading to steep price rises in Kabul as a result of foreign activity, and skewing of the local economy, making it even more difficult for women to make ends meet.
- Lack of structures for financing of projects to be carried out by non-governmental organisations and civil society in Afghanistan.
- Difficulties for local NGOs to receive money or carry out projects.

**Women and Decision Making**

- The importance of women's role in peace building, post

conflict reconstruction and political process is recognised and covered under UN Security Council Resolution 1325.

- The UN Secretary General has recommended that temporary special measures be taken, including targets and quotas, targeted at Afghan women to accelerate the de facto equality of women and men in decision making.
- Some acknowledgement that "when women are also at the peace table, better agreements result, reconstruction is more effective and the likelihood of the resumption of violence declines".
- NGOs and the UN are still not striving for gender balance in planning, implementation and evaluation meetings on reconstruction, development and humanitarian aid.
- UN working environments in-country are not gender sensitive – attitudes toward female staff are neither supportive nor equal, and expectations in this regard are usually vague or absent.
- Many UN agencies do not address gender in design, monitoring or evaluation of projects.
- The international political commitment to women's participation has been mainly verbal – legally binding documents such as the Bonn Agreement have very limited concrete commitment to women.
- Numerous reports on reconstruction either completely overlook issues around gender or continue to address women's concerns as part of minority interests
- No action has been taken by the UN Security Council to implement Resolution 1325. Without women's significant engagement Afghan security and stability will remain precarious well into the future.
- Representation of women – and particularly women from civil society – in peace negotiations in Afghanistan is virtually non-existent.
- Poor representation of women at senior decision-making levels such as UN management.
- No concrete use of UN Security Resolution 1325.
- Lack of evidence that any gender mainstreaming is actually being done at UN/NGO level: "planning implementation and evaluation meetings are attended primarily by men".

**Afghan Women and the International Media**

- The media has played a very important role in bringing women's issues onto the agenda, highlighting the concerns of "ordinary Afghan women" and mobilising support.
- Western media interest in Afghanistan's problems - and particularly the problems of women - has peaked and is now falling off. The result is that political attention is waning and the attendant monetary and other investments are moving on.
- Lack of searching questions from the outset on exactly what form support for Afghan women would take
- Lack of commitment from editors and proprietors to following through with stories about fulfilment of international promises to Afghan women.

With Soviet withdrawal in 1989, Afghan women experienced gender-specific violence and discrimination as armed groups struggled for territorial control. The parties that had fought the Soviet-backed government divided up the country while battling with each other to control the capital, Kabul. The United Front forces, a coalition of mainly Tajik, Uzbek, and ethnic Hazara parties, were part of this conflict. During this time the rule of law was virtually nonexistent in Kabul and large parts of the countryside, and three of the main factions of this coalition engaged in rape, summary executions, arbitrary arrest, torture, and "disappearances." During the short-lived and nominal rule of President Burhanuddin Rabbani, from 1992-1996, Kabul experienced full-scale civil war, with indiscriminate shelling of civilian areas causing heavy casualties and destruction. A number of the United Front's factions were responsible for perpetrating widespread rape during fighting in Kabul neighbourhoods in 1993 and 1995. In 1995, for example, a predominantly Tajik party, Jamiat-i Islami, a faction led by Commander Ahmed Shah Massoud and President Rabbani, conducted a punitive raid on a Hazara neighborhood of Kabul. Similarly, in instances documented by Human Rights Watch in 1998, violence against women was carried out by various warring factions, and in particular by the Taliban, as a means to punish and terrorize their perceived opponents.

**Assault on Human Rights**

Women in Afghanistan have suffered a catastrophic assault on their human rights during more than twenty years of war and under the repressive rule of the Taliban. Now, as women face further peril with the intensification of conflict following the September 11 attacks on the United States, the international community must make a firm commitment to uphold women's human rights in any post-conflict settlement.

The impunity that has characterized Afghanistan's civil war must not also come to characterize Afghanistan's post-conflict reconstruction and development. Throughout Afghanistan's civil war, the major armed factions - primarily the Taliban and the United National Islamic Front for the Salvation of Afghanistan (commonly known as the "United Front" or by its previous name, the Northern Alliance), a coalition of mainly Tajik, Uzbek, and ethnic Hazara parties - have repeatedly committed serious abuses of international human rights and humanitarian law.

Women have borne the brunt of this violence and discrimination. In the civil war, women have suffered massive, systematic, and unrelenting human rights abuses that have permeated every aspect of their lives. Both Taliban forces and forces now grouped in the United Front have sexually assaulted, abducted, and forcibly married women during the armed conflict, targeting them on the basis of both gender and ethnicity. Thousands of women have been physically assaulted and have had severe restrictions placed on their liberty and fundamental freedoms.

Moreover, the Taliban have sought to erase women from public life. They have banned women from employment in most sectors; banned education of girls beyond primary school; forbidden women from going out in public without the accompaniment of a close male relative (mahram); and banned women from appearing in public without wearing an all-enveloping chadari (a head-to-toe garment). These restrictions assault women's human dignity and threaten their very right to life.

The Taliban, which began as a religious movement of students educated in traditional Islamic schools in Pakistan and Afghanistan, emerged as a military force in 1994.

The Taliban draws its support primarily from the country's largest and historically dominant ethnic group, the Pashtuns. Concentrated in the eastern and southern areas of Afghanistan, the Pashtuns are, like their neighbours in Pakistan, overwhelmingly Sunni Muslims.

**Taliban Decrees**

Taliban decrees have greatly restricted women's movement, behaviour, and dress, and in fact, virtually all aspects of their lives. In public, women are required under threat of severe punishment to wear the chadari, and to be accompanied by a close male relative at all times. Violations of the dress code, in particular, can result in public beatings and lashing by the Religious Police, who wield leather batons reinforced with metal studs.

Women are not permitted to work outside the home except in the area of health care, and girls over eight years old are not permitted to attend school. According to reports on Afghanistan by the U.N. Special Rapporteur on violence against women, these decrees are generally more strictly enforced in urban areas, and are especially targeted against educated women who, before the Taliban took power, accounted for 70 percent of all teachers, about 50 percent of civil servants, and 40 percent of medical doctors in the country.

The restriction on women's mobility has meant that women do not enjoy satisfactory access to health care. As a result, an estimated forty-five women die everyday from pregnancy-related causes.

After the September 11 attacks, women in Afghanistan seek to escape the armed conflict, there will be a continued need for the international community, particularly United Nations (U.N.) agencies such as the United Nations High Commissioner for Refugees (UNHCR), to respond to the needs of Afghan refugees and internally displaced persons.

Women living in the camps in Pakistan expressed to Human Rights Watch their fears that even in Pakistan, their country of refuge, sympathizers with the Taliban may increasingly infiltrate the refugee camps and threaten the human rights of women. Any political or military solution to the situation in Afghanistan must include clear commitments by the international community to promote and protect women's human rights and fundamental freedoms.

The international community must insist on an end to impunity, for accountability for abuses of women's human rights committed during the civil war and for any violations that occur during the U.S.-led war on terrorism, and for full respect and protection for women's human rights as an integral part of any post-conflict reconstruction and development

The U.S.-led alliance Ensure that any military actions taken in Afghanistan comply with international human rights and humanitarian law and that specific protections afforded to women under international law in time of war are fully respected; and that all possible steps are taken to address the particular challenges that women encounter living in a conflict zone.

The Taliban and the United Front Immediately cease violations of humanitarian law, and in particular violations against women. Order the immediate cessation of any practice of rape or other forms of sexual assault.

The International Community Call for an immediate end to the systematic violations of women's human rights by the Taliban and other political factions in Afghanistan; Take all steps possible to ensure that adequate humanitarian assistance reaches all affected civilians inside Afghanistan, especially the internally displaced and female -headed households;

Support the efforts of international, domestic relief and Afghan women's rights agencies that are providing humanitarian and development assistance in Afghanistan, and ensure the inclusion of women both as recipients of aid and as equal partners in decision making regarding development and aid projects; Ensure that any government established in Afghanistan is committed to fully respect the human rights of all the people of Afghanistan and to repealing laws and ending practices that by their intent or consequence discriminate against women; As foreign aid is allocated to rebuild Afghanistan, ensure that development and reconstruction programs are structured to ensure that girls and women have full access to programs for education, health care, job training, and housing.

These programs must be crafted so that they reach

women who otherwise might not be aware of or be able to access the programs, including rural women, widows, and women who are disabled, internally displaced, or illiterate; Hold the Taliban and other political factions in Afghanistan accountable for their massive and systematic violations of women's human rights; and Hold the Taliban and the United Front accountable for violations of humanitarian law during the civil war, including extrajudicial executions of civilians, "disappearances", sexual violence, and gender-based persecution.

In light of the severe gender-based discrimination that has been a hallmark of the Taliban and other previous regimes in Afghanistan, U.N. agencies and programs working in Afghanistan should insist, and take all possible steps to ensure, that their programs in future function free from discrimination based on sex, and are tailored to guarantee to women meaningful access to humanitarian aid and other programs; and The U.N. should fill its vacant gender advisor position with the Office of the United Nations Coordinator for Afghanistan, and give the gender advisor the authority to monitor and ensure compliance with international human rights and humanitarian law, and also to undertake wide consultation with all interested groups so as to propose not only immediate measures of relief, but also measures to address the situation of women in a post-conflict Afghanistan.

According to a recent Taliban edict, aid agencies may only provide primary education to girls within the confines of a mosque. However, there has been an exception to the edict banning education for girls beyond primary level in the medical profession.

A limited number of women have been allowed to study for a medical degree, although Afghan education specialists questioned the standard of teaching and resources available. Widows, whose numbers after twenty-three years of war are significant, are acutely affected by the restrictions on women's employment and movement. Although the Taliban issued an edict in 1999 allowing widows with no other means of support to take paid work, employment opportunities remain extremely limited.

The Taliban has also allowed HABITAT, a U.N. agency,

to employ over 3,000 women in pasta processing centers in several urban areas. The general restrictions placed on women's employment have reportedly caused an increase in women begging on the streets and participating in prostitution. The anti-Taliban Forces After the Taliban captured Kabul in 1996, the opposing groups formed an alliance called the National Islamic United Front for the Salvation of Afghanistan, commonly known as the United Front.

The United Front supports the Faizabad-based government headed by President Burhanuddin Rabbani, known as the Islamic State of Afghanistan (ISA). However, the most powerful figure within the ISA was its defense minister, Ahmad Shah Massoud, who was assassinated on September 9, 2001. The membership of the United Front has varied over time, but all of its current major factions previously committed serious human rights abuses and violations of international humanitarian law, including rape of women. However, in some areas under United Front control, such as in Mazar-i-Sharif, women have had access to health care and been permitted to study up to university level.

Out of an estimated twenty two million 27 Afghans, most of those who depend on international assistance for their survival are women and children. The withdrawal of international aid workers and the disruption of foodshipments are likely to have a devastating effect, especially on widows who are the sole providers for their families.

Since the September 11 attacks, tens of thousands of Afghans have continued to flee Afghanistan, most of them towards Pakistan, but because of official border closures many thousands remain trapped at the border without any access to humanitarian assistance. Attacks on humanitarian relief agencies in Taliban-controlled areas of Afghanistan have been increasing since the weekend of September 22, 2001, when the Taliban cut off almost all communication between U.N. field offices inside Afghanistan and the outside world, and seized 1,400 tons of U.N. World Food Program (WFP) food stocks in Kandahar, in southern Afghanistan.

**Women Under Law**

Women living in Afghanistan have suffered massive and systematic violations of their human rights under the Taliban.

The Taliban have issued numerous edicts that control literally every aspect of women's behaviour in both the public and privates spheres. These edicts are officially issued by the Ministry for the Promotion of Virtue and the Prevention of Vice, and announced to the general public through the Taliban radio station, the Voice of Shariat (Islamic law). With a few exceptions, the Taliban have banned women from participating in the public sphere.

# 7

# Women in Politics

With Soviet withdrawal in 1989, Afghan women experienced gender-specific violence and discrimination as armed groups struggled for territorial control. The parties that had fought the Soviet-backed government divided up the country while battling with each other to control the capital, Kabul. The United Front forces, a coalition of mainly Tajik, Uzbek, and ethnic Hazara parties, were part of this conflict. During this time the rule of law was virtually nonexistent in Kabul and large parts of the countryside, and three of the main factions of this coalition engaged in rape, summary executions, arbitrary arrest, torture, and "disappearances." During the short-lived and nominal rule of President Burhanuddin Rabbani, from 1992-1996, Kabul experienced full-scale civil war, with indiscriminate shelling of civilian areas causing heavy casualties and destruction. A number of the United Front's factions were responsible for perpetrating widespread rape during fighting in Kabul neighbourhoods in 1993 and 1995. In 1995, for example, a predominantly Tajik party, Jamiat-i Islami, a faction led by Commander Ahmed Shah Massoud and President Rabbani, conducted a punitive raid on a Hazara neighborhood of Kabul. Similarly, in instances documented by Human Rights Watch in 1998, violence against women was carried out by various warring factions, and in particular by the Taliban, as a means to punish and terrorize their perceived opponents.

### Assallt on Human Rights

Women in Afghanistan have suffered a catastrophic assault on their human rights during more than twenty years of war and under the repressive rule of the Taliban. Now, as women face further peril with the intensification of conflict following the September 11 attacks on the United States, the international community must make a firm commitment to uphold women's human rights in any post-conflict settlement.

The impunity that has characterized Afghanistan's civil war must not also come to characterize Afghanistan's post-conflict reconstruction and development. Throughout Afghanistan's civil war, the major armed factions - primarily the Taliban and the United National Islamic Front for the Salvation of Afghanistan (commonly known as the "United Front" or by its previous name, the Northern Alliance), a coalition of mainly Tajik, Uzbek, and ethnic Hazara parties - have repeatedly committed serious abuses of international human rights and humanitarian law.

Women have borne the brunt of this violence and discrimination. In the civil war, women have suffered massive, systematic, and unrelenting human rights abuses that have permeated every aspect of their lives. Both Taliban forces and forces now grouped in the United Front have sexually assaulted, abducted, and forcibly married women during the armed conflict, targeting them on the basis of both gender and ethnicity. Thousands of women have been physically assaulted and have had severe restrictions placed on their liberty and fundamental freedoms.

Moreover, the Taliban have sought to erase women from public life. They have banned women from employment in most sectors; banned education of girls beyond primary school; forbidden women from going out in public without the accompaniment of a close male relative (mahram); and banned women from appearing in public without wearing an all-enveloping chadari (a head-to-toe garment). These restrictions assault women's human dignity and threaten their very right to life.

The Taliban, which began as a religious movement of students educated in traditional Islamic schools in Pakistan and Afghanistan, emerged as a military force in 1994.

The Taliban draws its support primarily from the country's largest and historically dominant ethnic group, the Pashtuns. Concentrated in the eastern and southern areas of

Afghanistan,. the Pashtuns are, like their neighbours in Pakistan, overwhelmingly Sunni Muslims.

**Taliban Decrees**

Taliban decrees have greatly restricted women's movement, behaviour, and dress, and in fact, virtually all aspects of their lives. In public, women are required under threat of severe punishment to wear the chadari, and to be accompanied by a close male relative at all times. Violations of the dress code, in particular, can result in public beatings and lashing by the Religious Police, who wield leather batons reinforced with metal studs.

Women are not permitted to work outside the home except in the area of health care, and girls over eight years old are not permitted to attend school. According to reports on Afghanistan by the U.N. Special Rapporteur on violence against women, these decrees are generally more strictly enforced in urban areas, and are especially targeted against educated women who, before the Taliban took power, accounted for 70 percent of all teachers, about 50 percent of civil servants, and 40 percent of medical doctors in the country.

The restriction on women's mobility has meant that women do not enjoy satisfactory access to health care. As a result, an estimated forty-five women die everyday from pregnancy-related causes.

After the September 11 attacks, women in Afghanistan seek to escape the armed conflict, there will be a continued need for the international community, particularly United Nations (U.N.) agencies such as the United Nations High Commissioner for Refugees (UNHCR), to respond to the needs of Afghan refugees and internally displaced persons.

Women living in the camps in Pakistan expressed to Human Rights Watch their fears that even in Pakistan, their country of refuge, sympathizers with the Taliban may increasingly infiltrate the refugee camps and threaten the human rights of women. Any political or military solution to the situation in Afghanistan must include clear commitments by the international community to promote and protect women's human rights and fundamental freedoms.

The international community must insist on an end to

impunity, for accountability for abuses of women's human rights committed during the civil war and for any violations that occur during the U.S.-led war on terrorism, and for full respect and protection for women's human rights as an integral part of any post-conflict reconstruction and development

The U.S.-led alliance Ensure that any military actions taken in Afghanistan comply with international human rights and humanitarian law and that specific protections afforded to women under international law in time of war are fully respected; and that all possible steps are taken to address the particular challenges that women encounter living in a conflict zone.

The Taliban and the United Front Immediately cease violations of humanitarian law, and in particular violations against women. Order the immediate cessation of any practice of rape or other forms of sexual assault.

The International Community Call for an immediate end to the systematic violations of women's human rights by the Taliban and other political factions in Afghanistan; Take all steps possible to ensure that adequate humanitarian assistance reaches all affected civilians inside Afghanistan, especially the internally displaced and female -headed households;

Support the efforts of international, domestic relief and Afghan women's rights agencies that are providing humanitarian and development assistance in Afghanistan, and ensure the inclusion of women both as recipients of aid and as equal partners in decision making regarding development and aid projects; Ensure that any government established in Afghanistan is committed to fully respect the human rights of all the people of Afghanistan and to repealing laws and ending practices that by their intent or consequence discriminate against women; As foreign aid is allocated to rebuild Afghanistan, ensure that development and reconstruction programs are structured to ensure that girls and women have full access to programs for education, health care, job training, and housing.

These programs must be crafted so that they reach women who otherwise might not be aware of or be able to access the programs, including rural women, widows, and women who are disabled, internally displaced, or illiterate;

Hold the Taliban and other political factions in Afghanistan accountable for their massive and systematic violations of women's human rights; and Hold the Taliban and the United Front accountable for violations of humanitarian law during the civil war, including extrajudicial executions of civilians, "disappearances", sexual violence, and gender-based persecution.

In light of the severe gender-based discrimination that has been a hallmark of the Taliban and other previous regimes in Afghanistan, U.N. agencies and programs working in Afghanistan should insist, and take all possible steps to ensure, that their programs in future function free from discrimination based on sex, and are tailored to guarantee to women meaningful access to humanitarian aid and other programs; and The U.N. should fill its vacant gender advisor position with the Office of the United Nations Coordinator for Afghanistan, and give the gender advisor the authority to monitor and ensure compliance with international human rights and humanitarian law, and also to undertake wide consultation with all interested groups so as to propose not only immediate measures of relief, but also measures to address the situation of women in a post-conflict Afghanistan.

According to a recent Taliban edict, aid agencies may only provide primary education to girls within the confines of a mosque. However, there has been an exception to the edict banning education for girls beyond primary level in the medical profession.

A limited number of women have been allowed to study for a medical degree, although Afghan education specialists questioned the standard of teaching and resources available. Widows, whose numbers after twenty-three years of war are significant, are acutely affected by the restrictions on women's employment and movement. Although the Taliban issued an edict in 1999 allowing widows with no other means of support to take paid work, employment opportunities remain extremely limited.

The Taliban has also allowed HABITAT, a U.N. agency, to employ over 3,000 women in pasta processing centers in several urban areas. The general restrictions placed on women's employment have reportedly caused an increase in women begging on the streets and participating in prostitution. The anti-Taliban Forces After the Taliban captured Kabul in 1996, the opposing groups formed an alliance called the National Islamic United Front for the Salvation of Afghanistan, commonly known as the United Front.

The United Front supports the Faizabad-based government headed by President Burhanuddin Rabbani, known as the Islamic State of Afghanistan (ISA). However, the most powerful figure within the ISA was its defense minister, Ahmad Shah Massoud, who was assassinated on September 9, 2001. The membership of the United Front has varied over time, but all of its current major factions previously committed serious human rights abuses and violations of international humanitarian law, including rape of women. However, in some areas under United Front control, such as in Mazar-i-Sharif, women have had access to health care and been permitted to study up to university level.

Out of an estimated twenty two million 27 Afghans, most of those who depend on international assistance for their survival are women and children. The withdrawal of international aid workers and the disruption of foodshipments are likely to have a devastating effect, especially on widows who are the sole providers for their families.

Since the September 11 attacks, tens of thousands of Afghans have continued to flee Afghanistan, most of them towards Pakistan, but because of official border closures many thousands remain trapped at the border without any access to humanitarian assistance. Attacks on humanitarian relief agencies in Taliban-controlled areas of Afghanistan have been increasing since the weekend of September 22, 2001, when the Taliban cut off almost all communication between U.N. field offices inside Afghanistan and the outside world, and seized 1,400 tons of U.N. World Food Program (WFP) food stocks in Kandahar, in southern Afghanistan.

Women are forbidden to take employment, to appear in public without a male relative, to participate in government or other public debate, and to receive secondary or higher education. The impact of this discrimination has been to silence women and strip them of all control over their lives. Afghan women do not experience these violations as separate and discrete incidents; rather, the discrimination is cumulative and so overwhelming that it is literally life threatening for many Afghan women.

**Policy of Taliban**

Women are deprived of the means to support themselves and their children. The Taliban enforce their discriminatory edicts through summary and arbitrary punishment of women by the Religious Police. By engaging in widespread discrimination and violence against women, the Taliban are daily violating international human rights law. The current Taliban regime, as well as all future regimes in Afghanistan, is bound by basic principles of international human rights law and, in particular, by the human rights treaties signed and acceded to by Afghanistan.

These rights violated by the Taliban's discriminatory policies include the right to freedom of expression, association, and assembly, the right to work, the right to education, freedom of movement, and the right to health care. International law guarantees all persons the right to freedom of expression. The Taliban's imposition of extreme types of restrictions on women's freedom cannot be reasonably construed as fitting within any of the exceptions to this right.

Afghanistan signed the Convention on the Elimination of All Forms of Discrimination against Women (CEDAW) on August 14, 1980 and the Convention on the Rights of the Child (CRC) on September 27, 1990. Afghanistan ratified the CRC on March 28, 1994. The two major human rights treaties, the ICCPR and the ICESCR, guarantee all persons the enjoyment of basic human rights, free from discrimination of any kind, including on the grounds of sex. Article 19 of the ICCPR.

Under Article 19(3) of the ICCPR, a state may limit this freedom only insofar as it is necessary for the protection of the rights of others, national security or public order, or public health or morals. These limitations must be expressly provided for by the law and must be strictly construed. "Public morals" is not defined in the ICCPR. The Human Rights Committee has stated, "public morals differ widely.

Women's right to equal access to health care services is a critical element of the right to health guaranteed under international law. CEDAW guarantees this right to all women, including women living in rural areas. The ICESCR provides equal rights to the "highest attainable standard of physical and mental health."

In Afghanistan, not only do women face Taliban decrees that are discriminatory, but they are also subjected to summary physical punishment without the protections of due process. Under international law, states are required to prosecute violations of bodily integrity, and to act to protect women from gender-based violence and discrimination. The ICCPR protects women from gender-based violence in its guarantees to the right to life, the right not to be subject to torture or cruel, inhuman or degrading treatment or punishment, the right to liberty and security, and the right to equality before the law, including effective protection against discrimination on the ground of sex.

Afghan women have symbolized their families' and societies' honour, and this concept of honour has been a potent source of political mobilization and manipulation by various competing forces. In particular, the seclusion of women and strict control over their movement is central to this honour code that is inextricably tied to the conduct of women. Under the Taliban, this control has been institutionalized by various edicts governing all aspects of women's public and private lives, by severely restricting women's freedom of movement and association, and their access to education, healthcare, and employment.

**Target on Women in Cities**

Women in the cities have been especially targeted and have borne the brunt of the zealous enforcement of these decrees by the Religious Police. But women in rural areas have also been adversely affected.

Women are effectively banished to the domestic sphere, and may not be seen in public unless they are almost totally concealed in a chadari or burqa and then only when accompanied by a mahram (a close male relative). Furthermore, women must not wear clothes that are decorated, brightly coloured, or form fitting, and women are not permitted to travel alone in a taxi. Even as regards access to healthcare, it is not only the structural consequences of continuing armed conflict, but the restrictions on women's movement, such as travelling with a mahram and wearing a veil in public, that severely constrain their ability to seek and receive medical treatment.

The very same discriminatory edicts inhibit the ability of female health care professionals to carry out their work safely and effectively and limit the few opportunities for professional development that women doctors hope to achieve. Similarly, access to education for women and girls has been further aggravated by discriminatory policies that ban girls from all but elementary levels of education, and ban women teachers from working. The punishment for violating these codes is severe. Typically, members of the Religious Police accost and may assault or imprison women who breach these restrictive requirements.

Women living under Taliban rule report being in a constant state of fear. The slightest infraction, real or perceived, of gender-specific norms or mores as expressed by Taliban edicts can and often does lead to summary beatings by the Religious Police. There is no defense or appeal. Punishment is immediate and harsh. The opinions, thoughts, expressions, resistance and very existence of women is effectively denied by the existing policies that seek to make Afghan women invisible, as the cases documented below illustrate. Women are not just beaten for violations of the dress code. They are beaten if they travel without a mahram. A woman doctor who left Kabul in January 2001 recounted the risks she had taken simply to get to work at her hospital. She worked long shifts and so took her infant son, whom she was breast-feeding, with her to her work.

Women from the cities, such as Kabul, Herat, and Kandahar, complained that these restrictions seriously affected their daily lives and caused them a great deal of stress. One Afghan man well informed about the conditions and their impact on women in Afghanistan said that for many, the restrictions are so great as to render them housebound and cause them to become extremely depressed, as there is nothing other than house work to occupy their time: "no television, no music, or videos. They have lost hope. ...They are oppressed by laws, by the state, and by the family."

Many urban-based women have a pervasive fear of the

Religious Police, having either been victims of their violence or having witnessed it. This fear further restricts their movements, forcing them to make arrangements to avoid leaving the home or travelling alone and to ensure that if they go out, they are accompanied either by their young sons, brothers, or a group of women.

For those women who do have a level of mobility because of their work as health care professionals, the challenge is in dealing with the rules governing such limited mobility. One Kabul doctor, who had fled Afghanistan six months earlier, spoke of the problems she had faced:

> We had problems less in the hospital than in our daily life. Going shopping, for example, was a problem. That is why my younger brother had to stay behind. He was fourteen, and when my parents left, he wanted to flee to Pakistan with them. But, if he had, I would have been unable to move around.

**General Decrees**

The general decrees controlling women's mobility also impair women's ability to access medical treatment. Women who must travel to seek medical attention may have to put off a visit to a clinic if they have no mahram who can accompany them. Even those women who do have a mahram may be reluctant to ask him to take time off from work to make the trip.

Local Afghan and international NGOs, struggling to rebuild the health care system throughout Afghanistan, were constrained by a lack of resources, continuing hostilities, restrictions on the training and supervision of female health care providers, and constant struggles in negotiating with Taliban authorities on programs and projects, especially those that involve women either as beneficiaries or as implementing partners.

Many of the most qualified doctors left Afghanistan because of the insecurity surrounding their work, which along with all other work for women had been banned by the Taliban. Later, as an exception, the Taliban allowed female medical staff to work. It appears that now some women have been allowed to study for a medical degree, while others have been allowed to receive training in nursing schools. This is an exception to the ban on educating girls beyond primary level. This ban virtually means that there will be no women doctors in the future.

Some educated women, especially former teachers, have continued to operate in secret home-based schools for girls. These schools have received support from international aid organizations operating in the country, sometimes with the tacit approval of local Taliban officials. But many such schools have been shut down when the Religious Police became aware of them. Teaching in such circumstances takes place in an atmosphere of tension and stress. A teacher working for an international aid organization that both secretly assisted home-based schools, and ran primary schools for girls in a number of provinces, described the situation in Nangarhar in eastern Afghanistan as typical: Girls' schools are only home-based schools, and some girls attend schools up to the age of eight or ten.

Until recently, it worked fine, but now there are more restrictions. The Taliban go to the teacher's husband and ask him to guarantee that she will not teach anymore. It is the same all over Afghanistan. Only very few women can teach. Teachers have had to be constantly alert to detection and so have evolved ways to conceal their activities, though these are not always effective. Often, family members are harassed as a way to punish or intimidate female teachers.

**Civil War**

In short Afghan women have borne the brunt of the civil war. On top of that, the Taliban have denied them fundamental rights and freedoms, including freedom of movement, association, and expression, and equal access to work and education, in all aspects of their lives. Now, as conflict intensifies with the U.S.-led war against terrorism, Afghan women face the likelihood of further suffering and deprivation of their human rights, fundamental freedoms, and personal dignity at the hands of warring factions.

Women are likely to endure some of the most serious humanitarian consequences of the military action. As the international community, and particularly the U.N., ponders the future of a post-conflict Afghanistan, accountability for past abuses and respect for women's rights - in law and in practice - must be a central feature of any reconstruction and development plan. To date, there has been no accountability for the human rights abuses committed during the civil war, nor for the additional violations of women's rights inflicted under the Taliban. Refugees, the majority of whom are women and children, continue to flee from Afghanistan, facing a bleak future and little assistance in Pakistan or other neighbouring countries.

The life for Afghan women and girls was a living nightmare, under the Taliban. The Taliban totally eradicated women from the public sphere and stripped them of power in the private sphere. Taliban decrees prohibited women from working outside the home and travelling in public without a mahram (husband or close male relative), and the requirement of the burqa was strictly enforced. Women and girls risked being beaten on the streets of most major cities for showing any part of their bodies, even by accident, for wearing the wrong kind of shoes or socks, or for making too much noise walking.

Women were barred from university and almost all girls schools were closed. One human rights group described the Taliban's restriction on women's rights as "one of the most deliberate forms of discrimination against women in recent history." Many Afghans-women and men-considered the Taliban's reactionary codes to be anachronistic and cruel.

Afghanistan has a diverse cultural, ethnic, and religious make-up, in which both women and men hold a variety of views on women's rights. The Taliban's interpretations of Islamic law were foreign to much of Afghanistan's people, especially those in urban areas. By imposing a monolithic and unified set of social standards on the whole country, they alienated huge sectors of the population. Refugee returns during Taliban rule slowed significantly in many places, and even reversed.

Some of the Taliban leadership skirted the rules, allowing local governments leeway on some issues and sending their own daughters to schools in Pakistan or Iran. Late in the 1990s, some of the finer points of the Taliban's many decrees were abandoned or were not enforced: female health workers were allowed to resume work in some cities, and in some areas schools were reopened. And in many rural areas, women continued to work and travel outside without the burqa or a mahram. In some areas, girls even went to school.

But until its demise in late 2001, the Taliban strictly enforcing most of its restrictions. When Taliban rule ended, many people within and outside of Afghanistan considered its collapse to be a "liberation" for Afghan women and girls, and for the population at large. There was much hope that Afghan women would soon enjoy increased freedoms and rights, denied to them under the Taliban. The rights of Afghan women and girls have been a contentious issue in Afghan politics and society for most of the last hundred years, while, for the most part, Afghan women themselves have been sidelined from public discussions and decision making about their rights and role in society. Women's rights have been used to polarize political and ideological conflicts, and reforms directed at women have often led to political instability. During the twentieth century, limited attempts by Afghanistan's male leaders to impose social reforms affecting women's rights contributed to political tensions and even revolutions.

In the late 1970s, when Soviet-backed communist leaders pushed new reforms including forced coeducation and the elimination of the "bride-price," these sent male rural leaders into open revolt, contributing to the Soviet Union's decision to invade Afghanistan in 1979.

In the 1990s, women's rights in Afghanistan remained a divisive issue. When Afghanistan's formerly Soviet-backed government collapsed in 1992 and the government of the Islamic State of Afghanistan (a loose coalition of mujahidin parties) was installed in Kabul, decrees were announced instructing women to observe hijab-covering of the head, arms, and legs. Local commanders in other cities announced similar decrees. Most of the urban female workforce continued at their workplaces but felt increasingly vulnerable to violence and attacks on their autonomy linked to political instability. Women in rural areas and returning refugees also faced restrictions. The Taliban took power in most of the country by 1996, introducing their notoriously repressive policies toward women.

## Struggle Continues

Women in Afghanistan have long struggled to claim full rights and freedoms, and under the Taliban, their position was undoubtedly worse than at any other time in recent history. Yet, one year after the Taliban's fall, women and girls in Afghanistan still face severe restrictions and violations of their human rights, for in many areas Taliban officials have been replaced by warlords, police officers, and local officials with similar attitudes toward women.

In some parts of the country, the same officials who administered the anti-women policies of the Taliban remain in their positions. This has meant the reimposition of extremely repressive social codes that typically have a devastating impact on women. Such restrictions severely undermine the most fundamental rights of women and girls in many areas of Afghanistan, including threatening their physical security.

International actors understood that in the short term their assistance would be vital. The international community's inability to fulfil its commitments toward women in Afghanistan threatens the promise of the post-Taliban era. And many women now are disillusioned about the reconstruction and peace processes set in motion by the Taliban's fall and the Bonn Agreement of December 2001. An area of special concern for women's rights is the province of Herat in the west of Afghanistan, which has a liberal literary and cultural tradition and a history of educating girls. But under the rule of the local governor, Ismail Khan, women's and girls' freedom of expression, association, movement, and rights to equality, work, education, and bodily integrity steadily deteriorated throughout 2002.

While conditions are undoubtedly better than under the Taliban-girls and women have better access to education and are not beaten by authorities in the streets-many Taliban-era restrictions remain in place. For women and girls in Herat, every decision of every day presents dangers or challenges from Ismail Khan's government: where they can go, how they can get there, whom they can go with, and how they can dress.

## Ban on Jobs

A Herati woman has little access to the public sphere, from employment to civic organizations or other forums where she can participate in public debate. In order to leave her home and reach what forums are available-such as school, work (in one of the few jobs open to women), a government-controlled civic organization, or simply to go to the market-she must overcome significant hurdles in the journey, travelling in a way that she will not be harassed, arrested, and taken off to the hospital to be subjected to an abusive "chastity" examination. Once she arrives at her destination, she must conform her speech, behaviour, and appearance to Ismail Khan's restrictions and edicts, which she has no way to challenge. When she returns home, she can expect no protection against violent or abusive family members-indeed, as in most parts of the country, fleeing from her home may result in her arrest and prosecution. Nor does she have any way to contest male family members' decisions about whom she will marry or whether she can attend school or work. She is effectively marginalized-politically, economically, and socially.

**Policy of Ismail Khan**

As it stands, Ismail Khan is not allowing women or men to take part in most decision-making processes, but this repression is falling doubly hard on women, who face both the general political repression of Ismail Khan's regime and his particular repression of women. Very few forums are open to women in Herat, and those that are open are heavily censored by Ismail Khan. Ismail Khan and his agents-almost all men-decide what rules govern women and girls' lives. Many rules are aimed at keeping the sexes segregated, which affects women and girls differently than men by excluding women and girls from bodies where decisions are made, from civic and cultural activities, from work, and from equal education. The consequences of breaking these rules are also different for women and girls than for men.

Women and girls who have challenged these policies have been publicly and privately castigated by government officials and called "un-Islamic," a serious charge in a climate of returning fundamentalism. They have also been prohibited from speaking publicly or to journalists about women's rights, and fired from their jobs or threatened with being fired. Women's participation in the reconstruction effort is severely constrained, leaving little hope for their broader political participation in the future.

Women and girls enjoy little freedom of movement in Herat. Unlike under the Taliban, women and girls can leave their homes during the day without being accompanied by a close male relative (mahram). However, they may not walk or ride in a car alone with a man who is not a close relative, even a taxi driver. A police task force now patrols Herat city, arresting men and women who are seen together and suspected of being unrelated or unmarried. Men are taken to jail; women and girls are taken to a hospital to undergo forced medical examinations to determine whether they have recently had sexual intercourse. When they leave their homes, women and older girls must wear a burqa or chadori, which impedes their ability to walk and see; if they go without it, they may be harassed and threatened by the police as well as private individuals. Unlike in neighbouring Iran, women are not permitted to drive cars, and they do not ride bicycles. (Even if these acts were permitted, they would be impossible wearing a burqa.) A public transportation system hardly exists, and where it does it is inadequate, leaving women and girls with few ways to get to school, work, or the market, or to seek medical care.

The Herat government discriminates against women in the right to work. Few jobs are open to women and those that are come with significant limitations from the government. Ismail Khan has pressured women not to work with international nongovernmental organizations (NGOs) or for the United Nations, although these agencies need women to administer many of their emergency aid and reconstruction programs. Women are also prohibited entirely from riding in cars with foreign men or from meeting alone with them. At least one Herati woman has been arrested and detained for her contact with foreign men during the course of her work with an international organization.

## New Laws

At the same time, almost no women have been invited to work in the Herat government. Ismail Khan has urged women instead to work at home or as girls' teachers. Government officials harass and threaten those who step outside of these narrow boundaries.

In public speeches and interviews with media, Ismail Khan often points to humanitarian and development needs, criticizing those who complain about human rights as indifferent to concerns about Afghans' day-to-day survival, whether they are safe from crime and have enough food. But there is no reason why development and reconstruction cannot be carried out at the same time that basic human rights are protected and respected. This is the responsibility of Ismail Khan and every other leader, in Afghanistan or any other country. Moreover, as Afghan women and NGO officials rightly point out, development and reconstruction cannot properly proceed without adequate participation of women-especially in staffing local government, NGOs, and U.N. offices.

Humanitarian and development assistance programs depend on women to determine what aid is needed, to ensure that it reaches women and children, and to administer programs that target women-for instance, programs for mothers and widows. But Ismail Khan has made it clear that he opposes women working for NGOs and the U.N., and he has made no meaningful efforts to promote female participation in government (or, for that matter, any independent participation).

Ismail Khan engages in recurrent double-talk about women-lauding the fact that women can go to school while telling them they should not use their education by working for foreign organizations or participating in the public debate about their rights. Women cannot take advantage of reconstruction, development, or education unless they are free to make choices about their employment and participation in civil society.

Many women in Herat who had recently returned from Iran and Pakistan told Human Rights Watch of the basic freedoms they gave up when they returned, including driving, discussing politics in the university, playing sports and music, and going without burqa or chadori. Some women told Human Rights Watch that they decided to return from Iran at least in part based on information that restrictions on women in Herat had eased.

Ismail Khan's abuses of women and girls' rights are

particularly severe. According to a U.N. official working with women's groups throughout the country, "Herat is the worst province for women in Afghanistan." And although the situation in Herat city is bad, conditions in rural areas of the province are likely worse. U.N. and NGO officials report that while the situation in Herat is particularly bad, it is not unique, and that restrictions on women and girls are again increasing all over Afghanistan.

In Kabul, a reconfigured Vice and Virtue Squad (renamed "Islamic Teaching") is now operating. A team of some ninety women under the Ministry of Religious Affairs harasses women in Kabul's streets for "un-Islamic behaviour," such as wearing make-up, and, in some instances, follows them home to castigate their parents or spouses. Women have reported being harassed and threatened by unidentified men for discarding particular aspects of the Taliban-mandated dress code.

**Serious Threats**

Outside of Kabul, women and girls have faced serious threats to their physical safety, including sexual violence. In the north, three rival forces have committed abuses against Pashtun civilians, including raping entire households and girls as young as fourteen. In the south during the loya jirga process in May and June, local commanders threatened women candidates and allowed their troops to harass women and girls in areas under their control.

During the loya jirga meeting itself, warlords from across the country monitored and threatened women delegates. Also in May and June around the northern city of Mazar-e Sharif, factional rivalry between local commanders contributed to targeted attacks on women aid workers and rapes of women and children in displacement camps that had become militarized. The very threat of this type of violence denies them the opportunity to exercise their basic human rights and to participate fully in the rebuilding of their country. Even the much lauded restoration of the right to education is under attack. Schools for girls have been attacked with rockets or set on fire in at least five provinces: Kandahar, Sar-e Pol, Zabul, Logar, and Wardak. Local forces have done little to prevent these attacks.

In some areas, troops under the control of current government officials-members of the Jamiat-e Islami party who are loyal to General Mohammed Fahim (the defense minister) or the former president of Afghanistan, Burhanuddin Rabbani-have been enforcing Taliban-era "moral" restrictions, for instance, forbidding families from playing music at weddings and from dancing, and in some cases arresting and beating musicians.

As in Herat, commanders in northern Afghanistan have pressured women not to work for foreign organizations. This type of social repression, enforced in some places by government troops, is a source of fear for many women, both because of what is happening now and for what it may signify for the future if restrictions on women and girls continue to increase.

While recent moves by the U.S. and U.N. mission suggest a new concern with human rights and security issues, this criticism for the most part still holds. The United States and other nations involved in Afghanistan have so far resisted repeated calls from the Afghan government, the U.N. mission, and numerous NGOs to expand the International Security Assistance Force (ISAF), the U.N.-mandated peacekeeping force for Afghanistan, outside of Kabul. The recent decision by the United States and United Kingdom (U.K.) to deploy additional troops outside of Kabul to work on security and disarmament issues, and the offer of the government of Japan to assist with monitoring of disarmament, are welcome signs. But much more needs to be done to increase human rights protections and decrease the stranglehold on power enjoyed by the warlords who rule most parts of Afghanistan.

As of December 2002, the U.S. and coalition military forces in Afghanistan are continuing to pursue a strategy of entrusting general security and policing to local forces with terrible records on women's rights. No governments involved in Afghanistan have offered adequate resources for expanded peacekeeping or police training throughout the country, despite the fact that most Afghans and diplomatic officials admit that these steps are a necessary precursor to reconstruction efforts and protection of human rights, and that the human rights situation in most parts of the country is deplorable.

There is a self-reinforcing obstructiveness about the issue: many European nations, asked about peacekeeping, condition their agreement to expanding ISAF on the U.S. setting aside its resistance to provide necessary logistical and intelligence backup; meanwhile, the U.S. claims it will offer the requisite assistance to other nations, if they would only offer troops.

**U.N. Mission**

The United Nations Assistance Mission to Afghanistan (UNAMA) has not placed sufficient emphasis on human rights monitoring and protection. Some expansions to monitoring and protection staff have been made: there are now one international and two Afghan staff devoted to human rights in each of the U.N. regional offices. However, the presence remains inadequate: UNAMA does not have the capacity to conduct large-scale investigations or deploy monitoring staff to many areas. Human Rights Watch believes that UNAMA's role in human rights monitoring, investigation, and protection must be significantly expanded.

Many Afghans, in Herat and elsewhere, expected the international community to stand up to warlords like Ismail Khan as they had stood up to the Taliban. Many are angry and disillusioned with the United States (U.S.), the United Nations (U.N.), and the international presence in Afghanistan generally.

The Afghan Human Rights Commission, which is mandated to monitor human rights conditions and investigate abuses, is not receiving sufficient political and moral support from the international community, including the U.N., to effectively investigate or monitor human rights conditions.

The commission is also suffering from serious staffing problems. Commission members' fear of political violence directly affects its work (at least two members of the commission have been threatened with violence, including the commission's leader, Sima Samar).

The Commission has not carried out general monitoring of human rights conditions, and has not conducted any major investigations outside of Kabul where its capacity is especially weak. International agencies and nations involved in Afghanistan have to do more to give the commission confidence.

Ismail Khan and his government control virtually all aspects of women's and girls' lives in Herat, on the street, in schools and workplaces, and even in their homes. By controlling the media, most civic organizations, most forms of employment that would be open to women, and education, Ismail Khan is able to dictate whether and how women and girls have access to these arenas. He has used this power to keep women and girls out of many forums, to suppress free speech and associations (especially related to women's rights), and to regulate women's and girls' dress and behaviour. By restricting their freedom of movement, he has also made it much more difficult for women and girls to access the few areas, such as schools and some jobs (teaching and a few other government posts), that are left open to them.

Ismail Khan dictates women's and girls' behaviour through announcements in public speeches, on Herat radio, television, and the only daily newspaper in Herat, Ittifaq-e Islam. His government officials-for example in the Department of Education, the Traffic Office, and the Department of Information and Culture-enforce restrictions on women and girls. In addition, police and teachers monitor women and girls' behaviour and appearance. Reminiscent of the Taliban's Ministry for the Promotion of Virtue and the Prevention of Vice, Herat police can arrest men and women whom they deem to be behaving immorally, and have trained squads of adolescent school boys to spy on women and girls.

Ismail Khan's government has denied women and girls the enjoyment of fundamental rights exercised by men and boys. Discrimination on the basis of sex is prohibited by the International Covenant on Civil and Political Rights (ICCPR), the International Covenant on Economic, Social and Cultural Rights (ICESCR) and the Convention on the Rights of the Child (CRC), to all of which Afghanistan is a party. The Convention on the Elimination of All Forms of Discrimination against Women (CEDAW), which Afghanistan has signed, defines discrimination against women as: any distinction, exclusion or restriction made on the basis of sex which has the effect or purpose of impairing or nullifying the recognition, enjoyment or exercise by women, irrespective of their marital status, on the basis of equality of men and women, of human rights and fundamental freedoms in the political, economic, social, cultural, civil or any other field.

CEDAW obliges states to "refrain from engaging in any act or practice of discrimination against women and to ensure that public authorities and institutions shall act in conformity with this obligation"; and to "take all appropriate measures to eliminate discrimination against women." In addition, Afghanistan is a party to the Convention on the Political Rights of Women, which provides that: "Women shall be entitled to hold public office and to exercise all public functions, established by national law, on equal terms with men, without any discrimination." Afghanistan's 1964 constitution provides in article 25: "The people of Afghanistan, without any discrimination or preference, have equal rights and obligations before the law."

Women and girls' freedom of movement is severely restricted in Herat city and has become even more so in the second half of 2002. Women and girls who break the rules risk being harassed, threatened, arrested, or, as an extreme consequence, being forced to undergo a gynecological examination. In order to leave their homes, women and girls face considerable hurdles.

Unlike under the Taliban, during the day they can go out without being accompanied by a close male relative (mahram). However, they may not walk or ride in a car alone with a man or men to whom they are not closely related. Women cannot drive cars, and they do not ride bicycles. (Even if these acts were permitted, they would be impossible wearing a burqa.) Ismail Khan has prohibited Herati women and girls from riding in cars with foreign men at all.

The impact of these restrictions is heightened by the fact that in Herat, public transportation is inadequate or nonexistent, leaving women and girls with almost no alternatives for moving around. In addition, when they leave their homes, women and older girls must wear a burqa or chadori, which impedes their ability to walk; if they go without it, they may be harassed and threatened by police, other government officials, and private individuals from whom they cannot expect police protection. Restrictions on freedom of movement significantly interfere with the ability to exercise a range of other human rights: to go to school, to work, or to the market to buy food and other goods, or to seek medical care.

Women and girls caught walking with men on the street, riding with men in cars, and alone with men in private homes are arrested by police. Arrest can be followed by an abusive gynecological examination at Herat hospital to look for evidence of recent sexual intercourse. Heratis report that with increasing frequency, police are arresting both young girls and married women, males and females in private homes, women travelling alone in taxis with the driver, and boys and girls seen talking or walking together on the street.

Ismail Khan not only enforces restrictions on women's and girls' freedom of movement with his own officials and the boys squads, he also encourages private citizens to do so as well. In November 2002, Ismail Khan announced on the radio and Herat television:

You must stop [unmarried] men and women who are together. . . . It is not only the business of the criminal branch and for Vice and Virtue-you must stop men and women who are unmarried from walking together on the street. According to Islam, you are obliged to beat them.

The ICCPR and the Convention Against Torture and Other Cruel, Inhuman or Degrading Treatment or Punishment protect individuals from cruel, inhuman, and degrading treatment; ensure the right to bodily integrity; and require states parties to protect these rights without discrimination of any kind. Under the Afghan Constitution the "state has the duty to respect and protect the liberty and dignity of the individual. . . . Imposing punishment incompatible with human dignity is not permissible."

Although most Herati women do not know how to drive, or do not have access to a car, those who do are still not permitted: the local government will not issue driver's licenses to women, and Herat city police have arrested women for driving. Although many women and girls hoped that with the Taliban's departure they would be permitted to drive, Ismail Khan's government has made it clear that it will tolerate no attempts to challenge the policy. Around late June 2002, a group of woman who knew how to drive applied to the Herat Traffic Office. As of September 2002, they had not been allowed to take the driver's test, and a government official informed them that they would not be allowed to do so. A widow with a disabled child and elderly mother-in-law, she had no one to drive her to work or to do shopping, or to take her children to school.

According to a witness, the woman was returning home in the late evening with her children when armed police forces stopped her in front of her house, asked her why she was driving, and confiscated her license. She was not wearing a burqa or chadori. A crowd gathered, her brother was notified, and he came to the scene and challenged the police. The police officers ordered them to go to the police station; the women went into her home and her brother went to the station. However, he was not able to persuade the police to return her license, and she stopped driving entirely. Many women and girls in Herat city expressed a strong desire to participate in their country's civil and political life, and to be able to speak freely, both publicly and privately. They want to participate in the political discourse and have a voice in governmental decisions-especially those that affect them. One of the most egregious aspects of the Taliban's rule was its attempt to erase women's participation in society. The situation has improved, but only slightly.

Ismail Khan is not allowing women or men to take part in most decision-making processes, but this repression is falling doubly hard on women, who face both the general political repression of Ismail Khan's regime, and his targeted repression of women. Very few forums are open to women in Herat, and those that are open are effectively controlled by Ismail Khan. He and his agents-almost all men-decide what rules govern women's and girls' lives.

Some rules are aimed at keeping the sexes separate. These affect women and girls differently than men because it is women and girls who are excluded from governing bodies where decisions are made, from civic and cultural activities, from work, and from equal education. Women and girls also face different consequences of breaking these rules than do men. Ismail Khan and his government have almost complete control of public speech-in the press, civic associations, the university, and the workplace.

Women who have challenged these policies have been publicly and privately castigated by government officials and been called "un-Islamic," a serious charge in the increasingly fundamentalist climate. They have also been prohibited from speaking publicly or to journalists about women's rights, and fired from their jobs or threatened with being fired. "We are very afraid," one woman said on the condition of anonymity.

Ismail Khan's government has barred or severely restricted women and girls from participating in many forums: it has denied them permission to form organizations, kept them out of most government positions, pressured them not to work for foreign organizations, and punished speech about women's rights. Ismail Khan has been particularly hostile to women and girls' organizations with some capacity to address even vaguely political issues, as opposed to strictly humanitarian organizations (such as those that teach literacy and handicrafts).

Within these organizations, Ismail Khan and his agents have especially targeted speech about women's rights. Symbolically, in March 2002, Ismail Khan cancelled a celebration of International Women's Day, to which five hundred guests were invited, the day before the event was scheduled to take place.

At the time of writing, the only women's organization in Herat permitted to be involved in any substantive political and social issues was the Herat Women's Shura (council), which was established in August 2002.

Many of Herat's professional women as well as students were eager for a forum to address issues related to women and girls, and participated in the shura's initial meetings. But despite some dedicated members who have elected to remain in the shura with the hope of using it to create more political space for women, the group is not independent of the government and has little prospect of fulfilling its original aims.

As with the Women's *Shura*, the government has pressured the literary society to avoid the subject of women's rights. In July or August 2002, there was a meeting of literary society members and officials from the Ministry of Social Affairs. Ismail Khan's son was also there. At the meeting, a literary society member read an article she had written about women's rights.

According to a person who was present, the member said that, "Men and women are the same, and their rights are the same, and women should go out and find jobs and live in society. There is no difference between women and men, and women should find jobs in the highest posts." Government officials responded by accusing her of being un-Islamic, a serious charge which implicates her honour and could potentially result in her being ostracized.

Women and girls are rarely shown on Herat television (controlled by Ismail Khan's government), and women explained to Human Rights Watch that they cannot be employed by the station or work as journalists. When women and older girls are shown, it is under the condition that they wear complete, conservative hijab with no hair showing; if they do not comply, they are excluded from the broadcast. For example, in late August or early September, the station broadcast a public meeting of the Women's Shura.

Almost all women and older girls in Herat city, when they go outside, wear a burqa, a floor length garment which entirely covers the face and body. The wearer sees through a small screen in front of the eyes but has no peripheral vision. Unlike during the Taliban, some women wear the front panel rolled up away from the face, and a few instead wear a floor-length cloth, which in Herat is called chadori, held under the chin, which also entirely covers the head and body but leaves the face exposed. Human Rights Watch researchers neither saw any women or older girls in Herat on the street without burqa or chadori nor interviewed any who said they would go out without either of the coverings.

The wearing of burqa or chadori is imposed by police, employers, and school administrators, as well as by some families and private individuals in the street. Women themselves may also elect to wear it; however, many told Human Rights Watch that their decision was motivated by the fear of harassment or even violence rather than meaningful choice. Laws or official policies that require women to wear burqas or chadori violate a number of fundamental rights protected under international law.

By applying only to women, the burqa requirement is discriminatory, in violation of articles 3 and 26 of the ICCPR. It is also an arbitrary infringement on the right to privacy under article 17 of the ICCPR, which "protects the special, individual qualities of human existence, a person's manner of appearance, [and] his or her identity." The burqa's restrictive nature also implicates the rights to freedom of expression, movement, and association.

Although women and girls are now, in small numbers, studying in Herat University, the discrimination they face there greatly constrains their participation and exemplifies the long catalogue of restrictions in Herat that combine to create an environment where their speech, behaviour, and appearance are controlled and where the free exchange of ideas, central to a university education, is very limited. In all of Afghanistan's universities, women and girls still do not enjoy access equal with men.

**Women at Risk**

US shifts its security policy in Afghanistan, American commitments to the human rights of Afghan women will amount to little more than rhetoric. Since Sept. 11, the US administration has repeatedly pledged its commitment to Afghan women. President Bush made the case strongly in his June commencement speech at West Point: "A thriving nation will respect the rights of women, because no society can prosper while denying opportunity to half its citizens." However, America's Afghan policy is, in effect, selling women out.

The United States has fostered the increasing power of the Afghan warlords and provided only minimal support to the fledgling Afghan government. Moreover, it has opposed the expansion of the International Security Force, which could neutralize the power of those with guns and allow other voices to be heard. A US- and UN-guided process helped ensure women a place at the table as ministers in the temporary Afghan administration and participants in the emergency grand council, or loya jirga, which met in Kabul in June.

During that assembly, women demonstrated why Afghanistan needs them to create democracy. Though a scant 10 percent of those assembled, with no troops or guns at their disposal, female delegates challenged with unparalleled candor the misogynist warrior ethos of both the Taliban and the warlords now in power and said they were looking for a leader who would make human rights a priority.

The lives of women remain vulnerable and there are reports of killings of women by their family members in the name of morality. Despite interventions by local NGOs the authorities have looked away, and have taken no action to investigate such murders. Such gender-based impunity by any State is a clear discrimination of the right to life of women

The female presidential candidate, Massouda Jalal, injected a modicum of democracy into the process, lining up the necessary signatures to run as male candidates fell by the wayside. The women's urgent need for accountable government drew them together in a unity that bridged tribal and ethnic differences. However, at the end of the day the men with guns had, with apparent US acquiescence, greatly increased their power within the Afghan administration and were escalating the intimidation of "dissenters."

During the loya jirga, the Afghan defense minister, Field Marshal Mohammed Fahim, assailed the husband of Massouda Jalal for his wife's temerity in running for president. Accusations of blasphemy pursued Former Vice President Sima Samar, who was driven from her post as women's affairs minister.

Interim government ministers with civilian rather than military credentials were dismissed, Chief Justice Shinwari, who publicly upbraided Samar and has called for full support of Sharia, or Islamic law, was reappointed; and the majority of the Judicial Commission, responsible for reconciling Islamic principles with other legal traditions, are graduates of religious schools, called madrassas, with no further education.

Returning home from the loya jirga, many women faced the threat of violent backlash. Their joy at the promise of freedom and pride in finding a public voice conflicts with the fear of pervasive lawlessness. Taliban-style sexual policing still thrives in a number of places under the aegis of the US Northern Alliance partners as well as in former Taliban strongholds.

Taliban pamphlets warn of reprisals for "spreading

indecency and vulgarity" by "sending women to offices and daughters to schools." In much of the country outside of Kabul, the crossfire of rival factions has left women immensely vulnerable and victimized anew by a wave of rapes and other forms of sexual violence. The US failure to support the Afghan administration materially or militarily has blighted early opportunities for women and the rule of law.

While spending more than $2 billion a month on its pursuit of Al Qaeda and the Taliban and channeling money and technical assistance to local military leaders, the United States pledged only $2 million this year to help the Afghan administration build a national army.

Most important, while anarchy grows, the United States has opposed the expansion of the international security force, essential for establishing national order outside of Kabul.

Afghan women continue to fear physical violence and insecurity even after the end of the Taliban regime in Afghanistan. Sexual violence by armed factions and public harassment tied to repressive Taliban-era edicts continue to restrict women in their movement, expression and dress. Women can only participate in the reconstruction of Afghanistan if they can be physically safe. Following the routing of the Taliban from power media coverage showed some women throwing off the *burqa*—an act which gave the impression that women were ready to show their faces in public and stop wearing the all-encompassing garment.

In fact, women in Kabul and Herat continue to wear burqas on the streets as of this writing. Many women interviewed said they were afraid to walk on the streets uncovered. Their reasons varied but the common response was fear "of the men with the guns". "Men with guns" refers to the former mujahidin or freedom fighters—those who fought under the commanders of the various warlords in the many phases of Afghanistan's wars. Many fighters buried their guns when the Taliban took over. As soon as the Taliban were driven out they dug up the buried weapons and some of them began robbing and looting homes. In Kabul there were over 1000 robberies in one month and a number of murders after the departure of the Taliban.

Most women do not remember when they did not feel

afraid. Their fear partly explains why women chose to continue wearing burqas even after the Taliban. Westerners have undeniably focused too much attention on the burqa issue. In the post-Taliban political climate the burqa has become a barometer of the level of insecurity women feel more than a women's rights issue.

**End of Taliban Rule**

Since the end of Taliban rule in Afghanistan in November 2001, women and girls have had growing access to education, health care, and employment. At the same time, many Afghan women still live in an environment in which personal physical security is constantly under threat. There are number of cases of sexual violence in the northern city of Mazar-i Sharif, including gang-rapes. Many women continue to limit their movements and to wear a burqa, the head-to-toe enveloping garment, for their physical security, even though the Taliban-era edict requiring women to wear the burqa is no longer in force.

In Kabul, Shazia is only 13. Her voice is barely audible. Around adults, she bites her nails and tugs at her black chiffon scarf, covering her face and hazel eyes. She is one of the hardened criminals inside the dank and forbidding walls of Kabul's Provincial Jail for women. Her crime: running away from the 45-year-old husband she was forced to marry.

In fact, the jail is filled with teenage girls accused of crimes ranging from falling in love to having illicit affairs, from leaving unbending parents to running away from abusive husbands. Taliban-style executions may be gone, but Islamic law and rigid cultural traditions persist in Afghanistan. The country still relies on Islamic law dating to the 7th Century.

The U.S.-supported government of interim Prime Minister Hamid Karzai says it still will uphold these laws, although perhaps not as strictly as the Taliban. Islamic laws allow women the right to turn down their parents' choice of husbands, but enforce harsh punishment for sex outside marriage. Tribal laws, on the other hand, allow relatives to imprison and even kill young women who lose their virginity, bring shame to their family by falling in love with unacceptable suitors or even seek a divorce.

**Severe Punishments**

In its zeal to enforce Islamic law, the Taliban chopped off the hands of thieves in public stadiums and had family members shoot down murderers. If a woman were to run away from her husband, she, too, would have been executed, said the deputy of security in Kabul, Lt. Gen. Mohammed Khalil Aminzada. A married woman who committed adultery would be stoned to death.

There is little information about AIDS here, but the World Health Organization reports 10 known cases in Afghanistan. Aminzada said Kabul's police don't go out of their way to arrest runaways or adulterers unless they feel it will create a threat to security or if family members turn them in.

Among its many tasks, Afghanistan's interim government was supposed to create a commission to plan the rebuilding of the criminal justice system and to restore human rights as part of the Bonn agreement last fall. The commission has yet to be established.

In the absence of new laws, the country's high court has gone back to using the old Shariah laws of Islam, those in place before the Taliban. But they say they will apply them more compassionately. Since the Taliban's departure, there have been no stonings or whippings. Those punishments could occur again some day, legal officials said, for repeat offenders or if the evidence is strong in a case. For example, under the strict standard set by Shariah law, a married man or woman will be stoned to death for committing adultery if the accusation can be substantiated by four male eyewitnesses. Under the Taliban, says the head of Afghanistan's high court, Fazal Hadi Shinwari, they didn't wait for four witnesses. "It's very difficult to find four witnesses who can confirm the act," said Shinwari, who has a long white beard, a copy of the Koran sitting on his desk and a leather whip hanging on his wall. "Of course the Taliban executed them without evidence, without any confirmation. They did not use the real Shariah. They just wanted to scare people. We're softer than them," he said.

So in the empty, dreary cells of the Kabul Provincial Jail sit young women like Farayba, 19. She and her lover went to the Taliban, hoping the former rulers would marry them against their families' wishes. Instead, Taliban officials gave them 5-year jail sentences. When the Taliban abandoned Kabul five months ago, Farayba escaped with 71 other women in the jail. Her family was relatively wealthy; her father had been a commander in the Ministry of Defense before the Taliban. When she chose to marry a poor man's son, Farayba brought shame to her family, who wanted her to marry a cousin. When she refused, her father, cousins and brothers beat her boyfriend's father. Fearing for their lives, the young lovers turned again to authorities, this time from the interim government. "The police officials told me to marry my cousin," she said. "I refused and so they said I should serve the rest of my 5-year sentence. I don't think there's any difference between this regime and the Taliban regime."

The western press has made so much of the idea that, as the Taliban left Kabul, the liberated women threw off their blue shrouds. But in Kabul, almost all the young women are still wearing the burka. This is not through force of tradition. There was a custom of wearing the burka among some ethnic groups in Afghanistan, but not among educated women in the cities.

**In Politics**

Some of the women who have taken off the *burka* are those now moving into politics. A woman in her early 30s, also called Zohal, talks enthusiastically about what this means to her. Her two-year-old daughter, silently playing with a wilted pink rose, sits on her lap as she talks. "The doors of everything have been closed to women for so long," she says. "Now we hope that the doors are swinging open. This loya jirga is only a first step, but in the future parliament there must be equal representation for women and for men."

Mindful that even in western countries women haven't achieved such representation, women make up more than half of the population of Afghanistan and that they have been the first victims of war. The literacy course in Sarasia is funded by the Revolutionary Association of the Women of Afghanistan. This extraordinary organisation has been going since 1977 and is a testament to the determined resilience of Afghan women.

The thousands of RAWA members have worked underground and in exile for nearly 30 years - against the

Soviet regime, the mujaheddin, the Taliban - and they are now stronger than ever. But although RAWA is beginning to operate more openly, most of its work is still anonymous and underground. Oddly, despite the west's much-touted support for a more liberal society, RAWA has never received support from any government. But RAWA's members are still agitating for women's equality and a secular government, and they are also passionately involved in rebuilding civil society.

But women in Afghanistan are not only struggling against the men who rule them. Many are simply struggling to survive.

Afghan women are thought to have the highest maternal mortality rates of women in any country, at around 1,700 per 100,000; life expectancy is about 46 years, and around 50% of children are stunted through malnutrition - yet donor fatigue is already a real danger. Dr Lynn Amowitz of Harvard Medical School, who is leading a new maternal mortality survey in Afghanistan, said recently, "Afghanistan is falling off people's radar screen and funding is becoming harder to find."

Kabul was not always a dystopian city - that once, in the 1970s and 1980s, it was cosmopolitan, with women walking down the streets in miniskirts, crowded jazz clubs and colourful parks. It's also important to remember that Afghan women were not always victims. In the 80s, 40% of doctors and 50% of university students in Kabul were women - and though such liberation did not extend throughout Afghanistan, many urban, educated women lived lives of relative freedom. Those women who have lived all their lives in the most traditional sections of society can still speak a language of resistance. Sarasia, a little village in west of Kabul, women here live close to the edge; even the village well, after three years of drought, is no longer working, so the women and children traipse across the fields to the neighbouring village every day to collect water. In one of the stark white houses, a literacy class is in progress. The women in this class couldn't be further from the educated elite. Soraya, for instance, is a widow of 50 and has been illiterate all her life. "If you are illiterate, it is as if you are blind," she says. Her eldest son doesn't want her to learn to read, but she has finally won his permission because this class is run by women for women in their own village. In this village, all the women wear *burkas*; they always have. None can leave the village without the permission of the men in her family, and none of the women in the room has had any formal education. And yet, somehow, they have kept alive the idea of a different society.

The literacy course in Sarasia is funded by the Revolutionary Association of the Women of Afghanistan. This extraordinary organisation has been going since 1977 and is a testament to the determined resilience of Afghan women. The thousands of RAWA members have worked underground and in exile for nearly 30 years - against the Soviet regime, the mujaheddin, the Taliban - and they are now stronger than ever. But although RAWA is beginning to operate more openly, most of its work is still anonymous and underground. Oddly, despite the west's much-touted support for a more liberal society, RAWA has never received support from any government.

But RAWA's members are still agitating for women's equality and a secular government, and they are also passionately involved in rebuilding civil society. On the street outside, it is the usual Kabul scene: heaps of rubbish, a blinding glare, dust-filled air. Then you push open a large blue door to a courtyard. Here, somebody is growing herbs and vegetables, and two white-and-yellow butterflies dip their wings over the thick green fronds of radish plants. Under awnings on the sides of the courtyard, one group of women is spelling out its Persian lesson and another is cutting bright cloth, learning to make shirts.

Britain will hand over command of the 18-nation UN security force in Afghanistan to Turkey. Meanwhile, with the political and financial support of the Bush Administration, Turkey will shortly assume command of the multi-nation UN security force in Afghanistan. In the past Turkey backed one of the worst Afghan warlords now being "rehabilitated" by the US, General Abdul Rashid Dostum. Dostum's troops were notorious violators of women and human rights across the board. Then again, Turkey's deplorable human rights record against its Kurdish citizens rivals that of Saddam Hussein's. Of course, former ally Saddam Hussein no longer receives massive US aid as does Turkey.

Turkey, though secular at government level, is a Muslim country with a large army and aspirations to enter the western fold. It is a long-standing member of Nato and an aspirant member of the EU. Washington was keen on Turkey's leadership of the International Security Assistance Force, not least because it allows the US to argue that the Afghan campaign is not, as is widely believed in the Muslim world, a war against Islam. President Bush asked Congress to pay Turkey $228m to take the job on. The vice-president, Dick Cheney, turning a blind eye to the State Department's own human rights report, felt moved to reiterate the administration's support for Turkey's application to join the EU.

**The Karzai Government**

The Karzai government has not hidden its anxieties about Turkey's support in the past for General Abdul Rashid Dostum, now deputy defence minister, whose passion for tying people to tank tracks was documented in painful detail by the journalist Ahmed Rashid. Gen Dostum's men, followers of Afghan affairs will remember, also had a remarkably poor record when it came to rape and sexual torture of Afghan women.

Turkish security forces systematically rape and sexually abuse women in Turkey. When victims complain, it is they, not the rapists, who face criminal prosecution. The document is a trial observation report - not, sadly, a trial of army or police officers for rape, but of women who spoke out and were then charged with undermining the unity of the state. The charges arose from a conference organised in June 2000 by several NGOs to address what they said was systematic sexual violence perpetrated by state officials against women in custody.

Revolutionary Association of the Women of Afghanistan (RAWA) condemned Turkey for declaring allegations of terrorism against Taliban as unjustified and baseless. A Turkish government special envoy Edymer Erman, who is visiting Kabul, said terrorism allegations against Taliban are unjustified and baseless and that there exists no evidence to prove the same.

The Turkish government's response to the powerful

evidence presented was to initiate investigations against 19 of the speakers and subsequently to bring legal proceedings against them for "denigrating" the security forces. A second investigation led to even more serious charges against five speakers, this time before the state security court, for daring to claim that Kurdish women were disproportionately the victims. By mentioning the fact that Kurdish women were raped in custody and during village raids, the state argued, the conference organisers, lawyers and victims had "incited people to enmity and hatred by pointing to class, racial, religious, confessional or regional differences". The charges before the state council carry a maximum sentence of six years.

It is no coincidence that many Kurdish women are raped. Rape, as the lesson of the Balkans reminds us, is a useful tool in the destruction of a rival ethnic group. Given the social and legal penalties for speaking out, it is a reasonable assumption that the documented cases of rape and sexual torture of Kurdish women represent the tip of the iceberg. Even so, they reveal that sexual torture is routinely used against women in custody, and frequently involves their children and other family members.

The Kurdish report has received little attention, but then the abuse of women in Afghanistan was scarcely a high priority in Washington before September 11. Afterwards, of course, even Laura Bush was moved to protest about the suffering of her Afghan sisters. Now that the Taliban have been ousted from Kabul, the continued suffering of the women of Afghanistan, like that of Kurdish women in Turkey, is no longer useful. The ongoing abuse is merely an embarrassment to Afghanistan's western "liberators", rather as the suffering of Kurdish women is an embarrassment as long as President Bush needs the Turkish military in charge of peacekeeping in Afghanistan.

**Prostitution Under the rule of Taliban**

Under the Taliban rule, prostitution was increased. The Kurdish report which follows only serves to highlight the following points:

- Contrary to the ludicrous assertions of Taliban and Jihadi criminals, the savageries of the "Islamic State" and of its substitute "Islamic Emirate" of Afghanistan have not only not had the slightest impact on reducing prostitution -this gross violation of women's rights- in the country, their "pious" criminality have increased the flesh trade by leaps and bounds.

– Once again, in contradiction of the Taliban and Jihadi fundamentalist bands' ridiculously childish opinionating, the scourge of AIDS knows no national or religious boundaries. HIV infection has long since infiltrated Afghan society and is rife especially among prostitutes where it claims unmarked and un-remarked silent victims. The fundamentalist rulers of Afghanistan are too insensibly ignorant to appreciate the threat of AIDS. In their puerile, arrogant "erudition", they believe that by chanting their refrain-word "Islam", their Sharia will perform a miracle and fundamentalist-contaminated Afghanistan will be AIDS-free!

– The "Islamic Emirate" with its perpetual pitching of the banner of "Islam" and "Sharia law" on each and every infamy, including stoning to death and arbitrary executions, can never hope to provide a cure for festering social ills, prostitution in particular. As we have asserted time and again, they can only worsen the situation.

– One of the unforgivable crimes of each and every stooge regime -from Taraki to Najib-is the propagation of prostitution and the physical, mental, and moral devastation of Afghan women. The Jihadi criminals elevated this disgrace to its acme. The more the Taliban hypocrites wrap themselves up in Islam and Sharia law, the more distinguished they become in shame and infamy. The fundamentalists and their sympathizers put prostitutes forward as a defiled, untouchable group in their "pure Islamic" society and believe that the "purity" of their illusory "pure" society lies in persecution and annihilation of prostitutes. It behoves our noble and patriotic intellectuals to point out in no uncertain terms that whatever ignominy that may be associated with the shameful flesh trade is a reflection of the mark of shame and disgrace branded onto the foreheads of fundamentalist rulers. These despicable rulers are most worthy of all contempt as they are the source and the cause of all social scourges, including prostitution, in our mortally wounded country.

Taliban arrival has increased the social and especially the economical problems of Afghan women. The women of Afghanistan live under monstrous oppression of both Jehadi and Taliban fundamentalists in disastrous situations where most of their basic human rights are denied of them. The Taliban denial of women to have a job has created a flood of unemployed women in Kabul.

These unemployed women face serious financial problems and as a natural consequence their children suffer from hunger, malnutrition, different illnesses and a chronic state of poverty. Most of them has have lost their last resorts of income and have sold most of their possession to buy food. Those who could afford leaving the country have done so, and those who could not are making the bulk of beggars in our country. A large number of these beggars are ex teachers and civil servants.

Bad state of economy especially in Kabul has hit hard the pity income of these beggars. The ban on female beggars to enter shops, inns and other trading premises is even further affected their income forcing a number of them to enter into prostitution for their survival, and survival of their children.

A large number of young widows who are the sole breadwinner of their families and with all doors of opportunity closed on their face are joining prostitution as well. According to a preliminary research on the problem there are hundreds of new prostitutes joining the ranks of professional ones. These women are mostly working from their houses termed as "Qala"s. As the income from begging is declining for women the number of prostitutes are increasing.

Only in Kabul city there are 25 to 30 brothels actively working which, for security reason, are constantly shifting residence every one or two months. Following is a brief report gathered form some of these brothels in Taimany, Hashuqan-o-Harifan, Qala-e-Zaman Kan, and qul-e-abchakan areas of Kabul:

Each of these brothels has three to five women working and living in them. Some of the terms they use are;

"Kharabati" for prostitute, "khala kharabati" for an old woman managing the work of the brothel, "Qala" for the brothel and "Qala dar" for their pimps. The environment is usually hostile and there are arguments and fights over clients. Each Qala has two to three Qala-dars and a khala-kharabati. The male pimps mediate between the prostitutes and their customers.

The old women are managing the internal affairs of the Qala; collect money from the clients, prepare food and do other chores around the Qala. Clients either come into the Qala or the women visit the clients house. A third way is through a taxi. Because of its security risk this way is more difficult as the Taliban has banned the use of a taxi without a "muharam". Therefore the prostitute take a 6-9 year old boy with them if they want to work through a taxi. These children are usually witnessing the acts. It has been said that these children are being asked for sexual acts as well.

Women who are not members of a Qala are considered a security risk as they may report them to Taliban. The women who work in a Qala usually carry three types of identity cards. One id, showing them as a widower with children, is used to get aid from UN offices or Red Cross. These Ids are not used a lot as they change place quickly and don't want to get involved with the local officials. Another id, showing them as a married woman, is used for renting houses and so on. If Taliban arrests them for Zena they use their third id showing them as a single women. Being single helps them avoid being stoned to death.

As an example last year a women, (SH), resident of Gala-e-Mussa was arrested for Zena. She spent two and half month in Taliban's jail. Finally she paid six million Afghanis bribe to the judge of military court (Abdur Rahman Aqa) and were freed after receiving eighty strokes of lashes. She said, "Mula Abdur Rahman (the military judge) receives bribes not only from prostitutes but from pick pockets and gamblers. Sharia (Islamic Law) is applied only on those who can not pay." 60% of the money that the clients of these women pay goes to their pimps and the old women working for them.

Fear of Taliban has reduced the number of clients. The average ages of these women are from 20 to 35 years. The hygiene of the their working environment is quite bad. A large number of these women are infected with chancre, syphilis, skin irritations and possibly aids.

AIDS might have been brought here by those traders who spend months in Arab countries and have visited brothels their. Due to present unfavorable conditions these women can not visit the doctors or use contraceptive pills. The traditional and old techniques put them in risk and often cause medical problems.

Most of the complaints are against "turban wearers" who are Pashto speaking Taliban. This is because of their rough manners, not paying enough or threatening as they leave the "Qala" and sometimes they enjoy torturing the women working there. The sixty years old women who keep around house call Ko-ko. She is an experienced woman who manages the affairs of the house. She keeps contact with other houses and gets her money from each woman. She was a cleaner in a Kabul hospital before and in her youth she was a prostitute.

She tells "during Najeeb's regime our Qala was discovered and I was put in jail. When they learned that I was a cleaner in one of the hospital they asked me to work as a spy for them which I accepted and they let me free. I was spying for them for a while when the ward manager asked me to solicit sex from the nurses for him, for which I received good money. A couple of nurses fell into his trap. Those nurses were later recruited into KHAD's 11th branch, however a third nursed reported the whole thing to the head of the hospital who then fired me." She added, "all the women who had worked with me have their own stories. Each had been forced to this line of work, no one is satisfied with this work"

With Ko-ko's help we listened to the stories of some of the women in one of the Qalas in Hashuqan-o-Harifan. There are a number of Qalas in Hazrat St in Hashuqan-o-Harifan. The professional prostitutes who work in brothels a number of women, because of family problems, can not work in brothels. These women work on the streets as beggars and invite clients to their houses. It is an undeniable and unarguable fact that young women in Kabul because of economical problems, poverty and hunger join the ranks of beggars and ultimately go toward prostitution. These women number in thousands and their numbers are increasing.

On May 25, 1997, five female employees of CARE, an international aid agency, were collectively beaten in public in Kabul for 'associating with foreigners' and 'bad hejabi', a fundamentalist term denoting female attire not conforming with strict Taliban-prescribed dress code for women and girls. The bruised and humiliated women all had official work permits issued by the Taliban authorities. The Taliban militia have further announced that all women working for foreign organisations are wanton. In protest against this outrage CARE suspended all its activities in Kabul until local Taliban authorities were forced to formally apologise for the incident, but Radio Shariat, the official mouthpiece of the Taliban, officially refuted this apology and announced that the Taliban had done nothing to apologise for.

# 8

# The Assessment

The report is submitted in accordance with the resolution 2001/3 by the Economic and Social Council (ECOSOC) on discrimination against women and girls in Afghanistan, in which the Council requested the Secretary-General to report to the Commission on the Status of Women at its forty-sixth session on progress made in the implementation of that resolution. This report draws on information of the UN system and other sources. Since the adoption of ECOSOC resolution 2001/3, the situation of women and girls in Afghanistan continued to deteriorate due to the ongoing conflict, the critical humanitarian situation, the continuing effects of a third year of drought, hunger, internal displacement and massive violations of human rights. Following the events of 11 September 2001, and the military intervention in Afghanistan by the United States of America and its allies in an effort to fight terrorism led to the fall of the Taliban regime. Significant changes then occurred in the political landscape of the country, but the immediate humanitarian crisis also increased. For the first time in many years, new opportunities were presented for women to reclaim their rights as active participants in the governance as well as in the rehabilitation and reconstruction of their country.

The report, which includes developments since the last report to the Commission at its forty-fifth session, focuses in sections II and III on developments prior to September 2001 in Afghanistan and UN activities; and in section IV on developments in the latter part of 2001. Section V contains conclusions and recommendations.

## Developments Prior to September 2001

Although the sanctions imposed following the adoption of Security Council resolution 1333 of 19 December 2000 were intended to reduce the flow of arms, the armed conflict continued during 2001, and intensified in May. Meanwhile, women and girls continued to be severely restricted in their access to education, health care facilities, and employment. Their right to movement and association were limited, and their access to recreational sites severely restricted.

Due to the ongoing armed conflict and the effects of the drought, the socio-economic situation forced large numbers of people to leave their homes in search for food, water, better livelihood and security. The unwillingness of the authorities to provide relief to its population combined with restrictions placed upon the assistance community made the provision of humanitarian assistance increasingly difficult, which affected women and girls disproportionately.

A mission to Afghanistan in April 2001 by the United Nations Senior Inter-Agency Network on Internal Displacement assessed the nature and magnitude of the crisis affecting internally displaced populations and related vulnerable populations. The mission report confirmed that the condition of women in Afghanistan was dramatic and that the Taliban had pursued a policy of marginalization of women and girls, but also noted that the application of. such restrictions had been inconsistent, allowing the humanitarian community to devise various entry points to reach some women and girls in need.

The fact that Afghanistan is one of the most heavily mined countries in the world exacerbated the difficult humanitarian situation. According to the UN Mine Action Programme Afghanistan has more than 732 million square kilometres of its territory mined and about 500 square kilometres of unexploded ordnance. Those particularly at risk are subsistence farmers, returnees, people in search of firewood, or those who take routes outside those regularly used.

## Intergovernmental and Expert Bodies

Throughout the reporting period, the situation in Afghanistan, in general, and the situation of women and girls in particular, remained under intense scrutiny by several UN bodies, including the Security Council, several of the ECOSOC's functional commissions and expert bodies, in particular, the Commission of Human Rights, the Commission on the Status of Women, the Sub-Commission on the Promotion and Protection of Human Rights, as well as the fifty-sixth session of the General Assembly.

Reports were submitted to the Security Council by the Secretary-General on the situation in Afghanistan and its implications for international peace and security and on the humanitarian implications of the measures imposed by Security Council resolutions 1267 (1999) and 1333 (2000) on Afghanistan. In so far as these reports referred to the situation of women and girls, they underlined the fact that officially sanctioned discrimination restricted women's access to the minimum opportunities available, in areas such as health, education and means of acquiring a livelihood.

The Special Rapporteur on the situation of human rights in Afghanistan noted in his report to the Commission on Human Rights, that the majority of internally displaced persons (IDPs) in Afghanistan were women and children and that many IDP compounds did not provide for the health needs of women. The Commission on Human Rights deplored, inter alia, the deteriorating economic and social conditions of women and girls in all areas of the country, in particular in areas under Taliban control and condemned the continuing grave violations of the human rights of women and girls.

Specific attention to the situation of women and girls was given by the Sub-Commission on the Promotion and Protection of Human Rights. In 2001, it considered a report of the Secretary-General on the situation of women and girls in Afghanistan, which noted that women and girls suffered disproportionately in the realization and enjoyment of all their rights.

The Sub-Commission considered it essential for the international community to continue to follow very closely the situation of women and girls and bring the necessary pressure to bear so as to remove all restrictions imposed on women. It also noted that the situation of women and girls was totally at variance with the precepts of Islam, which impose on Muslims the duty to acquire an education and pursue knowledge.

Following consideration of the report by the Special Rapporteur on the situation of human rights in Afghanistan at its fifty-sixth session, the General Assembly strongly, inter alia,. condemned the gross violations of the human rights of women and girls, including abductions and kidnappings, as well as accounts of many instances of forced marriage and trafficking.

**Socio-economic and Human Rights Situation of Women and Girls**

Throughout most of 2001, the systematic discrimination against women and girls continued in all parts of the country under Taliban control, but was particularly targeted at women in urban areas. Taliban policies were directed at the removal of women from public life, thus exacerbating traditional customs pre-dating the Taliban regime.

**Health**

According to data of the United Nations Children's Fund (UNICEF), the maternal mortality rate in Afghanistan is the second highest in the world, with an estimated 15,000 women dying each year from pregnancy-related causes. The infant mortality rate is 165 per 1,000; the under five mortality rate is 257 per 1,000, with one in four children dying before the age of five from preventable diseases. It is estimated that only 23 per cent of the population have access to safe water, and only 12 per cent have access to adequate sanitation, thereby increasing the incidence of diseases. 4 per cent of the population is disabled, many by landmines. Only about 15 per cent of births are attended by trained health workers, with more than 90 per cent of births taking place at home. At least 15,000 Afghans die of tuberculosis every year, of which 64 per cent are women. Malnutrition of women, which negatively affects pregnancies and deliveries as well as the health of children, is not only caused by the food scarcity linked to the conflict and the drought, but is also related to traditional preference for males which makes women reduce their own food allowance in favour of men and children.

With regard to mental health, the overall state of women's mental health was poor with more than 70 per cent of women exposed to Taliban policies meeting the criteria for major depression. Furthermore, women and girls were forced to attend public executions, floggings and other forms of cruel and inhuman treatment, which contributed to the psychological damage suffered by women and created a highly traumatized population with no access to mental health care. In addition, an increasing number of women was reported as drug addicts.

The poor health situation has been aggravated by the lack of basic health services and resources particularly in rural areas; the strict segregation of medical staff and the small number of trained women doctors, nurses and midwives that remained in the country.

**Education**

Twenty-three years of war destroyed the infrastructure of the educational system and further increased the illiteracy rate in Afghanistan. While the overall education of women and girls was at an extremely low level with only 5 per cent of women being able to read and write, it is worth noting that during the 1980s the female adult literacy rate was only 8 per cent.

During the Taliban regime, only about 3 per cent of girls received some form of primary education. The ban on women's employment also affected boy's education as the majority of teachers had been women. New curricula were introduced for the school year starting on 21 March 2001, which, in an effort to further advance the Taliban policy of Islamization, introduced subjects emphasizing Islamic and Arabic-language subjects to the detriment of arts and sciences.

**Employment**

The decree banning Afghan women from working in aid agencies, except in the health sector, issued by the Taliban in July 2000, remained in force throughout most of the year. In May 2001, a decree was issued which banned women, including female personnel from all aid agencies, from driving cars, thus limiting their activities severely. In July, the Taliban issued a decree formalizing restrictions on the activities of foreigners, and required foreign female Muslim workers to be accompanied by a male escort. Except for limited opportunities in the health sector and through income-generating activities, some women worked with the assistance community, but under severe limitations and often at risk of threats and harassment.

**Freedom of Movement and Association**

The Taliban systematically limited women's freedom of movement by demanding that women travel when accompanied by a male relative, which put a particular strain on female-headed households and widows. Women were harassed and beaten by Taliban if their public appearance was perceived to be in contradiction with Taliban edicts. The resulting seclusion of women to the home constituted a form of solitary confinement and created obstacles to women meeting with each other. Women's removal from the public space also meant that women could not play any role in the political process and were excluded from all forms of formal or informal governance.

**Human Rights Violations, Including Violence Against Women and Girls**

The Special Rapporteur on violence against women, its causes and consequences discussed instances of rape, sexual assault, forced prostitution and forced marriage. The war and the militarization of society led to an increased number of abductions of young girls and women by Taliban fighters. It is difficult to obtain exact numbers, as families have been reluctant to come forward and report cases of abductions for fear of reprisals and due to the social stigma attached to a daughter or sister kidnapped or sold for sex. 54 per cent of girls under the age of 18 were reported to be married. Families of girls and young women were reportedly forced to marry them to the Taliban or give them large amounts of money instead. Often families married young girls at an earlier age in order to use the bride price to assist in their family's survival. Another underreported crime, which requires further investigation, is the so-called "honour killings" of women and men who die at the hands of their relatives for having violated traditional codes of honour regarding the relations between the sexes. Sometimes killings are reported as "suicides" to prevent further investigation.

These massive abuses during the civil war and the Taliban regime constitute gross violations of international human rights law and standards to which Afghanistan is a

State party, such as the International Covenant on Economic, Social and Cultural Rights, the International. Covenant on Civil and Political Rights, and the Convention on the Rights of the Child. Afghanistan also signed the Convention on the Elimination of All Forms of Discrimination against Women in 1980.

**Activities of UN Entities**

During the period under review, the United Nations Resident/Humanitarian Coordinator, with the UN agencies on the ground, and United Nations senior staff within the United Nations Special Mission to Afghanistan (UNSMA) continued to address issues related to the discrimination against women and girls in all sectors. They made numerous efforts to negotiate the withdrawal of various discriminatory decrees, including those banning women's employment, which nevertheless remained in effect. Nevertheless, the assistance community was able to hold celebrations of International Women's Day in Afghanistan from 8 to 14 March 2001 in Kabul, Herat, Jalalabad, Mazar-i-Sharif, Kandahar and Faizabad. From mid-May 2001, UNSMA was forced to limit its presence in Taliban-held territory to Kabul. Civil Affairs Officers maintained contacts with political authorities, religious and community leaders, administrative officials, traditional assemblies, and representatives of youth and women's groups, as well as the media and the academic community.

The Afghanistan 2001 United Nations Consolidated Inter-Agency Appeal emphasized that the assistance community would collectively aim to expand access for Afghan women to education, health services and employment and income-generating activities. The Principled Common Programme focused on the activities both within UN agencies as well as international and national non-governmental organizations. It continued to address compliance of the provision of humanitarian assistance with agreed upon principles and guidelines through the use of such tools as the Strategic Monitoring Unit, the Gender Forum and regular inter-agency meetings. Despite the Principled Common Programme, consensus was not always reached among agencies as to how best to react to restrictions imposed by the Taliban on women.

The Taliban regime limited agencies' possibilities to reach

out to women and girls. The decrees restricting women's employment made it increasingly difficult to work with or access women as beneficiaries of humanitarian assistance, as only women aid workers could directly work with women beneficiaries. Male staff working for international agencies tended to focus on the needs of men and boys, but were also effectively limited in their access to women in need. The forced segregation of staff led to further disadvantages for women. While male Afghan workers travelled in UN vehicles, women had to rely on public transportation, which increased their exposure to violence. The situation was further complicated by the inconsistent approach taken by the Taliban on enforcement and conflicting information given to the assistance community.

Afghan women who worked for UN agencies and other international organizations, mostly restricted to urban areas, were at all times isolated from their male international and national colleagues as they were not allowed to interact with any males who were not direct relatives. Thus, women were often excluded from information sharing and decision-making processes. The World Food Programme (WFP), for example, reported that it continued to employ female national staff, who, however, had to work in a clandestine manner, particularly in. Kabul. The women were instructed not to come to the office, not to visit one another in their homes and not to draw attention to themselves when visiting project sites. Their employment, which was limited to urban areas only, took place with the knowledge and tacit approval of the authorities. Some WFP international and national staff, men and women, received threatening letters accusing them of being involved in activities supporting prostitution, an offense punishable by death in Afghanistan. In June 2001, four women employees were arrested and imprisoned for three days. The women subsequently fled to Islamabad.

WFP provided employment to women, primarily widows, through its bakery projects, which employed about 300 women in Kabul and 100 in Mazar-i-Sharif before September 2001. Taliban efforts to prevent employment of women in a survey of beneficiaries caused WFP to threaten to close down 130 bakeries that fed 280,000 people, including women and children. The situation was resolved by the authorities agreeing to allow women hired by the Taliban Health Ministry to conduct the survey. In Kabul, Mazar-i-Sharif and Herat, WFP supported large food-for-work activities that directly benefited women who were making quilts and pasta. Community fora financed by the United Nations Development Programme (UNDP) employed women in support of urban services through tailoring, kitchen gardening, embroidery, hat weaving, carpet weaving, needle work and schools. In Faizabad and Herat, women received vocational training for bee-keeping, backyard poultry, vegetable gardening and sericulture.

UNICEF worked with women in the health sector and organized home and community-based schools. With regard to the most vulnerable children and women, UNICEF focused on live-saving humanitarian assistance through immunization, nutrition, water and sanitation, emergency obstetric care and provision of non-food items. In north-eastern Afghanistan, WFP cooperated with UNICEF and non-governmental organizations in implementing a food-for education programme to reduce the drop-out rate of girls.

With regard to reducing the high maternal mortality and morbidity, the United Nations Population Fund (UNFPA) continued to reinforce support for safe delivery and emergency obstetric care inside Afghanistan and in refugee camps in Pakistan and Iran through local non-governmental organizations. WFP and the World Health Organization (WHO) trained male and female nurses in Kandahar and Herat and also continued their support for training and review courses for traditional birth attendant. In August 2001, the United Nations Drug Control Programme (UNDCP) launched a new drug demand reduction project targeting Afghan women in refugee camps in Pakistan with the goal to address the abuse and misuse of drugs and healthcare issues related to drug abuse. In order to address the increasing number of women drug addicts, UNDCP established self-help groups for women and conducted a detoxification programme in Afghanistan and in refugee camps in Pakistan 102 out of 230 drug addicts who successfully detoxified were women.

The United Nations Office for Project Services (UNOPS) Afghanistan Rural Rehabilitation Programme designed to enhance the capacity of women's organizations through revolving funds, micro-credit and income-generating activities, targeted female-headed households and provided support to communities in their points of origin. The United Nations Centre for Human Settlements (Habitat) continued to organize Community Fora as gathering places for consultation, participation and decision-making for women and men in ten districts of. Mazar-i-Sharif that were expanded to six other regions. The Fora covered activities related to social services, governance and business.

The UN Mine Action Service (UNMAS) supported the rehabilitation and social integration of the disabled Afghan population, including women and girls through vocational training and small financial credits. Women were also employed as community-based teachers.

**Developments after September 2001**

On 7 October 2001, the United States of America and its allies began a military intervention in Afghanistan to fight terrorism, particularly, the Al-Quaida network. The intensity of the aerial bombardment and the targeting of cities led to large-scale evacuations from urban areas and the loss of civilian lives, including those of women and children. It is estimated that the number of internally displaced people increased to more than one million and that about 7.5 million people inside Afghanistan would be in need of emergency assistance throughout the winter.

While assistance programmes had been hampered earlier due to repressive Taliban policies, which affected women disproportionately, the situation worsened when all international UN staff was withdrawn on 12 and 13 September and all foreigners were expelled by the Taliban on 14 September. In the absence of international staff, national staff continued their functions, including the distribution of humanitarian aid under difficult conditions. During the military intervention following the events of 11 September, the warehouses of the International Committee of the Red Cross in Kabul and offices of the UN Mine Action Programme were struck, and offices of UN agencies and international non-governmental organizations were looted by retreating Taliban forces and others, which affected the delivery of humanitarian aid.

The new operating environment led to intense discussions and preparations by the UN system in order to prepare for immediate, as well as medium- and long-term assistance priorities, for Afghanistan. On 3 October, Ambassador Lakhdar Brahimi was re-appointed Special Representative of the Secretary-General (SRSG) in charge of overseeing the political efforts of the United Nations in establishing an interim administration in Afghanistan. He also oversees the development of plans for the rehabilitation and reconstruction of the country. At UN headquarters, the first Integrated Mission Task Force (IMTF) has been established to advise the SRSG, and coordinate and prepare strategies, based on inputs from the Executive Committees and the field, through the Resident/Humanitarian Coordinator. The IMTF included a gender specialist from the Division on the Advancement of Women (DAW). Three Executive Committees, reporting to the Secretary-General, on Peace and Security, Humanitarian Affairs and the United Nations Development Group (UNDG), comprising clusters of agencies engaged in related work, met regularly and drew up strategic recovery plans on the political process, humanitarian assistance and reconstruction of the country, including gender perspectives. In addition, the UNDG and Executive Committee on Humanitarian Affairs formed a Sub-Group on Gender in Afghanistan to monitor developments on the ground in order to devise strategies to ensure that a gender perspective was mainstreamed in the peace negotiations and the reconstruction process, including the needs assessment for the Tokyo conference..

On 14 November 2001 in its resolution 1378, the Security Council expressed its strong support for the efforts of the Afghan people to establish a new and transitional administration leading to the formation of a government, which would be broad-based, multi-ethnic and fully representative of all the Afghan people, and should respect human rights regardless of gender, ethnicity or religion. In its resolution 1383 (2001) of 6 December 2001, the Security Council endorsed the Bonn Agreement establishing an Interim Authority. The Security Council authorized the establishment of an International Security Assistance Force in Afghanistan to assist the Afghan Interim Authority in the maintenance of security in Kabul and the surrounding areas in its resolution 1386 of 20 December 2001.

The Special Adviser to the Secretary-General on Gender Issues and Advancement of Women continued to address the situation of women's rights in Afghanistan in meetings with the SRSG and other senior officials within the United Nations system, in interagency consultations and in meetings with representatives of non-governmental organizations. She also facilitated contacts between Afghan women and women's organizations and the UN system and supported the organization of the Afghan Women's Summit in Brussels and follow-up meetings with the Secretary-General and members of the Security Council in an Arria Formula meeting. She also called on Afghan women to return to their country and former jobs, including in the civil service and elsewhere.

**United Nations Talks in Bonn and Establishment of the Interim Authority**

United Nations Talks on a transitional government for Afghanistan began in Bonn on 27 November under the leadership of SRSG Lakhdar Brahimi. Representatives of four Afghan groups participated representing the Rome process, linked to the former King; the United Front (also known as the Northern Alliance); the Cyprus Group and the Peshawar Group. All political groups had been encouraged by the UN to include women in their delegations and Afghan women's organizations were asked to contact the four groups for participation in the Talks.

Two women, Sima Wali and Rona Mansuri, participated as full delegates of the Rome process; Amena Afzali participated as a full delegate of the United Front; Seddiqa Balkhi participated as adviser to the Cyprus Group; and Fatana Gilani participated as adviser to the Peshawar Group.

The Agreement on Provisional Arrangements in Afghanistan pending the re-establishment of permanent government institutions (Agreement) was signed in Bonn on 5 December 2001. It noted that these interim arrangements were intended "as a first step toward the establishment of a broad-based, gender-sensitive, multi-ethnic and fully representative government." The Interim Authority consists of an Interim Administration, a Special Independent Commission for the convening of the Emergency Loya Jirga (a traditional assembly of elders) and a Supreme Court of Afghanistan. An Emergency Loya Jirga is to be convened within six months with the goal to set up a Transitional Authority. Elections are to be held within two years from the Emergency Loya Jirga. The Constitution of 1964, which had provided for the equality between women and men, will apply, to the extent that its provisions are not inconsistent with those of the Agreement..

The 21-member Special Independent Commission is to ensure that "due attention is paid to the representation in the Emergency Loya Jirga of a significant number of women." Furthermore the Agreement noted that the Interim Authority and the Special Independent Commission would "ensure the participation of women as well as the equitable representation of all ethnic and religious communities."

The Agreement called upon the United Nations to assist the Interim Administration in the establishment of a Judicial Commission; a Central Bank of Afghanistan; a Civil Service Commission; a Human Rights Commission; and in establishment of any other commissions not covered by the Agreement. With regard to human rights, the United Nations would have the right to investigate human rights violations and, where necessary, recommend corrective action. It would also be responsible for the development and implementation of a programme of human rights education to promote respect for and understanding of human rights. The United Nations would also assist in the registration of voters and a census of the population.

The Agreement set up a 29-member cabinet for six months headed by Hamid Karzai. The new Interim Administration, composed "with due regard to the ethnic, geographic and religious composition of Afghanistan and to the importance of the participation of women," took office on 22 December 2001 in Kabul. The Agreement provided that two Ministries, namely the Ministry of Women's Affairs, which had never existed before, and the Ministry of Public Health, would be run by women. The Ministry of Women's Affairs is headed by Sima Samar, a physician and founder of the Shuhada

Organization network of clinics, hospitals and schools in Pakistan and central Afghanistan. She is also one of five vice-presidents of the Interim Administration. Suhaila Siddiq, the Minister of Public Health, is a surgeon who continued to practise in Kabul throughout the Taliban regime.

The UN undertook to seek funds to cover administrative costs and essential rehabilitation of administrative facilities, including teachers' salaries to ensure that schools can re-open in March 2002, the Afghan New Year. Efforts were also undertaken to register former civil servants.

**Relief and Reconstruction**

The primary goals for the recovery and reconstruction of Afghanistan are to establish security and good governance; ownership of the process by the Afghan people; the re-establishment of basic services; and the reintegration of women in Afghan society and economy. The primary objective of the UN agencies and their partners is to provide immediate assistance to Afghans to survive the winter. Priority is being given to the provision of food, basic health services, water and sanitation, shelter and non-food relief such as blankets and winter clothing as well as the clearing of mines to support the humanitarian assistance.

During the military intervention, WFP national staff continued to deliver food to Afghanistan from the neighbouring countries. UNICEF managed to implement a massive polio eradication campaign, which reached over 10 million children under five years of age, and delivered life-saving humanitarian assistance, including nutrition, water and environmental sanitation, emergency obstetric care and provision of non-food items.

In mid-November, women national staff members of the Office of Humanitarian Affairs (OCHA), UNICEF, WFP and other agencies returned to work in Kabul and were expected to resume their posts in other urban areas as well. In December, WFP conducted a major survey on food needs in Kabul. Of 3,612 surveyors employed, some 2,400 were women, the first boost to women's employment since the fall of the Taliban.

WHO and UNICEF shipped emergency health kits into Afghanistan in October to serve more than a million people for three months. UNFPA supported by NGOs continued to provide its essential obstetric care services through a network of about 130 clinics.

The UN High Commissioner for Refugees (UNHCR) focused on assistance to IDPs inside Afghanistan and on the needs of refugees in neighboring countries, including the voluntary return of refugees. The United Nations Mine Action Programme initiated the clearing of an estimated 25,000 unexploded cluster bomblet units dropped on Afghanistan during the military intervention. A list of 103 sites of cluster bombs was provided by the United States and its allies.

In December, the Office of the High Commissioner for Human Rights deployed a needs-assessment mission in Pakistan and Afghanistan to assess the human rights situation, which paid particular attention to the systematic discrimination against women and girls.

Under the leadership of the World Bank, the Asian Development Bank (ADB) and the United Nations Development Programme (UNDP), a number of meetings took place, co-chaired by Japan and the United States of America and later joined by the European Union and Saudi Arabia, to prepare and coordinate the efforts of the assistance community and donors in the reconstruction and rehabilitation process of Afghanistan. Consultations were conducted with Afghans and a wide range of civil society representatives in Kabul, Pakistan and Iran as well as with the Afghan Interim Administration. The World Bank, ADB and UNDP conducted a preliminary needs assessment mission to Afghanistan in December 2001, which included consultations with Afghan NGOs.

The International Conference on Reconstruction Assistance to Afghanistan took place in Tokyo on 21 and 22 January 2002, to which the World Bank, ADB and UNDP submitted a joint assessment, "Afghanistan: Preliminary Needs Assessment for Recovery and Reconstruction", which included detailed funding requirements of Afghan authorities and UN activities during a one, two and a half, five and ten-year horizon. According to preliminary estimates, the reconstruction of Afghanistan would require about $15 billion over the next ten years. Given the lack of systematic data collection and the time and security constraints, the needs assessment provided indicative data and projections. It was expected that more consultations would be held with Afghan stakeholders to confirm priorities and medium and long-term funding requirements and to conduct a thorough needs assessment. The current assessment addressed gender equality as an important element for the overall reconstruction and development agenda, but the situation of women seemed to be reflected primarily on the area of social protection, health and education. While women's continued participation in the political and socio-economic processes was emphasized, there also seemed to be a tendency to perceive women primarily as victims of past. abuses and discrimination and as members of a vulnerable group rather than as active and full partners in all spheres of the reconstruction process. The Tokyo meeting, which highlighted education for girls as one of the key priorities for the reconstruction of the country, concluded with pledges and contributions of over 4.5 billion US dollars for the next few years, including 1.8. billion US dollars for 2002.

The United Nations system in consultation with the Interim Authority and international and national organizations and NGOs prepared a transitional assistance programme, "Immediate and Transitional Assistance Programme for Afghanistan, 2002," which was presented to the donor community following the Tokyo Ministerial Meeting. The programme outlined the immediate requirements, including quick impact recovery activities, support to the Interim Authority and humanitarian assistance.

**Women's rights reclaimed: activities by Afghan women**

Following the fall of the Taliban regime, Afghan women started to increase their activities. Numerous events were organized during the last few months by and with Afghan women's organizations inside and outside Afghanistan such as panel discussions, conferences and international meetings in order to ensure that the experiences and needs of Afghan women would receive the needed attention in all efforts directed at the post-Taliban Afghanistan. Schools for girls were reopened and women sought to return to their former jobs; and the first radio and television broadcast in Kabul featured a woman speaker. However, when the newly formed Union of Women in Afghanistan planned a march through Kabul on 20 and 27 November 2001, the organizers were informed by the then Minister of the Interior of the United Front, that the march could not proceed because of security concerns.

There were also reports about women left behind by retreating Taliban, who could become victims of anti-Taliban reactions, as well as women having been abducted from the Kabul area by fleeing Taliban. The fate of these women remains unclear. According to press reports, the Minister of Justice of the Interim Administration, promised to investigate cases of the kidnapping of women, but indicated that this would be difficult as some women were forced to marry Taliban officers or were trafficked outside of Afghanistan. According to the Minister, the Taliban regularly had sold women as sex slaves to fund its regime.

In response to requests from Afghan women, a number of non-governmental organizations convened the Afghan Women's Summit for Democracy in Brussels from 4 to 5 December 2001, in collaboration with the Office of the Special Adviser on Gender Issues and Advancement of Women and the United Nations Development Fund for Women (UNIFEM). About 40 Afghan women leaders from different ethnic, linguistic, and religious backgrounds participated, including three who had also attended the UN negotiations in Bonn. In a message to the Summit, the Secretary-General assured the participants of the full and unstinting support of the United Nations and emphasized that there could not be peace and recovery in Afghanistan without the restoration of the rights of women.

The Summit concluded with the adoption of the Brussels Proclamation, which included concrete demands for the recovery of Afghan society in the areas of education, media and. culture; health; human rights and the constitution; and refugees and internally displaced women. Its demands included: the right for women to vote and to equal pay; the right to equal access to health care, education and employment; an emergency plan for reopening schools by March 2002 for both girls and boys; training of teachers; the inclusion of Afghan women lawyers in the development of a new constitution; the rebuilding of hospitals and provision of health care, including psychological counselling; the inclusion of women in the Emergency Loya Jirga; the protection of women from forced under-age marriages and sexual harassment.

Participants of the Summit met with members of the European Parliament, members of the US Congress, members of the Security Council in an Arria Formula meeting, and women ambassadors to the United Nations. In their talks, the Afghan women called for measures to increase security in Afghanistan and facilitate the disarmament of all warring factions. The Secretary-General met with the Afghan women to hear their priorities and concerns.

UNIFEM organized a roundtable in Brussels from 10 to 11 December 2001 in cooperation with the Government of Belgium on "Building Women's Leadership in Afghanistan". The roundtable brought together Afghan women and UN agencies, the World Bank and donors, and issued an Action Plan calling for mechanisms to support the role and leadership of women in shaping the future of their country.

Other meetings were convened by Afghan women inside Afghanistan and Afghan refugee women, including a women's jirga (assembly of leaders) which was organized with the support of the Peshawar office of the International Human Rights Law Group in December in Pakistan. The jirga focused on peace and security and the importance of including women in next Emergency Loya Jirga.

In January 2002, Mr. Karzai, the head of the Interim Administration, demonstrated his support for women's rights by signing the "Declaration of the Essential Rights of Afghan Women", which affirmed the right to equality between men and women. The Declaration had been adopted by a meeting of Afghans in Dushanbe, Tajikistan, in 2000.

Even before 1979, Afghanistan was one of the poorest countries of the world with high maternal and child mortality rates and a very low literacy rate for women. Future plans and programmes for reconstruction and development of Afghanistan require an understanding of the country's past as well as its traditions and customs. Women had been discriminated against and marginalized before the Taliban came to power, where women's rights were severely limited through a system of traditional kinship where gender relations within the family unit as well as within the local community were dominated by males who were considered as guardians of the family honour.

Women's victimization during the civil war and, particularly, the Taliban regime, perpetuates a perception of women as victims and as members of a vulnerable group however. In reality, women assumed greater economic and social responsibilities during the years of conflict, which created a gap between the reality of women's lives, on the one hand, and generally. accepted norms based on traditional and customary models, on the other. This gap will have to be addressed in future interventions by the assistance community.

Afghan women should be seen as primary stake-holders and agents of change who have identified their own needs and priorities in all sectors of society and are ready to be full partners in the rebuilding of their society. The United Nations and the international assistance community should apply a consistent and principled approach and ensure that gender perspectives are mainstreamed in all its interventions while at the same time seeking to proceed in a sensitive way that gives Afghan women ownership of the process.

Afghan non-governmental organizations, including women's organizations, have been important partners in the provision of basic services and in the delivery of humanitarian assistance. The role of these organizations will continue to play a crucial role in the future recovery and reconstruction process, but should not be seen as the sole or main space for women's involvement, in particular, given the tendencies to equate civil society with women or to assign women a role in civil society only.

A safe environment, free from violence, discrimination and abuse for all Afghans is a first precondition for a viable and sustainable recovery and reconstruction process. The civil war and the militarization of society have fostered a culture of violence against women and girls, which is likely to continue to affect them during peace time. The current situation of change of power and instability may lead to increased violence against women in an atmosphere of impunity. Special measures need to be taken to protect women and girls from forced and under-age marriages and all other forms of violence.

Special attention should therefore be directed at the promotion and protection of the human rights of women and girls in Afghanistan, including the right to non-discrimination with regard to sex, age, religion, ethnicity, disability and political affiliation. Women's effective participation in civil, cultural, economic, political and social life should be promoted and protected throughout the country, including the right to life; respect for the right of women to work; the right to education, to security of person, to freedom of movement and association, freedom of opinion and expression, to equal access to facilities necessary to protect their right to highest attainable physical and mental health.

Although much attention was drawn to the imposition of the burqa on Afghan women as the perhaps most visible form of discrimination, Afghan women themselves considered other forms of discrimination such as the ban to employment and education of greater significance. Efforts by the United Nations and its partners to advance the status of women should therefore be based on a thorough understanding of the local culture and customs and on the priorities of Afghan women as defined by themselves. Furthermore, it will be crucial for the success of interventions on behalf of women to ensure that the assistance community acts consistently and leads by example in its own operations.

In order to support Afghan women in their full participation in the recovery and reconstruction of their country, the Commission on the Status of Women may wish to consider the following recommendations on governance, relief and reconstruction.

*Full participation in political decision-making*

The Afghan Interim and Transitional Authorities may be called upon to:

- ensure the full support for the participation of women in the Special Commission to convene the Emergency Loya Jirga and in the Loya Jirga itself;
- support fully the activities of the Ministry for Women's Affairs;
- ensure that all line ministries employ women, develop capacity to mainstream a gender perspective in their programmes, and that an inter-ministerial machinery is established to that end;

- ensure that women are well represented as members of the Judicial Commission, the Civil Service Commission and the Human Rights Commission, and that a gender perspective is taken into consideration when developing the mandates of these commissions;
- ensure that the work of the Human Rights Commission is underpinned by international human rights standards, including the Convention on the Elimination of All Forms of Discrimination against Women, and integrates women's rights in its mandate;
- ensure a safe environment free from violence to facilitate women's participation and the return of refugees;
- take urgent measures to repeal all legal and other orders that discriminate against women and to end all forms of discrimination against women; study and analyse the impact on women and girls of the existing legal system, including with regard to family law, divorce, property and inheritance rights; apply temporary special measures, including targets and quotas, targeted at Afghan women to accelerate the de facto equality of women and men in decision-making; take steps toward ratifying the Convention on the Elimination of All Forms of Discrimination against Women, in accordance with the Beijing Platform for Action and the outcome document of the twenty-third special session of the General Assembly;
- ensure the full participation of women in the assessment of short-, medium- and long-term priorities in all sectors.

The United Nations activities should be guided by Security Council resolution 1325 (2000) on women, peace and security. In its assistance programmes to the Afghan Interim and Transitional Authorities, the UN and its agencies should

- fully support the Interim Authority in its compliance with the commitments made in the Bonn Agreement regarding the participation of women;
- encourage steps to ensure that women become full participants at all levels of governance and decision-making, including in the Judicial Commission, the Civil Service Commission, and the Human Rights Commission;
- provide priority financial assistance to the Minister of

Women's Affairs in order to set up the Ministry, including hiring of staff, provision of office space and equipment and an adequate budget for recurrent and programme costs;

- provide support to all line ministries to develop capacity to mainstream a gender perspective in their programmes;
- support capacity-building for Afghan women to enable them to fully participate in all sectors;
- ensure that the judicial system has capacity to adhere to international standards of human rights;
- support measures to hold those accountable who are responsible for gross violations of women's human rights in the past, that full investigations are conducted and that perpetrators are brought to justice.

*Relief, reconstruction and development*

The United Nations system, donor governments and civil society, including NGOs, should:

- ensure a rights-based approach and gender-mainstreaming in all programmes and operations based on the principles of non-discrimination and the equality between women and men; and ensure that women benefit equally with men from such programmes in all sectors;
- develop comprehensive and coherent gender policy and programmes in Afghanistan, apply good practices of gender budgeting and strengthen interagency mechanisms for coordination and cooperation, including an interagency gender forum;
- re-appoint a Senior Gender Adviser in the office of the Resident/Humanitarian Coordinator or the office of the SRSG and ensure sufficient human and financial resources to that post, including the employment of Afghan women to ensure that traditional norms and values are taken into account in the programming; ensure the participation of Afghan women in all stages of programming, including planning, implementation and monitoring;
- employ Afghan women, including in management positions, and support women's freedom of movement and security in their employment with the assistance community;

- ensure equal access to funding for Afghan women's organizations; ensure that all UN international and national personnel, prior to the beginning of their service, receive a solid training on the history and traditions of Afghanistan and are fully familiar with and guided by international standards of the human rights of women and girls;
- ensure that international male staff work with national male staff on gender and human rights issues;
- give priority to the capacity building for professional Afghan women; encourage the involvement of Afghan women as well as of Afghan women's organizations based outside the country in all phases of peace-building and reconstruction, while assuring that such organizations have a constituency inside the country;
- develop indicators to measure progress and facilitate the monitoring and evaluation of all programmes and projects with regard to their contribution towards the achievement of gender equality goals;
- ensure that all reports to UN entities, including the Security Council, the General Assembly, the Commission on Human Rights and the Commission on the Status of.Women include sex-disaggregated data and statistics on the involvement of women in all sectors as staff, participants and beneficiaries.

# Bibliography


Afkhami, Mahnaz, "Introduction", *Faith and Freedom: Women's Human Rights in the Muslim World*, Syracuse, New York: Syracuse University Press.

Anwar, Raja, *The Tragedy of Afghanistan: A First-Hand Account*, translated by Khalid Hasan, London: Verso Press, 1988.

Bassiouni, Cherif, "A search for Islamic Criminal Justice: An Emerging Trend in Muslim States", in The Islamic Impulse, B.Stowasser (ed.) Centre for Contemporary Arab Studies, Georgetown University, Washington, D.C. 1987.

Cheryl Benard, *Veiled Courage: Inside the Afghan Women's Resistance,* New York: Broadway Books, 2002.

Eickelman, Dale, "Changing Interpretations of Islamic Movements", *Islam and the Political Economy of Meaning: Comparative Studies of Muslim Discourse,* (ed.) William R. Roff, London: Croom Helm, 1987.

Goodson, Larry P., *Afghanistan's Endless War: State Failure, Regional Politics, and the Rise of the Taliban*. Seattle, WA: University of Washington Press, 2001.

Griffin, Michael, *Reaping the Whirlwind: The Taliban Movement in Afghanistan,* London: Pluto Press, 2001.

Isby, David C., *War in a Distant Country: Afghanistan, Invasion and Resistance*. London: Arms and Armour Press, 1989.

Khan, Shahnaz, "Between Here and There: Feminist Solidarity and Afghan Women", *Genders,* Issue 33, Spring 2001.

Lindsey, Linda L., *The Health Status of Afghan Refugees: Focus on Women*. East Lansing: Michigan State University, Office of Women in International Development, 1990.

Lipson, J. & Miller, S., "Changing Roles of Afghan Refugee Women", in the U.S. Health Care for Women International 15, 1994.

Marsden, Peter, *The Taliban: War, Religion and the New Order in Afghanistan,* London: Zed Books, 1998.

Matinnudin, Kamal, *The Taliban Phenomenon: Afghanistan, 1994-1997*, Oxford: Oxford University Press, 1999.

Mernissi, Fatima, *Islam and Democracy: Fear of the Modern World*, translated by (Mary Jo Lakeland) USA: Addison-Wesley, 1992.

Skaine, Rosemariè, *The Women of Afghanistan Under the Taliban*, Jefferson, N.C.: McFarland & Company, November 2000.

Stowasser, B.F., *Women in the Qur'an, Traditions, and Interpretation*. New York, Oxford: Oxford University Press, 1994.

Wadud-Muhsin, A., *Qur'an and Women*, Kuala Lumpur: Penerbit Fajar Bakti Sdn Bhd, 1992.

# Index